Alice & Gerald

Alice
&
Gerald

A Homicidal Love Story

Ron Franscell

 Prometheus Books

59 John Glenn Drive
Amherst, New York 14228

Published 2019 by Prometheus Books

Cover design by Jacqueline Nasso Cooke
Cover background image taken by author; wedding image by Gerald Uden
Cover design © Prometheus Books

Inquiries should be addressed to
Prometheus Books
59 John Glenn Drive
Amherst, New York 14228
VOICE: 716–691–0133 • FAX: 716–691–0137
WWW.PROMETHEUSBOOKS.COM

23 22 21 20 19   5 4 3 2 1

Library of Congress Cataloging-in-Publication Data

Names: Franscell, Ron, 1957- author.
Title: Alice & Gerald : a homicidal love story / by Ron Franscell.
Other titles: Alice and Gerald
Description: Amherst, New York : Prometheus Books, 2019. | Includes bibliographical
    references.
Identifiers: LCCN 2018056204 (print) | LCCN 2018060132 (ebook) |
    ISBN 9781633885134 (ebook) | ISBN 9781633885127 (pbk.)
Subjects: LCSH: Uden, Alice. | Uden, Gerald. | Murder—Wyoming—Case studies.
Classification: LCC HV6533.W8 (ebook) | LCC HV6533.W8 F73 2019 (print) |
    DDC 364.152/30922787—dc23
LC record available at https://lccn.loc.gov/2018056204

Printed in the United States of America

To all who have known loss,
who waited for dawns that never came.
You're not alone.

"The attempt and not the deed
Confounds us."

—William Shakespeare, *Macbeth*

"She would have been a good woman . . . if there had been somebody there to shoot her every minute of her life."

**—Flannery O'Connor,
"A Good Man Is Hard to Find"**

"You fell in love with a storm. Did you really think you'd get out unscathed?"

—Nikita Gill

CONTENTS

Prologue

BROKEN COUNTRY

Somebody left the gate open.

In the 1960s, when the world seemed newly spacious, a whole generation saw a chance for a fresh start "out there." Like some quaint artifact of pioneer days, the words "west" and "opportunity" were synonymous. And deep down in the heart of the heart of the West was Wyoming.

So they came.

Wyoming was a place to land without baggage, where one could hide and never be found, a kingdom of dirt where giant hollows in the earth might swallow up a man (or woman) entirely, an ambiguous landscape of infertile dreams and pregnant hopes. The landscape was vast, desolate, and mysterious, festooned with hidey-holes that were forgotten or never known.

It was a spot on the edge of the Big Empty where your dog could bark forever or you could piss on the side of the road or shoot your gun at the moon or call yourself by another name. None of The World's ordinary rules applied. Whatever your badlands fetish, you could practice it unmolested in this impossibly empty place.

So they came on their blind, bad roads. It was as if some great spirit had folded the continent at the middle and every loose thing tumbled into the crease.

Not just pioneers, trailblazers, and visionaries who eventually made wealth and history, but also nonconformists, misfits, outriders, scatterlings, renegades, romantics, lost souls, pilgrims, rebels, drifters, insurgents, eccentrics, roughnecks, malcontents, escapees, wallflowers, mavericks, loners, rejects, outlaws, dissenters, mutineers, outcasts, deviants, heretics, free spirits, bohemians, oddballs, weirdos, freaks, desperadoes, black sheep, predators, odd ducks, underdogs, stragglers, round pegs, left-of-centers, delinquents and dropouts, slackers and runaways, and rule benders whose shadows would always be bigger than their light.

They came for the money, yes, but also for the extraordinary freedoms afforded by a lonely place where the next closest human might be someplace past the horizon. And that was the good part.

Naturally, many resisted domestication. The outside world held no fascination for them; intimacies were often fleeting. They were antipolitical, if not downright antisocial. But they weren't protesters. They just didn't want to be part of somebody else's revolution. Many didn't even want to be part of somebody else's family. Maybe they only sought easy chaos or temporary equilibrium, or a place on the edge where they could be happily distant from normal.

Or maybe they just wanted to be left alone.

So they gazed past the greener grass on the other side of the fence and fixed upon the other side of the metaphorical superhighway that divided civilization from the American outback, manicured lawns from scabby flats, downhill from uphill.

Ah, but any chicken will tell you that crossing a road is risky. Some found riches on the other side, and some became roadkill. Others got to the other side only to discover boarded-up gas stations, decaying motor courts, and empty beer cans, or found the other side to be indistinguishable from whatever wasteland they escaped. Some became citizens of a state with the highest per capita missing fingers. And some just fell deeper into the dark tomb their wretched lives had become.

In those days, the rest of America was unraveling, but in some ways, Wyoming had never raveled at all. It was as if the rest of the world lived in vivid Technicolor, while Wyoming flickered along in fuzzy black and white.

So they came.

Jobs were easy to find, careers not so much. Most folks weren't looking for careers. They followed the money and the work, which might lure them to a lot of jobsites in a very short time. They were oil patch gypsies who traveled light. There wasn't much room in their backpacks for perseverance or patience.

Few expected to settle down forever, and fewer still had the cash for a down payment, so they sought out cheap digs. Some rented mobile homes and travel trailers, or slept in their vans or tented in local parks. Eight or ten roughnecks might rent a cheap motel room, and who got the bed depended on which roommates were working a shift and which were getting drunk. Every eight hours, they just rotated.

People came and went here frequently, so it wouldn't be particularly noteworthy when they didn't show up one day. That was especially true in the boom times, when itinerants and drifters were common. Whole trailers vanished in the middle of the night, never seen again, and grand ambitions were unhorsed by an elusive, hundred-year wind.

The only social compact was that you pulled your own weight. Your color, sex, or religion didn't matter as long as you kept your promises and didn't add to the considerable burden such a place required everyone to bear. You plowed your own road; you dug your own holes. There was no room service. There was no 9-1-1, and even if there were, it would have been a while before the deputy arrived. Self-sufficiency was the key to everything.

All hoped for a better season. They didn't tell you in the brochure that Wyoming had three seasons that were too short and one that was too cruel. Natives were few, but one became an honorary native by surviving one winter. That was the only serious citizenship test required.

Many didn't pass. A lot of tomorrows never came. They went south before spring, or froze to death. Some accepted their own defective dreams. They either didn't find what they didn't know they were looking for, or they found it and realized it wasn't worth finding. They stopped waiting for spring, for someone good, for blue sky, for clear roads.

But some stayed. And come spring, they got a fresh start. Not redemption, exactly, but another chance to get it right. The day the river ice broke up and the remnant snow melted, every heart started beating again, as if for the first time.

Even the empty ones.

Chapter 1

A CRUEL SEASON

Gerald Uden liked girls who liked guns.

It was the summer of 1964. Like a lot of other unmoored floaters in that slack time, Gerald drifted to Wyoming to find himself. And maybe a job. Or a wife. Hell, he didn't know what he was looking for, really.

The ungainly, socially awkward farm kid had just been honorably discharged from the US Navy after four uneventful years as a radioman aboard the aircraft carrier USS *Independence*, and shore duty listening for Soviet submarines off the Carolina coast.

During his hitch, his mother and father—a onetime trucker turned jack-of-all-trades after miraculously surviving a terrible crash—had moved from Gerald's hometown, the tiny village of Harvard, Nebraska (pop. 774), to the scenic mountain town of Lander, Wyoming. Gerald's job-hopping dad took work in a lumberyard.

More than any other thing he dreamed for himself (or never dreamed), Gerald wanted to be part of a family. Until they died, his Nebraska grandparents had always lived on nearby farms, where Gerald learned to shoot guns and fix cars. The whole clan would fish, eat, and go to church together, and they lived in the same little houses when cash flow or bad health required it. Mom's side counted colonial rebels in its family tree and was proud (as only a family could be) to claim the irascible, anti-Semitic, sexist US Supreme Court justice James McReynolds as one of their own. Grandpa Uden had hunted buffalo on the high plains with Buffalo Bill himself.

It was Grandpa Uden who gave Gerald his first rifle and a stern lecture about gun safety he'd never forget. The first grader learned to shoot by plinking the sparrows' nests under the farmhouse's eaves, earning a penny a bird. Oh, there was that unfortunate incident when a country doctor had to remove a BB from a shocked playmate's forehead—but that was precisely where Gerald had aimed, so he had clearly become a good shot.

His parents, Lloyd and Betty Uden, believed in God and went to church on Sunday, but they weren't zealots. Lloyd sensed God's presence more in the trees than in the pews. To Lloyd, church was mostly about dollars, not deliverance.

The elder Udens considered drinking and cussing signs of ignorance. They never argued in front of the kids. They expected decent behavior from Gerald and his two younger siblings, but they didn't hover. Life had too many other priorities, and small towns had a way of keeping an eye on kids.

It didn't matter much. Among the many odd jobs his father had held was town marshal, and he once warned if Gerald ever got in trouble with the law, his father would side with the cops. Despite his feelings about church, right and wrong weren't fuzzy concepts for Lloyd Uden.

For some kids, a small town feels like being buried alive in a claustrophobic casket. They run away to the big city. But not Gerald. Quite the opposite. At seventeen, he ran west from Nebraska to become a cowboy someplace where nobody would bother him. He only turned around when his '48 Chrysler spluttered and gasped halfway up the Rockies— which was about the same time he realized it was all a brainless fantasy. He only got halfway home before the junker crapped out, and his father rescued him in Ogallala, Nebraska. On the long drive home, Lloyd didn't say much until a chastened Gerald broke the silence.

"I didn't know" is all he said.

His father just stared down the endless road ahead.

"Well, next time," he said, his voice frighteningly calm, "you best just keep on going."

A few months later, Gerald joined the navy. Still only seventeen, he needed Lloyd's permission, but in June 1960, he swore an oath to defend America and Ike from all enemies, foreign and domestic. He learned to swim, qualified as a sharpshooter, saw the world, bought a new rifle and a used car, listened for phantom Russians, got dumped by his girlfriend back home, went to Cuba during the Bay of Pigs debacle, and almost stepped on African soil once. Then the big adventure was over. Vietnam was not yet a thing, and the navy had no further use for him.

So with nobody left in the old hometown and no place better to land, Gerald lit out for Wyoming, for the comfort of family. His clunker '59 Ford sedan had blown up just before his discharge, so he hopped on a Greyhound bus with his seaman's bag—his life's possessions—for the long journey.

In Lander, he paid his parents fifty bucks a month in rent. But grass didn't grow under Gerald's feet. He quickly found work as a $2.29-an-hour maintenance man at US Steel's taconite mine out near the old hard-rock camp of Atlantic City, fixing equipment, oiling machines, welding whatever needed welding, and painting whatever needed painting.

His weekends were for hunting. Birds, deer, rabbits, elk, prairie dogs, anything that gave him a moving target. Some of it was for the meat, some just to keep his eye sharp. The blood didn't bother him. Blood reminded a man he was alive.

Gerald's childhood interest in guns had blossomed in the navy. He became a collector and a student of firearms. He knew their worth, loaded his own ammunition, read all the gun magazines, kept his weapons immaculately clean, and could identify most guns on sight the way some men knew the make, model, and engine specs of any car at a glance.

His fascination with guns didn't hurt Gerald's love life. Maybe it even helped.

In the fall of 1965, he bagged a trophy bull elk in the badlands below Limestone Mountain, not far from the abandoned Lewiston mining district, where fevered turn-of-the-century prospectors left a thousand holes as they hunted gold. Once considered rich pay dirt where dreams could come true, this desert scrubland was now just a honeycomb of panned-out pits, cavities, and burrows in the middle of nowhere. Weathered head frames and tumbledown shacks marked the spots, few and far between, where men had once staked their best claims. Nobody had lived here for almost a hundred years. Now, except for hungry predators and a few weekend prospectors who scraped in holes first dug by dead men, it was a miserable landscape more brutal than any human who ever walked on it.

Gerald hauled the elk's enormous carcass home and butchered it on a telephone pole in his dad's alley. He splayed the bloody hide across a patch of dirt in back, where he flensed the fat and flesh from the skin, thinking it might be tanned into a supple piece of leather by a guy he knew.

Out of nowhere, a girl appeared.

Barbara Ann Phillips was, literally, the girl next door. Gerald had seen her before, but she was just a small-town high school kid, too young for a worldly twentysomething like him. Not worth a second look. Now, as the slim teenager strolled across the threadbare yard, though, Gerald saw her differently. She had darker eyes than he remembered, and dark shoulder-length hair. A nice smile too. Not a movie star, but Gerald—who wasn't exactly a matinee idol himself—had flirted with much uglier girls.

And she knew her big game.

"Where'd you get him?" she asked.

"Twin Creek, below Limestone Mountain," Gerald said, continuing to flense the skin.

"How big?"

"Five by five."

"Nice. How much did he weigh?"

"Maybe seven hundred."

"What did you get him with?"

"Winchester .264 Magnum."

"I got a .270 myself. Long shot?"

"Hundred yards. Once through the heart. Went down like I hit him in the head with a hammer—and stayed down."

"Whaddya gonna do with the hide?"

"I dunno," he said. "Blanket, maybe."

Barbara Ann was impressed. Her parents were avid hunters. She knew a good shot, and she knew the big bull would fill the freezer with good meat for a year. But she also thought this guy was cute.

Gerald was impressed too: a girl who wasn't squeamish about the dirty work of butchery.

They talked small for a while, until Gerald worked up the nerve to ask Barbara Ann to "the show." She said yes. That night, they went to Lander's only movie house and saw some second-run flick that had already played everywhere else.

Overnight, Gerald was ass over teakettle in love. Problem was, Barbara Ann was still only a seventeen-year-old schoolgirl, although she'd turn eighteen in a few weeks and planned to graduate when the semester ended. He sought her father's permission and got it, though it was reluctant. Barbara Ann's preacher uncle married them around Christmas, and the newlyweds settled into a $75-a-month apartment over the J. C. Penney store—until they realized the landlady was sneaking in to "fix" the young wife's housework. That's when they bought a cramped used trailer and parked it in Gerald's parents' backyard. Home sweet home.

Cabin fever wasn't a problem: they spent much of their first year outdoors, hunting or fishing together. If anybody had asked Gerald to describe his perfect mate, Gerald would have painted a girl who loved campfire smoke, baited her own hooks, owned her own hunting rifle and had a keen eye, cooked like a chef in the open air, loved sex, and slept on a leaky air mattress without complaining—like Barbara Ann. It was idyllic.

But the marriage got overcrowded. The impatient mothers-in-law started lobbying for grandkids, which turned to some home-brewed medical advice, which turned to a serious health crisis caused by birth control pills that put Barbara Ann in the hospital with life-threatening blood clots. After a painfully short recovery period in which she simply didn't recover, the old-fashioned rube Gerald wanted his wife back on her feet, doing chores and servicing his needs. He demanded that she buck up, even though she'd nearly died only two weeks before.

Barbara Ann got up, all right. She went straight from her bed to divorce court, and Gerald was roadkill.

For the next five years, he played the field damned hard. The game was afoot.

In the spring of 1973, he met Wanda, a mercurial wild child with some nasty habits he could overlook. And she liked to shoot guns. A dishwater blonde with a feral streak, she loved motorcycles and the wild thing. Another dust-devil romance, another hasty wedding, another trailer (this one behind a bowling alley) . . . and another painful divorce after only six weeks of wedded bliss. Wanda took off, and the thunderstruck Gerald lay in his empty trailer-house bed wondering if he was just snakebit when it came to women. Alone at his angle of repose, he was on the verge of sliding right off the damn mountain.

Still, Gerald refused to surrender. He still yearned for his own family. He knew he had to change, to evolve, to become the kind of man that could keep the kind of woman he desired. Yeah, maybe he could be less demanding, less controlling—more solicitous. But it wasn't a completely conscious choice for him. Loneliness made his marrow ache, like a below-zero morning before the sun came up. It didn't require a lot of navel-gazing to wiggle away from the pain to find a posture that didn't hurt so much. He wasn't that deep.

Whether he knew it or not, Gerald didn't just want to be wanted. He *needed* to be wanted.

So he was back on the market, a two-time loser at thirty, a glorified janitor at a hard-rock mine, back at square one on the family thing. A guy who never seemed to walk under the right cloud. In those slow-water days before online dating, Gerald spread the word the old-fashioned way: he told Fran, the landlady who'd rented him and Wanda a vacant lot where he could park their mobile home.

Fran was a good ol' gal, a rodeo queen in her day, and she knew darn near everybody in the county. She adopted all kinds of strays and took special pity on the busted ones. She liked Gerald and hated to see a good man go to waste.

A few days later, there came a knock at Gerald's door.

It was a dark-haired, dark-eyed woman, in her midtwenties, a little chunky but not bad looking. She wore saucer-sized glasses and had a nice smile.

And a gun.

"You Gerald?" she asked.

"Yeah."

"My name's Virginia. Fran said you might be able to help me," she said. "Would you take a look at this rifle and maybe tell me what it's worth?"

A good-looking piece, Gerald thought. He fancied himself to be a crackerjack gun guy and a fine ladies' man, to boot, so he invited her in.

Inside his dismal trailer, Virginia handed him the little rifle. It was an old Winchester slide-action .22 that had been in her family for a long time. It was a Depression-era takedown model that came apart for easy storage. Gerald examined the polished bird's-eye maple stock—definitely not original, but it had "S. Dear" carved in it. It was her late grandfather Stacy Dear's gun.

Nice gun, Gerald said, but not a museum piece. Without the original stock, he reckoned it wasn't worth much more than the $35 somebody paid for it back in the 1930s.

"Sorry," he said as he handed it back.

Virginia smiled wanly and shrugged. She was hoping it'd be worth more, she said. She was a single mom moving back to town with two young sons and—it all tumbled out—an ex-husband who wasn't paying child support, a series of tedious odd jobs, not enough cash for rent, her own mom getting older and living alone, more and more chores going undone, drab prospects for the future, winter coming. She seemed stressed, angry, broke, and sad all at the same time.

Gerald felt sorry for her. He actually coveted the gun for himself and even thought about making an offer, but he wasn't sure she came to sell it. In fact, he thought her visit might not be about the old gun at all. It made him smile.

Equal parts handy and horny, the gallant Gerald offered to help Virginia with some of the chores at her little house in nearby Hudson, a onetime coal camp on the Riverton road with a few hundred people and a couple nice restaurants he couldn't afford but no real modern reason to exist.

The next weekend, he drove out to Hudson, nestled in a river draw twelve miles from Lander. Virginia had rented a sturdy stone-block bungalow off one of the town's few paved streets. It was one of Hudson's oldest homes, built years before women could vote, but it hadn't been kept up. Now dog-eared and dreary, it bore only traces of grand ambitions gone awry. Hell, a lot of hopes and houses caved in here, and, in time, the land always swallowed them back up.

Virginia shared the cluttered two-bedroom cottage with her two young sons, Richard and Reagan. At four and six, with a flustered mom and no dad, they lived in perpetual little-boy motion. They were full of energy, and it spilled out in great spasms of daylong chaos. Gerald looked around the shabby-cozy place—he guessed no more than five hundred square feet—and it was a shambles.

It looked like Virginia's hands were more than full. They were spilling over. Alone with Gerald, she had been reserved, soft-spoken, not especially assertive. But around her boys, she clenched.

Virginia simply never learned how to deal with the pandemonium two little boys could wreak. The only child of an adventuresome single mom herself, she snapped at them, wrangled them like wildcats, shoved them toward any open door, ignored them when she could. She didn't discipline them so much as she surrendered to her anger. And she felt perpetually guilty.

Her face changed around them. She couldn't enjoy her own kids, who looked to Gerald like . . . little boys. Today, they might be diagnosed with attention deficit disorder or hyperactivity, but back then, they were just rambunctious kids.

They just need a man in their life, Gerald thought.

She'd graduated in a paltry class at a trifling high school in tiny Pavillion, a "ceded" town comprising a couple hundred white people and some surrounding farmers inside the Wind River Indian Reservation, a checkerboard landscape of mostly white men's towns, government land, sovereign Indian land, and non-Indian landowners. Pavillion, named for a distinctive nearby butte, was one of those cobbled towns.

Virginia supported herself with menial (often brief) jobs and reselling junk she picked up at garage sales. She moved around a lot, so her life had been stripped down to the bare essentials. Her furniture was sparse and scuffed. The cupboards weren't overstocked, but no week ended with spare cash. The only reason the boys wore clean clothes was that her mom ran a local Laundromat.

The source of her fluster wasn't just her rambunctious sons.

At twenty, she'd gotten pregnant and been briefly married—just six months and a week in 1968—to a Korean War vet who was cutting federal timber in Idaho. He kicked her out after she called one of his children from a previous marriage a "son of a bitch." The kid was a toddler.

Her son Richard was born two months later, and her ex-husband regularly paid $75 a month in child support. (Reagan came along two years later, and even though he went by the same last name as Richard, he was the product of Virginia's fling with a curly-headed bartender in Jackson Hole, Gerald would later learn.)

But six years later, in 1974, with two kids and no prospects in the midst of a recession, there was always too much month left at the end of the paycheck. She lamented to Gerald that her asshole ex-husband was skipping payments and refusing to pay more; in reality, she received the money like clockwork every month from the state, and she'd never asked for more. And if Gerald had taken Virginia's ex-husband out for a beer, the old soldier might even have said he wasn't completely convinced Richard was his son either.

Virginia wasn't telling Gerald a lot. That her deep, secret insecurity caused her to seek lovers who made her feel valued, at least for a moment. That she had no real friends. That she feared dying alone. That she chafed under the mysterious burden of motherhood.

It wouldn't have mattered much. Gerald had already locked on his target.

Another romantic dust devil barreled in. It blew Virginia's skirt up, and Gerald fell hard, again.

First came sex, then came fishing. Virginia loved being outdoors, which made her all the more attractive to Gerald. A couple times, they even went plinking with her antique gun. Soon enough, they hauled along the boys, who seemed to thrive when there were no walls against which they might bounce.

More important, he got to know the boys, and they got to know him. Suddenly they were outgunned at the dinner table, so meals were more relaxing. And they felt safer with a big man in the house, especially when Gerald made a big show of slaying the monsters under the bed.

Richard, the older boy, was mellow and studious for a first grader. He wore big black plastic glasses to correct his crossed eyes, liked sports, and built radio-controlled models. But Reagan, two years younger, was different. The gap-toothed kid was rowdy and high-strung, probably hyperactive before it was commonly diagnosed. He was a handful, and Virginia didn't have enough hands.

Dinnertime was a nightly struggle. The boys refused to eat, or demanded to eat something else, or threw their food, or screamed bloody murder about everything. They wanted fast food burgers for every meal, and Virginia often obliged them because it was easier than tussling with them every night. She wasn't the best cook, but it wasn't always about the food.

Bedtime was worse. Richard and Reagan fought sleep. They feared everything: the smothering dark, the melancholy sounds of wind, headlights scampering across the wall, monsters in the closet or under the bed. They wept to think they might actually die before they woke.

Virginia couldn't soothe their irrational fears. She could barely tolerate them. She just prayed for exhaustion—hers or theirs—and closed the door. She wasn't a bad mom, just a swamped one.

She needed a partner.

Just as the boys started to trust Gerald, then to depend on him, so did Virginia.

And Gerald was falling for them too. As the days passed, he increasingly believed he'd stumbled into the perfect, ready-made brood.

She needs me, and those boys need a dad, Gerald thought. *And I need a family.*

It wasn't long before Virginia introduced him to her mother, Claire Martin, who managed the Laundromat in Riverton. She was unlike her beloved only daughter, Virginia, whom she knew could be high-maintenance. Claire was an outgoing, free-spirited former Pennsylvania factory worker, a wartime Rosie the Riveter and independent woman who hadn't needed a man around after she divorced the infant Virginia's father. She didn't take crap from anybody, even a husband. So in 1949, she'd loaded up her sedan and trundled west to Wyoming with her baby, determined never to let somebody else run her life. Out here, she could ride her motorcycle or paddle her scull on a mountain lake or lie down beside a creek and never have to explain it to anybody.

The laundry's owner let Claire park a trailer in a vacant lot behind the shop, where the drifting Virginia occasionally crashed, customers came for coffee while their loads tumbled, and Claire often babysat Richard and Reagan. Now she was happy that Virginia had found somebody.

Gerald and Virginia's courtship was torrid and short. Technically, they were only dating, but neither had any doubt that this was, finally, the real thing. They were old enough to know what they wanted, young enough to chase it enthusiastically. Virginia could hump ten miles in hard country and still cook a fair supper; Gerald's paycheck and closet-monster killing took the edge off her desperation. It passed for a perfect match in these parts.

So three months after they met on Gerald's trailer-house step, he asked her to marry him. Virginia quickly, delightedly agreed. A few days later, the impromptu wedding on July 3, 1974, was short and sweet. Gerald wore a gray-brown suit with a boutonniere, Virginia a paisley smock with flowers in her hair, and the boys wore new suits for the first—and last—time. A day later, Gerald stowed his trailer behind Virginia's bungalow, and they moved into the house together.

Finally, a family.

It was a dream come true.

The first family project was a new coat of yellow paint for Virginia's cheerless stone house. It made everything seem brighter, even the people inside.

Virginia supplemented their household income by selling second-hand furniture out of their garage and knocking on doors with her Amway stuff, but Gerald was making good money at US Steel. They weren't rich, but suddenly they both felt like the sky was the limit.

She was also an amateur astronomer, and on some nights, they went out to count the stars. The northern lights were rare at this latitude, but one night, on a hill away from the polluting lights of town, they watched them dance across the sky. It was a good omen, they told each other. They made love right there on a hill under the aurora borealis.

Although Virginia wasn't impulsive, nor even overtly passionate about much, she giggled like a schoolgirl when Gerald took her for rides on his Honda 750 motorcycle. The rushing wind washed away her fears, worries, and insecurities for a while, like every ride was a cleansing adventure. She held on for dear life.

With the boys, everything was an adventure. They tagged along on hikes, fishing and hunting trips, and grocery shopping in town. They especially loved to venture out into the sagebrush flats to shoot at cans and the occasional scavenger bird. Gerald taught them outdoor skills and kept all their indoor demons at bay.

Richard and Reagan began to call him Dad, and it swelled his heart every time. They'd never known a father, and Gerald never knew one word could be so powerful.

Once, as a snowstorm approached, they found some motherless ducklings down by the creek. They rounded them up and took them home, where they drew a bath so the ducklings could ride out the storm, safe and warm. Virginia hated to see any family destroyed.

One last entanglement remained. Virginia could wriggle free from her ex-husband, Richard's father, if Gerald would adopt the boys. No more fighting over child support, no more monthly reminders of past bad choices, if only Gerald would officially accept the role he already played: Dad.

Gerald happily accepted the job. A lawyer drew up the papers, Richard's father signed off, and in March 1975, Gerald instantly became the father of two. He couldn't have been happier if they'd come from his own loins. He promised them a proper upbringing. And they'd never miss their real dad's $75 a month.

In the summer of 1975, about to celebrate an idyllic year of marriage, they embarked on their first big road trip together. Two thousand miles to Mechanicsburg, Pennsylvania, where Virginia's estranged father and stepmom were houseparents at a Hershey home for needy kids. *Too decent to get dumped*, Gerald thought when he met his father-in-law. But then, Gerald obviously wasn't adept at marriage's complex emotional calculus, for himself or anybody else. Whether it was luck or perseverance, he was glad his current marriage was working out so nicely.

After a few pleasant days in the sticks, Virginia caught a wild hare. She told Gerald she had decided to drive down to Philly to see some distant relatives. Alone.

Gerald was perplexed. It was almost time to start the long journey back to Wyoming, so Virginia bought him a plane ticket home and she stayed in Pennsylvania with the boys. When Gerald landed, he wired some pocket money to her and counted the lonesome last days of summer until Richard and Reagan would start school.

But they didn't return.

It was September, and the air had turned suddenly cold. Gerald called Virginia and they argued. He demanded that she come home. She refused at first but finally surrendered.

Back in Hudson, she wasn't the stargazing, duck-saving, motorcycle-riding young mom he'd married. She'd changed. She wouldn't sleep in his bed. She barely spoke to him. Their bright little yellow house fell dimmer and darker all of a sudden.

What happened in Philly? Gerald wondered. *Did she ever love me? Did she meet another man? Or had she simply gotten all she needed from me?*

The boys had changed too. The happiness had seeped out of them. Maybe taking an unspoken cue from their mother, they started calling him Gerald, not Dad.

It was happening again, like a sudden cloudburst that blows up before you know it. Three witchy wives, and three times Gerald had been blown down by a sudden squall he never saw coming.

A dispirited month passed before Virginia finally pulled the trigger: she asked Gerald for a divorce. Confused, angry, and clueless, he didn't put up much of a fight.

Virginia filed the divorce paperwork—"intolerable indignities," she claimed with legal vagueness—while Gerald hooked up his old trailer and hauled it back to Lander. They agreed he could keep his truck, his motorcycle, and their accumulated debts, but she kept everything else. He promised to keep the boys on his US Steel health insurance and pay $150 a month in child support out of his $8-an-hour paycheck from the mine.

The split stunned Claire Martin. She liked Gerald. Virginia never complained about how he treated her. Sure, maybe he was a little old-fashioned about marriage and wives, but to be fair, Claire, ever the bohemian (and mother-in-law), already believed that about most men.

While Gerald occasionally saw his adopted sons and things remained cordial with Virginia during the separation, the only real tie that truly bound them was his $150 every month.

Maybe it's always about the money, Gerald chafed as he slunk away. *What a chump I am.*

Chump or not, Gerald sunk again into a dark depression and thought about shooting himself with one of his guns. He was alone again, unshaven, holed up in his trailer, no seat covers in his old pickup, stuck between a hard place and harder women.

But not for long.

One morning, a new neighbor showed up in the space next to Gerald's. A bigger trailer than his. No big deal, since folks who lived in mobile home parks voluntarily gave up panoramas and privacy. Once Gerald's pathetic view was blocked, it wasn't long before there came another metallic rap on his front door.

It was the trailer park manager. Hanging back on the bare ground behind her was a big-breasted, comely woman with long dark hair, dressed like a dollar-store buckle bunny in a Western pantsuit, cowboy boots, and dangling turquoise earrings. *Not bad,* Gerald thought. Two kids stood nearby, a towheaded toddler and an indifferent teenager who looked as if she might like to be anywhere else at that moment.

They needed some help. A *man's* help.

Their trailer's electrical plug was 110, but the park's hookups were 220. The manager knew Gerald was a handyman at the mine, so she thought he might be able to save everybody an electrician's bill (and a city inspection) with some under-the-table quick fix. Gerald took a look, consulted with the power company, and got to work.

It was lunchtime when he finished, so Gerald offered to buy burgers at the Husky Truck Stop cafe. Their conversation was heavier than the usual get-acquainted banter.

Her name was Alice Prunty. Her same story had been told in a thousand other trailer parks every day: She was a widowed nurse and single mom scrabbling for a fresh start. Although she was only in her thirties, she'd been married twice and borne five kids, three of whom were still school age or younger. She divorced her first husband, a cop in her native Illinois, and her second—a philandering World War II vet who drifted from midwestern grain elevators to Wyoming ranch work—died from alcoholism, leaving her a pile of debt, an infant daughter, and a piddling widows-and-orphans pension from the US Army.

Since that guy, Don Prunty, had died a couple years ago, she'd filed for bankruptcy, toiled as a barmaid and bus driver, nursed a few months in a small-town psychiatric hospital, and farmed out the kids to relatives back East when things got tight, which was frequently. To hear her tell it, just another star-crossed mom busting her ass to hang on to the edge of a savage earth hurtling through time and space.

Nice boobs, Gerald mooned to himself.

"You like to fish?" he asked her.

"I love it," Alice replied.

"I know a place," he said. He told her about Atlantic Creek, way up in the Shoshone National Forest, up above the old mining camps of South Pass and Atlantic City. It was barely wider than his truck but chock-full of little brook trout. They made a date to meet the next morning for a day of hiking and fishing up in the mountains. Alice was giddy.

Maybe Gerald was a sucker for love, but he was hooked. Alice was easy on the eyes, earned her own paychecks, seemed like a resourceful gal, already had kids and a trailer, and liked to fish. *Damn.* He barely slept.

The next morning dawned sunny and warm. Alice showed up outside the trailer with her sprightly three-year-old, Eliza,[1] and her own fishing rod. That impressed the hell out of Gerald. They all piled into Gerald's old truck and headed up the mountain with a can of worms and a picnic lunch, and they fished all day. Alice frowned upon the scrappy little brookies—she liked 'em bigger—but she was a good sport about it. She also kept a tight leash on Eliza, who never acted up once. Alice was in complete control—unlike Virginia—and that turned Gerald on.

For his part, Gerald recited jokes from old comedy LPs he'd memorized. Alice laughed at all his stolen humor.

Over a picnic of cold cut sandwiches, Gerald listened patiently as Alice skipped through her life's arduous tale, never pausing long at any painful memory or giving much detail. She'd been born to an unwed teenage mother in Denver, adopted by a young soldier and his wife, and raised in an Illinois farm town. She got pregnant and married at sixteen; birthed four kids in quick succession; got divorced; got married again to the boozer who dragged her to Wyoming to be caretakers of a historic ranch, then abruptly died, stranding her and their new baby in this beautiful, godforsaken place at the end of the earth. But there was nothing more for her back East. Her only chance to climb out of her hole, to make her own way, was here.

There by Atlantic Creek, he felt Alice's pain. She was still young and earnest, and Gerald didn't think she deserved all the pain she'd already endured. But she was a survivor, not a straggler—unlike Virginia. He reckoned, if things worked out the way he hoped, that he could make Alice's life better. He could give her what she deserved.

Later, they packed up their rods and their creels full of brookies and hiked out. On the bumpy pickup ride home, Gerald knew he had a keeper. Any woman confident enough to venture into the boondocks with a stranger and bare her soul was a woman he wanted to ride with, he thought.

In that long, hot bicentennial summer of 1976, Gerald and Alice fell in love. Hard and fast.

On one of their first real dates—playing pool at a Main Street tavern—Alice confessed that she too had been immediately attracted to Gerald when she first laid eyes on him. Then she beat him soundly at a game he thought he could win.

After a couple more dates, they tumbled into bed. Not one of those forbidden teenager liaisons, but a full-on fuckfest between two consenting adults who'd already bumped a lot of other uglies. And Alice especially knew what she was doing. If Gerald had any reservations about her before he saw her naked, they now lay in a crumpled heap on the bedroom floor.

It was dark outside when the grunting stopped and they slumped back on the wet sheets. Alice cuddled against him. It was the part of love-making he didn't like so much: talking.

But Alice had a story to tell, and she told it softly.

There had been another husband. Her third. After the alcoholic one. A crazy man, a junkie, a door gunner in Vietnam who'd been kicked out of the army for being nuts. Named Ron Holtz. She met him in a small-town Veterans Administration psych ward where she'd taken a nursing job. They fell in love and ran off together to get married, even though she knew it was wrong. They rented a trailer house in Cheyenne, where he drove a cab to support his habit. Then he started beating her and threatening the baby when she cried. He boasted that he'd killed babies in 'Nam and he'd kill her too.

One night around Christmas, Ronnie Holtz went berserk, and Alice shot him before he could harm the baby. It was self-defense. She didn't have a choice. She stuffed the brute's body in a cardboard storage barrel and drove her Pinto into the frigid blackness to drop it down a remote, abandoned mine shaft on the historic ranch she'd managed with her other late husband. She raced home, hurriedly packed up her possessions, and left town before anybody missed either of them.

And nobody ever did. They'd barely cast a shadow in Cheyenne. A few months later, she filed for divorce, claiming abandonment. It was granted when Ron Holtz failed to show up in court.

Alice wept on her new lover. A speechless Gerald, dumbfounded by the confession, just hugged her tight. She told him she wasn't sure if he could love her now, but he promised he'd never tell a soul. *Never.* He also reassured her that some assholes, like Ron Holtz, just needed killing, although he secretly wondered why she didn't just run away.

Either way, as they lay there in the dark, naked and laid bare, Alice's secret became their bond.

He didn't know why she picked that particular moment to reveal it. Maybe she felt safe with him. Maybe to test him, or to nudge him a little off-balance. Or maybe it was a warning shot in case he ever raised a hand to her.

But Gerald swore to himself he'd never let Alice go. She was a keeper.

And although he wasn't especially well churched, it all felt to him like Adam and Eve, after Eve confessed to biting the apple but before the clueless Adam knew what it all meant.

Sure, Gerald sensed Alice's backstory was far more complicated than she let on. Maybe more complicated than he wanted to know.

It didn't matter. He was dead set on this woman.

They'd met on July 7, 1976, while Gerald's divorce from Virginia was still wending through court. Three months later, in mid-October, a judge finally signed the divorce papers. It was done.

So two weeks after the divorce from his third wife was final, an impatient Gerald married his fourth. Their marriage license listed Alice as a "widow." Gerald couldn't afford a ring, but in her three previous trips down the aisle, Alice claimed, she'd never gotten a ring anyway. Hell, it wasn't like either of them needed a marital Miranda warning; with six previous weddings between them, they knew the drill. On November 5, 1976, they celebrated with a church wedding—Gerald wore a sad boutonniere with the same shiny gray-brown suit he wore at his wedding to Virginia, Alice a secondhand Gunne Sax cotton dress—but almost nobody came.

With no money for a proper bridal suite, they spent their frozen wedding night in sleeping bags in the bed of Alice's Chevy pickup during a Jackson Hole snowstorm. In fact, their honeymoon was really just an elk-hunting trip. That was just one of the things he loved about Alice: she was a real carnivore. They came to kill something.

But such romance can't last forever. When the wintry weekend ended, Gerald went back to his broken machines at the mine, and Alice returned to her new nursing job at the little Lander hospital.

Gerald tried his damnedest to keep Alice happy. In those first few months, he spent his last penny on a month-late diamond wedding ring that doubled as a Christmas gift. When a crocked Alice stumbled in after a girls' night out, so drunk she couldn't even fall into bed, he spread a blanket on the trailer floor so he could sleep beside her. And he constantly promised her he'd someday buy her a piece of land where he'd build her a proper house, raising milk cows, chickens, and turkeys out in the country, a farm away from all the people neither of them really liked much.

Alice basked in Gerald's fawning. She couldn't get enough. It was her drug.

When she and Gerald attended her employer's New Year's Eve party, they'd hardly taken a seat when Gerald's first ex-wife, Barbara Ann— now a hospital employee too—unexpectedly appeared. She scurried to their table, introduced herself to Alice, and started babbling fondly with Gerald about their good ol' days, as if they were still best friends.

When Barbara Ann finally left, a seething Alice erupted. *Who the hell does she think she is? Old lovers can't come back,* she said. *Old love affairs shouldn't be discussed, and ex-wives should disappear forever!*

Gerald had never seen Alice so furious. He got the message loud and clear. *More fawning,* he thought.

That spring, he paid $1000 an acre for a twenty-acre patch of unde- veloped greasewood hardpan on an unpaved county road east of Pavillion, Wyoming, a place so small that even people in Wyoming didn't know where it was. A perfect place to escape.

They moved Alice's trailer out there—it was bigger than Gerald's—and drilled a water well in the impossibly deep, dry earth. That made it official. Gerald didn't mind the well water's high alkalinity, but it gave Alice the shits. So they also dug another hole for the septic tank.

Soon enough, they plopped down a propane tank for fuel, bartered for used lumber to build a barn, and traded Alice's truck for a new Ford Pinto so they could afford it all.

They settled into a comfortable rhythm: Gerald worked and tended to the property, while Alice handled the money, paid the bills, and made all the decisions.

After a short time, one of Alice's younger sons, Michael, moved in with them. He'd been farmed out with his two brothers and a sister to relatives in Illinois during Alice's turbulent nomadic days and her romance with Gerald, but now he was coming home to his mother's care. At least until he could be farmed out again.

Bored, or maybe just looking to belong, Michael joined his school's Future Farmers of America chapter, in which every member was required to undertake an agribusiness project. Michael picked pigs. So Gerald built a hog pen and filled it with swine, all for Alice's boy.

And since no impossibly dry patch of land is complete without a boat, Gerald bought one of those too. A sixteen-foot aluminum baby with a fifty-five-horsepower outboard, a walk-through windshield, room for eight, and seats that converted to beds. With the trailer, just $4200 and easy payments. Alice loved it.

The fun really started that summer when Alice and Gerald invited friends to a chicken-slaughtering party. They set up a fetid, grim assembly line: Gerald whacked off their heads, Alice scalded them, the kids picked off the feathers, and the guests singed the pinfeathers, before everybody pitched in with the butchering and freezer-wrapping. City folk never had this kind of fun.

Eventually, the Udens invited Alice's adoptive parents, Sam and Vivian Barbier, to drag their own trailer onto the place. For a while, nearly the whole family—Alice's family—was all together again. Alice was even happier.

Life was good.

That is, until Virginia popped into their lives again. Since the divorce, she'd been unmoored, job-hopping and floating casually out West and back East, and cashing Gerald's mostly regular child support checks.

Legally, Gerald had unrestricted visitation rights with the boys, but it always made Alice uncomfortable when they were around, so Gerald's visits quickly tapered off to nothing after he courted and married Alice. When he occasionally encountered them on the street—especially if Alice was with him—he acted as if he didn't know them. Once, the boys asked him to attend a school program, and Gerald told them he couldn't because Alice wouldn't allow it.

Sadly, Richard and Reagan often asked about their "daddy," but Virginia had no gracious answers.

As a single mom, Virginia was easily annoyed by her kids most of the time. Away from the kids, she was relaxed and fun. She wasn't a bad mother, really. They were clean, had food and clean clothes, but she'd sometimes yank their pants down and spank them.

And the boys weren't bad, just … boys. Richard would bring little gifts home to Virginia and Claire, things he'd picked up on his walk home from school. But he could also get profane and talk back in blue streaks. Devil and angel at the same time.

Reagan was Virginia's secret favorite, probably because he required less energy. He wasn't a perfect kid by any means, but he wasn't constantly bubbling over.

In June 1978, Virginia finally had enough—of everything. She borrowed some cash, loaded up the boys, and headed to her native Pennsylvania, far away from Wyoming. For three years, she had bounced around from apartment to apartment, job to job, and eventually out of Pennsylvania altogether. She landed in New Jersey, with no great prospects and no real improvement in her life.

Money was always a problem. Even with minimum wage jobs and occasional unemployment checks, she could no longer stretch Gerald's $150-a-month child support payment.

Worse, the boys got sick a lot, especially Richard. It didn't help that when they most needed medical help, something was always fouled up with Gerald's insurance. She suspected Gerald and Alice of secret schemes and just grew angrier every time it happened.

And when she was angry, she vented in great acidic gusts.

Sinking into depression and gaining weight at an astounding rate, Virginia started calling collect and writing nasty letters to Gerald, partly to clear up the insurance mess and partly to demand more child support. And maybe partly to be a pain in his ass.

What she got back was the venomous wrath of Alice Uden:

Virginia,

Gerald and I enjoyed your letter, as we always do.

It appears to me that you have the idea that I try to keep your messages (letters and phone calls) from my husband. We keep no secrets from one another. . . . We have a lot of laughs at your expense. It is very difficult for either one of us to understand how any human being can be as brainless as you are.

If you get the idea that I don't like you, you're very correct.

I have no use for any woman that does not have the mind, backbone or guts to stand on her own two feet and take care of herself and her kids, by herself, without raping some poor man's pocket. Any woman that can't do that is a worthless piece of garbage.

I worked, supported 5 children, and also had to give my tax money to support leeches like you, who are too lazy to go out and get a good enough job to take care of your own. . . .

You are worse than most of your kind. Everyone in the family knows how you hounded Gerald to adopt your kids, so he could wind up supporting them, since their father wouldn't. . . .

You're quite a con artist. Most lazy trash are. Gerald must have really tried to hold his marriage together by adopting your boys, because he doesn't even like kids. He swallowed your line: hook, line and sinker, and now he pays for it. . . .

He was hoping the power plant [Three Mile Island nuclear plant, then in crisis, was very near Virginia's Pennsylvania apartment] would explode and take you with it. It's really a shame that it didn't.

The long, handwritten letter closed with more nastiness from Alice about a child support payment that Virginia claimed hadn't arrived. It was unsigned and undated, but on the back, Virginia—intending to document all her correspondence with the Udens—wrote, "Alice, Spring, 1979."

Virginia's next letter is lost, but judging by Alice's response, it skewered her parenting skills, among other cruelties. The reply, dated January 26, 1980, displayed more of Alice's malice:

> Box 117
> Pavillion, Wyo 82523
> January 26, 1980

> Virginia,

> I'm afraid I owe you an apology. When I stated in my last letter last spring that Gerald didn't like children and did not want to be a father, I was mistaken. Gerald never told me that he did not like children and did not want to be a father. I only assumed that since he didn't go to see his sons that he didn't like them. . . . We discussed this recently and I found out that the reason he stopped seeing them was because he thought I didn't want him to.

> He knows now that this is not accurate and he does want to see them.

> Now for the part of your letter that is directed at me:

Each and every one of my children . . . made their childhood mistakes. Because they were given proper parental guidance, they rose above their mistakes.

[At this point in her letter, Alice responded point by point to a series of allegations about her kids with equally malicious allegations about Virginia's kids. Further, she threatened to report Virginia to federal postal investigators for opening insurance checks that were made out to Gerald.]

My opinion of you has changed. Unfortunately, I gave you credit for a little more intelligence than you actually have. Not only are you now (or have been in the past) a parasite on the taxpayers, you are a snoop that breaks federal laws.

One thing that Gerald forgot to mention. Your half of the boys' fare is (at present time) $572. You can either send it to us before their return flight or you can pay it from your end. Their reservations for a return flight are made for April 13.

I guess you aren't capable of reading a return address to see who a letter is from [a reference to the insurance check snafu] so I will spell it out.

Alice

Once more, Virginia scrawled "Alice, Jan. 1980" on the back of the letter and filed it away. She didn't have $572, but she knew there were no airline reservations. It was just Alice's way of reminding Virginia that her life sucked.

A few days later, another letter arrived in Virginia's mailbox. Five pages long, it was also unsigned and undated. It was Gerald's handwriting, but oozed with Alice's unmistakable vitriol and lacerating style. Had she drafted the letter for Gerald to copy in his own hand? Why would she even try to make it appear that somebody else had written it?

Regardless, the letter took a direct shot at Virginia's heart. In unambiguous terms, it outlined the Udens' plan to take what was most valuable to Virginia: her money and her sons. Ironically, Alice had zealously avoided meeting the boys or Virginia when she had several chances. Now she purposely played the role of a benevolent stepmother who'd be better for children than their wicked mother. It was a calculated slap in Virginia's face.

Virginia,

Our records show that we made the Sept payment. It seems to me that every time you move anymore you forget to leave a forwarding address. I can't help it if the mail gets lost because you want to hide.

I guess it's time I have a say about the harassment we have received in the last 3½ years. Up till now I have been easy going and let things slide, Every time I turn around any more you are threatening to go to court for something so I guess that's what I'm going to do also. I have never liked the idea of not seeing the boys or contacting them. . . . This *will* change.

I have never been around a more selfish, domineering, scheming person than you. You never had any intention of wanting a father for the boys. Your only interest is in the money. . . .

I'm not sure you are a good influence on the boys, or mentally capable where they are concerned. You seem to have some pretty sick ideas about a father-son relationship.

It may interest you to know I have been seeing an attorney for some months now to see what we can do to straighten this mess out. I have been reluctant to start proceedings because of possible harm it could do to my sons. Since you insist on this course of action I am proceeding also.

I will insist on visitation rights. You live too far away for weekly visits so they will have to come for the summer and holidays such as Christmas and Easter. Of course while they are here the support money would stop. My attorney feels a judge would be very interested in your dirty, underhanded dealing.

I want the chance to be the dad to my boys that I was not allowed to be. Having the boys here will give me the chance to help them grow up and become men, instead of street bums or mama's boys tied to her apron strings. Richard & Reagan carry my name (I think) and I intend that they do so with honor. . . .

When a child reaches the age of 14 [Reagan and Richard were 10 and 11 at the time] they can choose to live with either parent and there isn't anything the other can do about it. Alice and I intend to do everything we can to show my sons that they would be much happier living with us. We have so much more to offer them than you ever will. . . . I intend to see my boys grow up having some real fun in life. . . .

We are really looking forward to their coming to be with us and having the time so that Alice can get to know her two new sons. Alice is really good with kids and I'm sure that she will have them loving her in no time. . . . There is nothing that will give me more pleasure than watching them grow up just like me.

There is one way you could stop all of this and that is to have the adoption set aside and declared null and void. I don't think you'll do that. You worked and schemed too hard to give up now.

You have no honor or self-respect. No one on welfare does.

Gerald's (or Alice's) letter ends with a sarcastic "Happy New Year" and adds a postscript reminding Virginia to send the boys' Easter vacation dates so airline reservations could be finalized. And a final dig: "Did you get permission from a court to take the boys out of Wyo? Because I never gave [my permission]."

And, again, Virginia wrote Gerald's name on the back.

Before she could reply, another letter arrived. This time, Alice heaped more insult on the intentional injuries of Gerald's (?) last letter, in her inimitable slashing style. She knew just how to efficiently disembowel another mother, like slaughtering a chicken.

Virginia,

Just wanted you to know we sent you a money order in September. Since it was never returned to us, I will have to assume you received it and are trying to hold us up for more money. You will have to furnish more proof that you didn't get it. . . .

I'm looking forward to meeting my new sons. I know the three of us will get along just fine and will love one another in no time at all. With the experience I've had of raising five children, three of them sons, I know just what boys need to make them happy. They will love their new mother.

We are going to have our boys for part of every year and hopefully in the future *on a permanent basis* for as many years as Gerald is their legal father. That is the only way we can mold them to be like their father. We have to have some influence in their lives if they are ever to bring honor to Gerald's name. We know that you haven't the ability to do so, as your past record shows.

If you think we're bluffing then you are in for a big shock come Easter. The boys will come to Wyoming or you'll go to court on contempt charges. . . .

If you try to disappear to avoid this, you will lose the support money.

As Gerald says,

Happy New Year

In surprisingly short order, more letters arrived in January from the Udens, all of them reiterating the same noxious threats about visitation, lost child support checks, lawsuits, and name-calling. On each, Virginia scribbled the name of the sender, whether Gerald or Alice, and put it in a box with the others.

It overwhelmed Virginia. In mid-February 1980, she composed a long, desperate letter to the district judge in Lander, asking if anything the Udens had threatened to do to her would stand up in court.

In the letter, she described her abortive marriage to Gerald, which seemed to implode after he adopted her two sons. He occasionally swatted them both with a belt, but he had a special animosity toward Richard, she said. The little boy was not allowed in the same room with Gerald, except at dinner, she claimed. And when the slightly odd Richard was bullied by kids at school, Gerald only said that the kid probably had it coming.

Another time, Reagan developed a serious eye infection while Virginia was out of town, she told the judge. The eyeball swelled with blood, but Gerald refused to take him to the doctor.

She also recounted how Gerald once shot a bird, and, knowing Richard was inordinately sensitive about innocent animals, he tossed the carcass to the cat, which tore it to pieces in front of Richard. The child became hysterical and incoherent ... which made Gerald mad.

The boys knew about the recent nasty letters, which upset them terribly, she said. Reagan cried most of the time now, and Richard—who now attended a special school—suffered with bad grades, persistent ulcers, and possible Hodgkin's disease or leukemia. Sending them to Gerald and Alice would be disastrous, she said.

"Could you tell me if the court would make me send them or return to Wyo?" Virginia pleaded with the judge. "Can you tell me if [Gerald] has taken any action yet, or let me know when he does? And does he have to pay support if I don't send them?"

In a two-page response, the judge told Virginia that he couldn't say much. The costs of visitation are ordinarily paid entirely by the visitor, not the custodian, he wrote, but it simply "would not be appropriate for the Court to offer advice or consolation." He sent a copy of his letter to the Udens too.

In April 1980, with her hope and options dwindling, Virginia filed a last-ditch complaint in New Jersey's Domestic Relations Court. She claimed Gerald's $150-a-month child support was sporadic and inadequate. But when Gerald's lawyer showed receipts that proved he'd paid it faithfully every month, as ordered in the divorce decree, the judge ruled against Virginia.

Alone, empty, and stranded emotionally, Virginia had reached the end of her road and herself. It was time to turn back. As soon as the school year ended, she decided she would return to Wyoming, where she could live with her mom in the trailer behind the Riverton laundry, find a job, and have some help with the boys.

And maybe regain a little equilibrium.

The journey to Wyoming from the Jersey shore took three days.

Virginia's crappy little car was barely big enough for her, the boys, and all their clothes. It broke down several times on the weeklong journey. She left furniture, toys, kitchenware, and everything else behind in New Jersey, hoping she could rent a cheap trailer in Wyoming and go back to pick it up later. It was just stuff. She had her boys and they were the most important things in her life.

And in the summer of 1980, she had her mom again. Claire Martin was overjoyed when her prodigal daughter and grandsons pulled up in the alley beside Superior Laundry.

Virginia still had second thoughts. She wasn't sure Wyoming should be more than a rest stop. New Jersey simply offered more chances to succeed . . . or fail. There were special schools for Richard that Wyoming didn't have. And the boys themselves embodied her indecision: one wanted to stay, and one wanted to go back.

Virginia had never stayed anywhere long. Her idea of "home" was where her mom and kids were.

For now, they were all home. For now.

Life could restart.

Gerald and Alice learned Virginia was back in town when she called to tell them where to send the next child support check. It put them in a predicament: After making such a big deal about visitation, they couldn't very well continue to ignore Richard and Reagan.

As much as Alice believed ex-lovers, ex-wives, and ex-families should be invisible, Virginia and the boys weren't disappearing.

They hadn't been back very long before Gerald made the first move. He called Virginia to arrange a sleepover for the boys at his house. Virginia consented, and they arranged a time to pick the boys up.

Gerald arrived at the appointed time, but Virginia asked if she could meet Alice first. After all, if her boys were to spend the night in somebody else's house, she wanted to know who'd be watching them.

Gerald agreed, but as Virginia and the boys went out to the car where Alice waited, Alice quickly ducked down in the seat.

"No, no," Gerald blurted. "Never mind. That's not gonna work."

"But I want to know who—" Virginia started to say.

"Well, you know me," he said. "That's enough."

"But—"

"No, that's enough."

The boys jumped in the car, and Gerald drove away, Alice still hiding. And it became the routine every time Gerald picked them up—there were several times—that he'd go to the door alone while Alice stayed out of sight. She adamantly refused to meet Virginia.

No matter. Virginia had been busy fussing with her future.

She'd put a $50 deposit on a decrepit old mobile home where she and the boys could live. She withdrew her last thousand dollars from the bank for the trip to retrieve her furniture and home goods from New Jersey, and Claire kept it safe for her in a Mason jar on the shelf. Virginia called the insurance company about the checks that never seemed to get to her. She and Gerald spoke a few times, and he didn't seem to know about all the nasty letters she'd gotten while she was back East. And she secretly planned to sue Gerald for more child support money to cover the boys' considerable medical expenses, which swamped her.

Still, the bad mojo never stopped. Richard had been hospitalized three times since they got back. Just a couple mornings before, he'd awakened with another scary lump on his neck. It'd happened before. Virginia rushed him to the hospital, where he was admitted for an overnight biopsy. Gerald even visited, and Virginia took her chance to ask if he knew of anybody who'd let her borrow a sizable trailer that she might use to retrieve her possessions in New Jersey.

It was almost sweet. She told her mother Gerald had been cordial, maybe pleasant, since she'd returned to Wyoming. Alice still remained distant and, in Virginia's mind, evil.

Although the sleepovers were mostly uneventful, the boys came home from one and told their grandmother Claire that Gerald and Alice had locked them in an unused travel trailer overnight. They slept on a dirty mattress on the floor.

But the real highlight of that weekend was a fishing trip to a nearby reservoir in Gerald's boat. Stopping at the deepest, coldest part of the lake, Gerald commanded the boys to strip down to their underwear and jump into the water to practice swimming.

"Sink or swim," he said.

Richard and Reagan leaped into the stunningly cold water and immediately dog-paddled back toward the boat. But Gerald wouldn't let them in. In fact, he motored away from them, shouting that it'd make them better swimmers.

Reagan freaked out and started crying. Richard treaded water beside his brother and tried to calm him as they watched the boat motor farther and farther away. When it seemed impossibly far, they both frantically screamed for help.

Alice caved first. She ordered Gerald to rescue them, so Gerald turned around, drew the boat alongside the terrified boys, and hoisted their skinny-stiff little bodies onto the deck, where they whimpered and shivered for a long time.

The fishing trip was over.

Free will is a funny thing. A man might say he's doing what he wants to do when he's actually only doing what he's told—because he only wants to do what he's told to do. He believes in the myth of choice because he has no choice.

Such a man is at the mercy of his master . . . or mistress.

It was a Thursday night, September 11, 1980, when Gerald called Virginia at her mom's mobile home. Good news, he said: The guy who sold him hay had a flatbed trailer he'd loan Virginia to haul her New Jersey possessions back to Wyoming, if she wanted it. She could check it out tomorrow out near his place. In fact, he told her he had the next day, Friday, off and invited the boys bird hunting, which the boys loved.

They arranged to meet at two Friday afternoon at the isolated corner of Tunnel Hill and Williams Roads, a half mile from the Udens' place but visible from their house, because Alice still wouldn't allow Virginia on her property. Virginia could see the trailer, drop the boys in Gerald's care, and return to town to help her mom at the laundry for the afternoon. Sounded like a plan, and they hung up.

A free trailer was happy news. She found her mother at the laundry.

"Guess who just called me," she said.

"I can't imagine," Claire replied.

"Gerald."

Claire sat up. That was unexpected.

"He told me he can get me a trailer," Virginia continued. "You know, to go back and get my things from New Jersey. It belongs to a man who sells him hay that was going to loan the trailer, but he didn't mention any names."

Claire was a tad befuddled. Even if the nastiness had abated lately, Virginia would never ask Gerald for anything except more child support and money for doctor bills. Certainly no favors.

Maybe Virginia was a little befuddled too.

"I can't imagine Gerald doing me any favors at this point," she confessed. "But if I can get a trailer that won't cost me anything, it'll save me some money."

Claire understood what her only child had endured for the past few years, and it broke her heart. She knew the map of loneliness like the web of scars and veins on the back of her hand. She saw that Virginia was aching, broke, and confused. A thirty-two-year-old single mom, her daughter feared life had passed her by like a freight train passes a bum, and there was no catching up. She didn't date or hold any real job very long. If things were thawing with her ex-husband, maybe it wasn't the worst thing happening in her life, but Claire couldn't help being suspicious.

It was curious timing to Virginia too. She planned to call a lawyer the next morning to start the paperwork for more money from Gerald, but she was willing to give him a chance to redeem himself a little. And the boys still loved their dad, even if she didn't.

"He also asked me to bring the boys along," she told Claire. "He said he'd take them bird hunting. He asked me to bring your old .22. That OK?"

Shooting birds with a .22? Claire had never heard of such a thing, but Virginia seemed intent to keep the date. Reluctant to set off Virginia's hair-trigger rage, she didn't say anything more that night.

The next morning, as promised, Virginia called her lawyer's office and told the secretary to start the paperwork. Richard and Reagan, old enough to sense the coming storm, overheard her and were distressed. They told her they didn't want their bird-hunting trip to be ruined by another argument between Virginia and Gerald. They begged her not to upset him or start a fight.

"Isn't there another way you could do this?" Claire asked her after the boys made their tearful case. "Rather than go through court . . ."

"I'm just tired of arguing with him," a melancholy Virginia said. "I want to do something definite about it right now, before it goes farther."

Claire understood the desire for finality but worried for the boys. She knew Virginia planned to confront Gerald, probably today. The timing was bad. It wouldn't end pretty.

"Please don't go out there with the thought in your mind that you're going to fight with Gerald—in front of the boys."

Virginia slumped. "I've had it. I'm just tired of the whole thing."

They let it go. Claire went to the sporting goods store that morning and bought a box of .22 shells for the outing. The day was cloudy but warm. No jackets would be needed.

After lunch, the boys were so excited to see Gerald and shoot guns that they cleaned out Claire's old Country Squire station wagon. They sat inside a half hour before they were to leave, fingering Claire's old .22, fantasizing about bull's-eyes and impatiently waiting for their grand safari to start.

Finally, it was one thirty. Time to hit the road. Claire gave her daughter five bucks for gas and told her to drive safely.

After some grandmotherly gun-safety warnings to the boys from Claire, Virginia started up the car. She pulled slowly past the laundry's back entry and tooted her horn. Standing in the doorway, Claire waved goodbye to her daughter and grandsons, who were bouncing like crazy kids in the back seat, excited to be with their father again.

Chapter 2

LAST SEEN

SEPTEMBER 12, 1980

Virginia and the boys arrived a few minutes early, but Gerald was already there.

Just him, no truck.

He stood alone beside the fat, dusty delta of Williams Road, where impatient country drivers with their horse trailers and hay loads on Tunnel Hill Road had cut the corners clean off. Even so, Gerald just called it "the corner," even if there wasn't a single corner at the whole intersection.

Virginia pulled up, and Gerald slid into the passenger seat and greeted the boys warmly. They were wired and could hardly wait. Virginia asked him about the loaner trailer, but he told her the guy was running late and they could see it on the way back. Gerald then directed Virginia to drive another few miles, maybe five or six, to a spot he knew was perfect for shooting.

The old Country Squire trailed a plume of ocher road dust north while Gerald continued to stoke the boys' excitement. Virginia didn't say much, just drove.

Dry clouds slid across the sky. There was no sign of rain, no smell of snow, just a bleak cast on the bruise-colored landscape. The whole landscape, normally just drab, was now also flat and shadowless. Only the corpse-white hardpan stood out in the tattletale gray air.

Gerald knew exactly where he wanted to stop to shoot. Up around a big bend, where the irrigation canal passes under a low-slung, two-lane beam bridge. In a natural bowl hidden from passersby. No houses nearby. Just past the sandstone hoodoos that stood like broken bad teeth, some bearing ancient petroglyphs by long-dead natives, some bearing not-so-ancient markings by drunken teenagers and rabbit hunters. A remote spot nobody was likely to pass, at least not without being seen a long way off.

"Here," Gerald said. "This is it."

Virginia pulled off into the cheatgrass shoulder this side of the canal. The water ran sluggish and buckskin brown, full of sandrock dust, caliche, horseshit, and other high plains compost. There was so much dirt in the channel that you could damn near plow it.

They spilled out of the station wagon, boys first. Richard and Reagan clamored to start the shooting, arguing who'd get the first shot, but Gerald told them he still had to build the collapsible .22 rifle and test-fire it first.

While Gerald put the gun together and loaded it, the boys jacked around. Virginia kept only half an eye on them. Claire had bought .22 short shells, less stopping power than a long shell. Probably didn't matter much when the game was small.

Gerald fired a couple shots into the salt sage, at nothing in particular, just to make sure the gun wouldn't jam. When the crack of the shots faded away, he listened for cars that might be coming.

Virginia had her back to him, looking across the road, when he put the muzzle of the gun against the back of her head and fired. She dropped like a sack of grain right where she stood.

Eleven-year-old Richard was farting around with some bullets on the open tailgate, not paying attention, when Gerald shot him behind the left ear. He, too, crumpled where he stood.

Reagan, though, had seen his older brother die. Terrified, he dashed toward the canal, screaming. At the water's edge, he stumbled and fell into the muddy water. Gerald followed him calmly, as if he were stalking a wounded animal. He stretched out his gun hand and shot the ten-year-old child behind his ear too.

The killing was easier than it should be. It wasn't at all like Hollywood, with great gusts of blood and brain matter. The little .22 bullets just ricocheted like a deadly pinball in the skull. No twitching. The boys didn't bleed as much as Virginia, but they probably didn't die instantly. Their little hearts probably beat for ten seconds, maybe more. Their lungs breathed. Gerald killed their brains, but the rest of them struggled to survive a little longer. Alive but no longer living.

Gerald shoved their bodies into the back of the station wagon. The boys' corpses were light, thank God, but he didn't notice Virginia's head wound was still leaking as he heaved her in. He just wanted to get them home before some yokel came along and ruined everything.

On the road home, three dead bodies in back, Gerald tried to think straight. Did he leave any clues? Might somebody find the bloody stain from Virginia's wound beside the road? He felt confused, cold-blooded, guilty, paranoid.

And oddly relieved.

That no cars passed while he was slaughtering three people.

That his plan worked. The funny part was there had never been a free trailer to borrow. But if he let her go back to New Jersey, he'd have missed his chance.

That he only had to tell one lie. *They never arrived,* he'd say. Cops couldn't prove otherwise. Stupid people got caught because they had to juggle a lot of lies.

That he was such a good shot they didn't seem to suffer. He really didn't want to track any of them like a gutshot deer dragging its own intestines across the prairie.

That the carnage had been efficient. Less than a half minute.

That he wasn't forced to use his father's .45 semiautomatic army pistol, which he'd hidden in his waistband and expected to use. That saved him the heartache of destroying a cherished family gun just because it was an incriminating murder weapon.

That he hadn't gotten any blood on his good jeans.

That he had the courage to overcome his fear of killing a woman whom he'd once loved and bedded and two little boys who called him Daddy . . . not long before they died, in fact.

That what he did was evil, not who he was.

That he saved himself just shy of $14,000 it would have cost him in child support before Reagan, the youngest, was an adult. He knew because he'd added it up: $150 for ninety-two more months. His thirty pieces of silver.

That he solved the problem of Virginia.

And that Alice would stay with him forever now that Virginia had disappeared, like ex-wives should.

Alice would be pleased.

Now, Virginia and the boys were past caring. Gerald, though, had plenty to worry about.

He drove them back to the house. According to plan, Alice was at her parents' trailer, playing cards, so she could distract them if they got suspicious. Gerald parked the station wagon on the other side of his '68 Ford pickup so if the in-laws were watching, their view would be blocked.

He first hefted the boys' limp bodies into the pickup's bed, then dragged Virginia to the station wagon's tailgate.

Oh, shit.

Virginia had been leaking worse than he thought. Her bright red blood stained the car's cheap cargo mat, the floorboards, and the back of the seat. After dumping her in the back of the truck, he tried to hose out the blood but only made a bigger mess. *To hell with it*, he thought.

Gerald retrieved some empty feed sacks from the barn to hide the bodies, weighting them down with rocks and other heavy crap in the back of the truck. All the jostling had restarted a steady trickle of blood from Virginia's punctured skull, but now it didn't matter. Nobody would think twice about old blood in his truck. A lot of deer and antelope carcasses had bled out back there.

The next ruse: After hiding the Country Squire behind the pig barn, he went inside to fetch his Weatherby hunting rifle and a shotgun, which he displayed openly in the pickup's gun rack, even though he had no intention of firing them. He stopped at his in-laws' trailer on his way off the property and announced he was going sage chicken hunting. He'd be back by dark, he said. Maybe a Friday afternoon hunting trip sounded like an odd, impulsive idea, but Gerald was an odd, impulsive guy. Nobody batted an eye. Especially Alice, who called more shots than Gerald would admit.

On the road by two thirty, Gerald knew exactly where he was going, a couple hours away. He stuck to the little back roads to avoid people as much as possible.

He needed to top off his tank, or risk running out of gas with three dead bodies in back. He didn't want some gas monkey eyeballing his cargo, but only a couple stations in the county offered self-serve. One of them was the Milford Store, a dowdy little mercantile with a few pumps on the edge of the reservation. The whitewashed mom-and-pop market sat at a secluded crossroads where traffic and questions were sparse. The perfect place for local farm kids to redeem old bottles for ice cream in the summer, and for a mass murderer to gas up.

It was almost three o'clock when Gerald's pickup rolled off the highway across the gravel to the Milford Store's pumps. Just as he'd hoped, he was alone out there. He got out of the truck and quickly checked to see that his grim cargo hadn't been uncovered.

Oh, shit.

The pump was jammed.

Before he could jump back in the cab and speed away, the store's teenage attendant came out to reset it. Gerald froze.

Since the kid was there, he graciously pumped Gerald's gas. While he stood beside the truck, the pump clicking, he looked down to see some reddish fluid dripping from the bed onto the gravel.

"Hey, you got a leak or something," he said, pointing at a trickly blotch just under the bed.

Gerald thought fast.

"Transmission fluid," he sputtered. The dumb kid bought it, even though it wasn't the right shade of red and wasn't coming from anywhere near the transmission.

Good enough, Gerald said. He shoved seven bucks in the kid's hand and got out of there before the kid got wise.

Virginia's wound had continued to ooze. He had a god-awful mess back there. So he stopped at a hidden swale on the road and shoveled some shoulder dirt in the bed, just to soak up as much gore as possible.

Gerald still needed gas, so he backtracked to town, where he found a cheap self-serve station. He topped off his tank and, for good measure, filled a five-gallon jerry can that had been rattling around in back with the bodies.

Finally, he was ready for the last, long leg of his ghastly run.

In the late nineteenth century, the old Hidden Hand mine was dug in a vast wasteland known today as the Lewiston gold-mining district. It surrounded South Pass City, a thriving Oregon Trail stop that had been a ghost town since the Great Depression.

Mining in the 1800s was freewheeling, risky, and dangerous. Most little mines were dug by one or two prospectors, maybe a family operation. Big commercial operations needed the right time, the right people, the right science, the right technology to dig; lone prospectors could buy a claim on Monday and be digging on Tuesday . . . and walk away by Friday. Thus, the district was pockmarked with abandoned mines, big and small—from dents in the soil that exuded lost hopes to great, deep holes that suggested played-out hopes.

The Hidden Hand was one of those. In its day—roughly 1885 to 1930—the Hidden Hand produced a lot of gold. Its shaft plunged a hundred feet deep into Wyoming earth, but sometimes the richest ore came when miners excavated horizontal offshoots ("drifts") or rooms ("stopes") off the main shaft.

Gerald had recently hunted out there, the emptiest corner of the Big Empty. He slept one night in a decaying Hidden Hand cabin that had been built with timbers salvaged from a decommissioned 1870s US Army cavalry fort nearby. Once, he even went down in the Hidden Hand mine, such as it was, and crawled into one of its side rooms, which couldn't be seen from above.

By that time, though, what was once pay dirt was now just dirt. Much of the mine's vertical shaft had collapsed in on itself. Getting there was a four-wheeling adventure on a tangled snake's nest of rough, two-track roads. If one happened to get there, one shouldn't expect to see another human for weeks, maybe months.

A perfect place to hide a body, Gerald thought.

Oh, there were other ways. He'd thought about where to stash Virginia and the boys ever since he decided to kill them less than a week before.

He considered tossing them in the waste dump at US Steel, but that was too risky.

He considered incinerating them in the mine's 2,200-degree blast furnace, which he could operate. But he worried about a telltale smell of burned human flesh. Again, too risky.

He considered dumping them in a burning underground coal seam out by the village of Hudson, where he'd once lived with Virginia. But if something went wrong, he couldn't very well go down there and fix it. Again, too risky.

He considered feeding them to his hogs, bit by bit. That would require butchering them, probably on his kitchen table. He'd only have to collect the teeth—the only body part the hogs couldn't digest—and destroy or hide them. Too messy . . . and too risky.

He considered, briefly, barbecuing them and . . . no, no, not that. He shook off the notion quicker than the grisly scene popped into his brain. Gerald was a lot of things, but he wasn't a cannibal.

The Hidden Hand mine was perfect, and not just for its ironic name. It was unlikely anybody would stumble upon the corpses out there, much less his actual dumping. Wild animals and bugs would destroy the evidence soon enough. And Alice had dumped her abusive husband's body in an old mine shaft, and nobody was likely to ever find it.

Perfect.

Gerald found the Hidden Hand while it was still daylight. He scanned the horizon with his rifle scope. Nobody for five miles in any direction, probably a lot farther. *Nobody.*

He backed his wretched pickup to the edge of the mine and opened the tailgate. He dragged the three bodies out of the bed, then let gravity suck their dead weight into the deep hole.

Then he climbed down to the bottom, now maybe only twenty feet, and dragged them, one by one, into a stope. The claustrophobic little side room wasn't big—just barely enough space for a big guy like Gerald to maneuver around on his hands and knees while arranging three dead people so they couldn't be spotted by a hunter or prospector passing above. Luckily for him, rigor mortis hadn't yet made them awkward to move. But he had to get real close to them, close enough to smell their blood.

Back where he'd killed them, Gerald had picked up Richard's glasses and put them in his pocket. He left them with the body in the mine.

Finally, he clambered out of the old hole, their new grave. It was like climbing a river because its sloping wall was slippery with loose dirt and stones. Standing on the rim, he looked back down into the mine. Maybe it could be deeper, but his little hidey-hole worked.

He briefly contemplated stealing some dynamite from US Steel, collapsing the Hidden Hand, and burying the dead in one thunderous blast, but that felt like overkill. Nobody would ever find Virginia and the boys now, so why risk drawing unwanted attention with a big explosion or blowing himself up?

Gerald just walked away. No goodbyes, no prayers, no regrets. The weight of heaven didn't burden him at all.

He had to hit the road. It was past four o'clock, and the trip home to Pavillion and his beloved Alice would take two hours. He had plenty of gas, he could stick to main roads, and it'd be dark when he got there.

But this tragedy had one last act.

After nine, Claire Martin started to worry, even if she wouldn't admit it to herself. After all, she was a mother.

Virginia was a big girl, and she didn't have any childhood curfews, Claire told herself. She could afford to take the boys out for dinner, and maybe they went to the movies afterward. Maybe she ran into friends, or stopped to see a girlfriend, or had a flat tire, or . . . just to be sure, Claire picked up the phone and dialed Gerald's number.

The pleasantries were brief.

"Where's Virginia?" Gerald asked. He was mad.

"What do you mean, 'Where's Virginia?'" Claire responded.

"She never came."

"You were going to bring the boys back, weren't you?"

"I haven't seen any of them!" he said. "They never got here."

"What do you mean?"

"They were supposed to meet me at two o'clock, but they never showed up. I haven't seen any of them today."

"Did you wait at the corner, like you were supposed to? You were supposed to meet her at the corner, weren't you?"

"Yeah, I waited."

"How long?"

"A long time."

"Just how long? Did you give her time to get there, in case she had a flat tire or a breakdown or something?"

"I was there for at least an hour. Maybe longer."

"Are you sure they didn't show up, Gerald?"

"I haven't seen anything of them, at all."

Claire was flummoxed. "You didn't see my car in the neighborhood or anything?"

"Nothing."

"Well, I don't know what might have happened."

"Me neither," Gerald told her. "Maybe Virginia changed her plans or something. You know, just decided that she didn't want to see me."

Claire expected Virginia to call any minute, but she wasn't going to sit and wait.

"I'm about to close up the laundry," she said. "I think I'll get a friend to go out with me to look around."

Gerald quickly volunteered to help.

"No need. Why don't I come to town and pick you up?" he offered. "We'll go around and look for her."

"Oh, it really isn't necessary, Gerald," she said, still trying to convince herself that Virginia had probably just changed plans. "I'm here now. I'll just go look for them."

"No, no, you just wait there," he insisted. "I'll come in to town and pick you up."

Claire closed up the laundry, as usual, at ten. She called her friend Marie Roskowske and asked Marie to drive her around to help search for Virginia. Marie knew both Virginia (whom she liked) and Gerald (whom she hated), and she knew about the friction between them. Claire recounted the strange phone call with Gerald, how Virginia and the boys never showed up for the hunting trip that afternoon.

"That son of a bitch did something to them," Marie said.

Claire brushed it off. She still wanted to believe the whole situation was all more worry than it was worth. Virginia would show up, and they'd laugh after they cried.

Together, they waited for Gerald to show up. And waited. Long after the boys' usual bedtime, Claire admitted aloud to Marie she was getting genuinely a little worried.

Finally, around eleven o'clock, they decided to go out and search, just the two of them, without the undependable Gerald. Claire locked up, and they got into Marie's little sedan. Marie pulled out of the laundry's driveway onto the street, where her headlights lit up a passing red Pinto—with Gerald inside.

Marie honked. Gerald parked and jumped in the front passenger seat of Marie's car. Claire sat in back, behind Gerald. He squirmed a lot, leaning curiously forward in the seat. He shuffled his feet until the floor mat doubled over. In fact, he fidgeted so much that Marie thought he might rub a worry hole in the knee of his jeans.

He told them, again, how Virginia and the boys never showed up. The point needed to be made. They quizzed him about the details, but he stuck to his story: *They never came.*

The three of them went to Riverton's drive-in theater first, because Virginia had earlier mused about taking the boys there. The kid at the box office let them drive inside, where they prowled up and down the rows of cars while somebody broadcast a message on the window speakers. But Virginia and the boys weren't there.

Outside the drive-in, they found a pay phone and called the town's two indoor theaters. No luck.

They weren't at the hospital either.

The three of them rolled past all the places with big public parking lots, drive-throughs, convenience stores, and fast food joints, but most of the town's sidewalks were already rolled up, even on a Friday night. Virginia wasn't at a bar because when she drank, she just fell asleep. If they passed a place that was open, Claire or Marie would go inside to ask if anybody had seen Virginia or the boys, but Gerald never got out of the car.

Out of the blue, Claire asked what Alice thought about Gerald looking for his ex-wife.

"She's out looking too," he said.

"I can't imagine that, Gerald," Claire said. How Alice felt about Virginia wasn't exactly a secret.

"No, I talked to her," he said. "I asked her just this one time to help us find Virginia because something might have happened to her."

Alice planned to meet him at midnight at the Montgomery Ward if the search petered out, Gerald said.

They drove around town two or three times but found no sign of Virginia, the boys, or the Country Squire. It was just before midnight when they ended up back at the laundry, tired and distressed.

"I've had enough," Claire said from the back seat. She began to cry for the first time. "Let's go to the sheriff."

Gerald quickly got out of the car.

"If you girls are going to the sheriff," he said, slightly piqued, "I'm gonna find my wife and go home."

"Why don't you come with us?" Claire asked.

"No, no. I'm going home."

Gerald got in his car and drove away. Claire and Marie went to the Fremont County Sheriff's Office, but it was locked up for the night. They made one last fruitless pass through town and headed back to the laundry—where they saw Gerald again in his red Pinto, cruising along slowly. Maybe he was still looking.

Back at Claire's trailer, they arranged to file a missing person report at the sheriff in the morning. Marie left, and Claire began to call family and friends—anybody she could think of—to ask about Virginia. Nobody had seen her.

But Marie wasn't done. She parked on a side street near the Montgomery Ward, where Gerald said he'd meet Alice at midnight, and watched. Neither of them showed.

Claire didn't sleep that night.

She listened for the door to open.

She watched for a light to come on in the other room.

She waited for the phone to ring.

She stared into the darkness that smothered her, unwilling to expect the worst and unable to hope for the best.

The sun eventually came up, but the phone never rang, and a new day never came.

Just a sliver of the waxing moon occasionally shone between the clouds that dark night. Midnight was an accomplice.

Back at the Pavillion place, Gerald transferred some personal stuff—Virginia's purse, some coats and bloody clothing, and the murder gun—out of the station wagon into his shed.

Leaving Eliza asleep in her bed, he drove the Country Squire toward the mountains east of town, while Alice followed closely in her Pinto. His truck would have been better, but she hated driving it. He knew a spot on the barely maintained Dickinson Park Road, way up, far beyond where the pavement ended. He'd been there many times, hunting and picnicking. There, he could roll the car into the mile-deep Trout Creek Canyon, where nobody went and where it'd never be found.

It was the deep end of night when they arrived. Gerald steered the station wagon off the one-lane dirt road and parked it facing down a little slope toward the black canyon. Alice parked the Pinto on the road above so her headlights illuminated Gerald's sinister work. She didn't get out.

Gerald shifted the gear handle into neutral and pushed the car toward the gorge. When it started to roll faster on its own, he just stood back and admired his own nefarious brilliance. He wanted to hear a few seconds of silence before it crashed a thousand feet below, as if this were all a Saturday-morning cartoon.

The station wagon picked up speed, jounced over some sagebrush, and . . . veered away from the canyon's edge. To his dismay, it caromed toward some trees and, with a metallic crunch, lodged on a huge boulder.

A hundred feet from the road.

In plain sight.

Oh, shit.

How could the damn thing take a wrong turn on its own? Gerald stood there in the blackness, recalculating.

Maybe he could back up and start over. He got in and turned the key. The engine came on, but the car wouldn't budge. It was good and stuck.

Maybe he could push it off the rock. Nope, not even with Alice's help.

Maybe he could yank it off with the . . . Pinto? Dammit. Maybe with his truck, but not with Alice's gutless little piece of crap.

Maybe come back tomorrow, in daylight, with the truck. Nah, too risky.

Maybe he could burn it into unrecognizability. *Yeah, that's a good idea,* he thought. He looked around for some paper and found an empty paper bag in the back of the station wagon. He removed the gas cap, wadded it into the gas tank's filler neck, and lit it with some matches. But while the flame slowly grew, he worried the fire might get out of control, or burn so bright that it could be seen in the valley below. He quickly doused the burning sack.

The Country Squire was going nowhere tonight. The best plan might be to hide it as well as possible, maybe slow down any snoopers, and contrive a plausible story about why his fingerprints were all over the damn car.

With only the Pinto's headlights to light the dark, Gerald locked up Virginia's car. He unscrewed the vehicle's license plates and busted its reflective turning lights with his camping hatchet; no need to make it easy for a passing car's headlights to light it up. Then he hacked some pine boughs to camouflage the vehicle from the road.

Because he'd hunted so often up there—that's why he picked the place—Gerald drove Alice's Pinto down the mountain's rough roads. At a particularly bumpy patch, he scraped the undercarriage on some rocks, knocking the plug off the oil pan. They drove home with only enough oil to keep the engine from seizing up.

When they finally got home, it was only a few hours until dawn. It had been a long, eventful day. Shit had happened. They both felt unburdened, even a little giddy about getting away with murder, but also bone-tired, so they didn't have sex.

They just fell asleep in each other's arms.

Chapter 3

TOMORROW . . .

Claire and Marie closed the laundry Saturday morning and resumed their search before breakfast. They drove out to a nearby lake, where they explored irrigation ditches, campgrounds, rest areas, under bridges, everywhere. They even shined flashlights into fetid outhouse toilets because, God forbid, a corpse might fit in there.

They also scoured a vast, hilly district known as Sand Draw, looking for evidence of . . . anything. The car, its tracks, familiar artifacts dropped on the ground, blood spots, footprints, shallow graves, anything.

Arid and sandy, nobody lived out there, just jackrabbits, deer, antelope, and a few elk. A few decent two-tracks allowed teenagers and the occasional hunter easy access to arroyos and draws that afforded privacy for anyone seeking to shoot, drink, or screw out there. Or to kill somebody, themselves maybe.

Claire and Marie found nothing.

Back in town by midmorning, they went to the sheriff's office. A young deputy asked perfunctory missing-person questions—Virginia was an unemployed white female, thirty-two, five-six, one-seventy, blue-green eyes, brown hair, medium complexion, a blood clot in her left eye, and upper and lower dentures. The car was a "1973 Ford stwgn (brown) Lic WY 22-1331."

The deputy dutifully filled out his form, adding under "Additional Information" that Virginia and her two sons were last seen going hunting with ex-husband Gerald Uden and had a .22 rifle in the car.

He checked his watch and wrote "9/13/1980" and "1123" next to his signature, and told Claire to be patient.

"I'll just hold onto this until tomorrow," the deputy said. "Then I'll come over, and we'll go over it."

"Well, that does me a lot of good," Claire fumed. "You're not gonna search or anything, and you're not gonna help us search?"

"No," he replied as if a distraught grandmother who'd been up all night wasn't a big deal. "Instead of searching for your family, we'll first try to find the car."

Claire was confused.

"Don't the people in the car matter?"

"This is the way we do it," he tried to assure her. "They'll probably be in the car."

"Not necessarily. You don't know what happened to them at this point. You have no idea. You don't know what happened to the car. You could find the car empty somewhere, and then where are you? My family is still missing."

It went like that for a while, but the deputy wasn't budging.

Claire persisted. She suggested places to search for the car, but the deputy didn't seem interested.

"We'll just have to wait until we find the car."

They can't look for the car until they find it. It was a real-life Abbott and Costello routine, Claire thought.

"Why don't you start out at Sand Draw?" she suggested. "Virginia and Gerald used to take the kids looking for rocks. The kids used to love it. Why don't you look out there?"

What she didn't mention was the possibility of suicide. *Maybe Virginia got into an argle-bargle with Alice and couldn't handle it. Maybe this was her final exit. Maybe she killed herself and the boys with the .22 rifle. Maybe she is out there right now. Dead.*

"Look, ma'am," the deputy said. "We have it covered. We'll look everywhere."

"How about Dickinson Park Road?" she pressed further.

"Why would we search way up there?"

"We used to go up there and picnic a lot," she said. "We didn't know there was a road up that mountain until Gerald showed us. He used to take us up there on picnics, take the boys through the woods, fishing and all that. I don't know, maybe Gerald and Virginia got to talking or something, and he took them up there."

Or maybe she decided to kill herself and the kids, and you'll find the car parked up there with all three of 'em in it. Who knows? Claire was descending into her own internal darkness.

But she was done trying to convince Fremont County that something was wrong. Claire was on her own.

"I can't sit here waiting for you guys to find a car that could be out of state, or anywhere," she said as she stormed out of the sheriff's office, frustrated, to continue her own search.

She went home and put together some posters with Virginia and the boys' pictures, which she copied at the drug store. She hung them in every bar, shop, and gas station that'd let her, tacked them to power poles and fences, and gave them to cops. She wanted every set of eyes in town looking.

A few days later, a deputy stopped by the Uden place. They weren't home, but he wandered around. Nothing looked unusual except some fresh concrete in the well house. The deputy didn't make a report, and nothing further was done.

Unknown to Claire, four days after Virginia and the boys went missing, a deputy added a note to the missing person report at the Fremont County Sheriff's Office. A Mrs. Hart had called to say that Virginia had given her a $50 deposit to rent a mobile home and mentioned that she was going back to New Jersey for her belongings. She expected to be back by midmonth.

To the local cops, the whole disappearance appeared to be a tempest in an overly dramatic grandmother's teapot.

Gerald rose refreshed, happy. Another day, another dodge.

First things first. After a leisurely breakfast, he burned all the clothes and blankets from Virginia's car in his trash barrel.

He rummaged through Virginia's purse, which contained the usual detritus of a woman's life, and burned everything except for $27 she had in her wallet. He needed gas money.

He also removed Virginia's granddad's antique .22 rifle—the murder weapon—from its handmade, velvet-lined wooden carrying case, which he then burned too. Gerald loved that old gun, but he couldn't risk being caught with it. He busted its fancy bird's-eye maple stock from its metal parts, which he cut up with an acetylene torch and, a few days later, turned to slag in US Steel's blast furnace. He buried the stock out in a dry creek bed near his house (although when he went to dig it up later, he'd either forgotten the exact spot or it had vanished).

He'd thrown the car keys out the window in the dark, left Richard's glasses with his body, washed the muddy blood out of his truck, hidden the station wagon's license plates—and still came out twenty-seven bucks ahead.

Just like that, he erased his last connection to Virginia and the boys. In fact, he felt kind of virtuous. Sure, he felt guilty about killing three people who'd once (and in the boys' case, still) loved him, but they'd become nuisances, and he had a new family to raise.

Just keep telling that one lie, he thought, *and you're home free.*

One problem remained: Claire was a tough old bird and wouldn't give up without a fight. She could turn up the heat enough to force local cops to get off their asses.

Yeah, they needed a plan to keep Claire quiet.

Eight days after Virginia and the boys vanished, the postman delivered unexpected good news: Virginia was alive.

On September 20, a Mailgram arrived at Claire's trailer. It had been sent the afternoon before by "V. U. Martin"—an unfamiliar rendering of Virginia Uden's name—from 556 Carola, Creve Coeur, Illinois. It was addressed to "C. Martin" in Riverton, Wyoming.

> Mom: Sorry I have worried you. I am in trouble.
> The boys are okay. Cover for me. Say I am in California. Will write when possible.

Claire was simultaneously relieved and bewildered. Virginia wasn't dead, and the boys were safe—but it just didn't feel right.

"Trouble"? She'd never been in any kind of "trouble." Virginia had no ties to California at all, so why would that seem like a credible cover story to anyone? Would she take off on a wild cross-country escapade with $5 worth of gas and leave $1,000 in a jar back home? And she was a rambling letter writer who'd jam four or five sentences behind one period—never clipped telegram language, even in a telegram.

But what really perplexed her was the signature. Virginia had never signed her full name to any correspondence with her mother. In hundreds of letters and cards, she simply signed "Gin."

Claire replied with her own Mailgram, asking Virginia to contact her directly. She sent it to 556 Carola in Creve Coeur, Illinois, begging Virginia to contact her.

Then she waited.

A Mailgram never came, but Gerald showed up unannounced the next morning, September 21.

"Don't you answer your phone anymore?" he asked as Claire invited him in. "I've been trying to call you all morning."

Claire picked up her phone. It was dead.

Together, they went outside to look for the problem. Claire traced the overhead phone wires from the pole and followed them across the parking lot because, you know, the wind could blow down the alley pretty good. Nothing seemed amiss.

Gerald, though, went directly to the junction box, where phone lines ducked under the trailer.

"Here's your trouble right here," he said. "The wires have been cut."

Sure enough, Claire saw a neat slice across the cable.

"If you'll get me some tools, I'll have it fixed in just a minute," the ever-helpful Gerald offered.

While he worked on the line, he opened his heart to Claire. He worried that she didn't think he cared enough about Virginia's disappearance. Fact is, he told her, he'd been endlessly searching for her on his own, and that was why he'd been trying to call. He had a new idea, he said.

The boys loved to hunt for agates out in Sand Draw, he said. Maybe they went out there. He asked Claire to go with him. They could cover more ground as two, he said.

"I've already been out there," she said. "And now I'm just waiting for friends to take me out to the reservation to look around out there."

For some reason, she didn't tell him about the Mailgram from Virginia.

That same night, around ten thirty, one of Riverton's more observant citizens called the police. There was a scruffy, unshaven guy smoking a cigarette in a red pickup parked crazy a block west of Superior Laundry on Federal Boulevard. It was dark, the caller said, but this guy was watching somebody or something with binoculars.

A city cop rolled slowly past the red pickup, and the driver ducked down in the seat. The cop lit him up.

The driver was Gerald Uden. The cop patted him down and found a lead weight attached to a short yellow rope in his coat pocket.

"What's this?" the cop asked.

"For my own protection," Gerald told him. "I think my ex-wife is in the laundry. She ran up some gambling debts in the casinos in New Jersey, and there's Mafia people around looking for her."

The cop had only a vague recollection of some trouble involving Gerald and the laundry. He'd seen a flyer or something, but it didn't seem relevant at the moment. What mattered was that at the time, it was against the law in Riverton to carry a concealed weapon of any kind— and a homemade sap was a weapon. Gerald was ticketed and released.

The next day, he went to the courthouse, pleaded guilty to a clerk, and paid a $25 fine. Nobody ever connected the strange incident to the open missing persons case, or told Claire Martin that a curiously armed Gerald had been watching her.

Gerald smiled as he left. Such a small price to pay for dodging an attempted murder rap.

Two days later, on September 23, a typed letter arrived in Claire's mailbox. Oddly, the postmark indicated it had been mailed from Riverton the day before, but there was no return address this time.

Mom,

Hope I haven't worried you too much. Am in trouble. It's best if you don't know about it. I had to leave in a hurry. There wasn't time to tell you.

Last Wed. I stopped at a drug store in Illinois long enough to buy some things. I gave one of the clerks some money to send you a message. Hope you got it. I couldn't take time to do it myself.

We're with friends in Penn. Now. You don't know them. I think we'll be alright for a while. I have money for now. That's why I'm in trouble.

I'm sending this in a way that can't give away my location. They may be watching you. It is safer for you if you don't know exactly where we are right now. If anyone asks tell them we're in California.

I need to figure out how to get our things and money from our house in N.J. and how to get support money. When I do I'll let you know.

We're safe for now but have to keep going. Will be in touch when possible. It's important that we don't attract attention so we'll have to be careful. I'm counting on you to cover for me. Take good care of Freddie and George. The kids miss them and you.

Virginia

Again, Claire immediately responded with a Mailgram to the Carola address: *How can I help? Urgent you call home or laundry. Mom.*

Without waiting for a reply, Claire took the Mailgram and letter down to the sheriff's office. Captain Larry Mathews, head of the sheriff's investigation division, read it and smiled.

"There you go," he said. "All your worrying for nothing. She'll be in touch with you when she gets the chance."

Claire shook her head. "No, something's not right."

"Is that her signature?" the investigator asked.

"She never signs anything to me with her full name. 'Gin' or 'Ginny,' maybe. Not that."

Mathews was unsold. He knew that anxious families imagined the worst before their missing loved ones walked back in, perfectly alive. And they almost always walked back in.

"Well, I don't know about that," he said. "That's her signature, right?"

Claire was flustered. She admitted it was Virginia's signature and promptly left.

Later that day, Claire received a phone call from a Joyce Johnson in Illinois, who told her that Virginia had borrowed enough money from her to get to New Jersey and made her promise to call Claire and the cops to settle their fears. Nothing to worry about. She and her sons were all safe.

So Mathews added a page to the missing person report, explaining that Virginia Uden and her boys had been located alive and well in Illinois. He scrawled a big "10-66" across the front: *Report canceled.*

Officially, less than two weeks after their disappearance, nobody in law enforcement was looking for Virginia, Richard, and Reagan Uden anymore.

Case closed.

But Claire's topsy-turvy week wasn't done.

A couple days later, September 25, another letter arrived. Not from Virginia, but from the Carola address in Illinois. It bore no postmark. It was handwritten and dated September 24 but not signed. It contained the two urgent Mailgrams Claire had sent to Virginia.

> Enclosed are two telegrams that have been sent to my address. There is no one by the name of V. U. Martin at this address. A lady came in the place where I work & asked if I would send this telegram for her. She gave me some money & the message & left. That was my only contact.
>
> I would appreciate no further messages be sent to this address. It is very annoying.
>
> Thank you.

Now more than ever, Claire believed the telegram and letters were part of a cruel hoax. Even if Virginia was alive and safe, she had no part in this correspondence, Claire was sure.

She gathered it all and went to the sheriff's office again. She gave them all to the detective. She made a passionate case that it was *possible* they weren't from her missing daughter. Too many things didn't feel right. All he had to do was have somebody knock on the door at the Carola Street address and ask a few questions. Could he please do that?

The detective relented. He'd confidently dealt with some of the worst liars, shitheads, and creeps society had to offer, but a stubborn grandma had worn him down.

That afternoon, he called the Creve Coeur Police Department, which was smaller than Riverton's. He told them he was working a missing persons case and asked if they could check out 556 Carola, maybe get the owner's name and number for him.

The house was vacant. But it wasn't hard to find the last tenant, a twentysomething woman named Thea Thomas.

As a professional courtesy two weeks later, two agents from Illinois's Division of Criminal Investigation knocked on the door at Thea Thomas's new apartment in Peoria Heights. They had a few questions.

Did she know V. U. Martin? *No.*

Did she send a Mailgram to Claire Martin? *Yes.*

Why did she send it? *Because her mother had called and asked her to do it.*

Did she say why? *Because she had a friend in trouble, and she needed to get a message to her mother in the form of a telegram.*

Did her mother tell her exactly what to say? *Yes.*

Did she sign it "V. U. Martin"? *Yes.*

Did she know that "V. U. Martin" and Virginia Uden were the same person, and she was a missing person? *Not at the time. She did now.*

What happened next? *She received two telegrams from Claire Martin.*

What did she do with them? *She called her mother.*

What did her mother tell her to do? *Send the telegrams to her mom with an unsigned note telling Claire to stop sending them. She'd take care of it.*

What happened next? *She learned the story of Virginia and her boys' disappearance. She was shocked.*

What did she do next? *She called her mom, enraged that she'd been dragged into some weird sham-thing about missing people she'd never met. Her mom promised to visit the sheriff and straighten this misunderstanding out.*

And what was her mother's name? *Alice Uden.*

That same afternoon, Gerald and Alice walked into the Fremont County Sheriff's Office on their own. Captain Larry Mathews took them into an interview room.

Up front, the Udens confessed to sending the bogus telegram and subsequent letters to Claire . . . but not to the disappearance of Virginia and the boys. Alice denied being the caller "Joyce Johnson from Illinois," but Mathews secretly wondered what the chances were that a random woman would unwittingly join such a cruel prank with an identical story at the precisely perfect moment.

Alice wept. For her part, she admitted finagling the sham correspondence without Gerald or Thea's knowledge because she believed Claire was trying to frame them for a crime. She had no intention of frustrating the investigation. Confessing now was the honest thing to do, Alice said, and she wanted to protect her husband and daughter from any trouble that she alone deserved. It all seemed like a great idea at the time, she conceded, but now it was embarrassing and dumb.

She didn't mention she'd recently been out to Oregon to buy a few acres of land. She and Gerald hoped to move themselves and her parents there soon. It might not look good to the cops if they appeared to be planning an escape.

The chivalrous Gerald quickly leaped to his beloved and beleaguered wife's defense. He repeated how Virginia had never shown up for their hunting trip and how he believed Claire Martin herself warranted more scrutiny. She was, after all, the last person to see Virginia, Richard, and Reagan alive.

That word "alive" struck Mathews as odd, but he said nothing.

Up to now, nobody had talked about Virginia and the boys as being dead.

A couple days after Gerald abandoned Virginia's station wagon on the lip of Trout Creek Canyon, a weekend woodcutter and his wife spotted it off the road. They walked around it, but it was locked. It had no license plates, no keys in the ignition, no people inside. The husband, whose day job was surveying construction jobs, tied a piece of fluorescent surveyor's tape on a branch to mark the spot.

When they got back to town, they called the sheriff's office to report an abandoned vehicle way up the Dickinson Park Road. The dispatcher thanked them and hung up.

A week later, a tribal cop on patrol stumbled upon the station wagon. He took a closer look and found an old grocery bag stuffed in the gas filler, partly burned. He also saw some kind of stain in the back. Back at the reservation office, he filed a report, but nobody took it further.

On October 4—more than three weeks after the disappearance—a rancher and his eleven-year-old son were looking for stray cows when they saw a glint up ahead. When they investigated, they found an old brown Ford station wagon, partially covered with pine boughs. The father opened one of the doors, and the dome light lit up.

The rancher and his son immediately went back to town to report the car to the sheriff.

This time, the third reported sighting, somebody finally took notice. The sheriff himself told the rancher to keep a sharp lookout when he drove in that area, and take his dogs. He didn't explain further, but he didn't need to. The warning was ominous enough.

The sheriff sent a deputy and one of his sergeants up Dickinson Park Road that afternoon. The Country Squire was exactly where the rancher said, hopelessly stuck on a rock. Unlocked, windows rolled up, no keys. An old title in the glove box confirmed it was Claire Martin's car, missing since September 12.

The deputy and his sergeant—and another tribal cop who showed up later—searched the car and found no signs of violence, no blood, no clothing. They combed the area around the car but found nothing except shards of the busted taillights.

A wrecker arrived and pulled the car off the rock onto the road. Again, the cops searched it and found nothing troublesome.

One of the deputies radioed the sheriff directly for instructions. Did he want FCSO's crime lab or anybody else to check it further? Negative, came the reply. Take it to the owner.

Incredibly, without any fingerprinting or forensic examinations for blood, flesh, or fiber evidence, the tow truck off-loaded the station wagon beside Claire's trailer. The chain of custody was broken, and any incriminating evidence the car might contain was made instantly doubtful. But to be fair, nobody yet suspected foul play, no matter how much they should have.

There it sat until Claire screwed up the courage to look inside. Except for a slightly twisted bumper where it had lodged on the rock, the car didn't *look* any different, but it *felt* different. Sure, the deputies said they had found nothing, but after her experience with the sheriff's office over the past few weeks, she didn't trust deputies.

Claire first opened the tailgate. She immediately saw a stray piece of raw wood on the spare tire box. It hadn't been there before. Richard and Reagan always picked up stuff like that because, well, they were boys who imagined all the things they could do with a godforsaken piece of wood.

There was a roll of duct tape and an unfamiliar cardboard box back there, too, like a grocery store castoff. But otherwise, nothing she didn't recognize.

She opened the front passenger door and looked around. Two Popsicle sticks were on the dashboard, and she reckoned the boys must have had ice cream on the trip. She saw nothing else odd or obviously out of place. But then she reached under the seat.

She pulled out an empty cardboard ammunition box.

Fergawdsakes, how thoroughly could the cops have searched if they didn't find an empty box of shells under the seat in a missing woman's car? Claire was pissed.

Claire then slid into the rear passenger seat and saw nothing . . . until she looked over the seat into the cargo area.

There, up against the back of the back seat, was a faint, brownish stain. Looking closer, she saw a few splatters of something dark on the back of the seat.

Was it blood?

Claire's heart quickened.

It looks like blood.

She ran inside and called the sheriff's office.

A couple county detectives, Captain Mathews and Sergeant Ed McAuslin, soon arrived at Claire's trailer in an unmarked car. "Show us what you saw," Mathews said. To Claire, it seemed almost like a courtesy call, not a genuine fact-finding mission. *Are they just humoring an old lady?* she wondered.

She swung the tailgate open.

"There." She pointed. "That looks like blood to me."

McAuslin and Mathews looked inside but said nothing.

Claire then opened the rear passenger door and glanced down the back of the seat.

"And here," she said. "I'm sure this is blood up here too."

The detectives looked even closer.

"And here," she said, gesturing to some little splatters on the door.

McAuslin's demeanor pivoted.

"Don't touch anything," he said.

Suddenly, she had a brainstorm.

"Here, let's lift up this rug and see what's under there . . ."

Before McAuslin or Mathews could stop her, Claire folded the back seat down and lifted the mat.

Under the cargo mat was a circular smear of something that looked like diluted, old, dried blood, as if somebody had frantically tried to wipe it away. Without saying anything, without fancy tests, the two seasoned detectives knew what it probably was.

But before he could stop her, Claire dug even deeper. She unlatched the back seat and tipped it forward so they could see underneath. McAuslin quickly shoved his face down close.

Down in the crack where the seat closed and nobody would think to clean, something awful had dribbled. McAuslin told—no, ordered—Claire to stand back.

To him, it looked like crusty blood, bone, and brain matter. Suddenly, three goddamned weeks later, this was real.

"Stand back," Mathews said. "Don't touch anything. Don't take anything out. Give me your keys."

McAuslin locked up the car. Mathews called back the tow truck. The car that nobody seemed to care about for so long was now a crime scene.

Back at the sheriff's impound lot, crime scene technicians fell on the car like carrion eaters.

They found more than any naked eye had seen. Blood on the cargo area's tailgate plate. Blood splashed on the seat back and passenger door. Blood splattered inside that grocery box. Biological material leaked down under the back seat. Bloodstains in the rear cargo mat that somebody had tried to wash out. Blood under the mat.

They found more fingerprints than they could ever identify. They didn't have Virginia's or the boys' prints for comparison, and maybe a dozen or more people had touched the car since it was left on the mountain, including passersby, deputies, and the tow truck driver—as well as countless people before the disappearance. If Gerald's fingerprints were among them, it was meaningless evidence because he had touched the car on several occasions.

It had all been mostly invisible to casual observers, but apparently not to one mule-headed grandma.

The blood was human. And it matched Virginia's, type A positive.[1]

And the sheer volume of blood evidence—although mostly microscopic—suggested it wasn't just a minor nick. She lost a lot of blood. Somebody had done a ham-handed job of trying to wash it out but left enough for scientists with microscopes.

The question was no longer where. Now it was: *Who?*

The crime scene techs had been over the car with a fine-tooth comb. They had what they needed. When McAuslin called Claire to tell her she could pick it up from the impound lot, she balked. She didn't want to drive it. It wasn't the machine but the ghastly remnants it contained . . . and the ghosts. Not ethereal, semitransparent phantasms at the top of the stairs, but the knowledge of what must have happened in that car.

Marie Roskowske gave her a ride to fetch the car. She got in and sat there for a minute. She couldn't get the image of that blood and the . . . She cried. Eventually, she slow-rolled out of the impound lot, onto the street, heading for home. Marie followed.

Claire had a death grip on the steering wheel. Her car crawled along, well under the speed limit. Somebody behind her started honking, then laid on it with a perpetual blare. *Go around,* she thought, but the horn still blew. She just kept her hands locked on the wheel and stared straight ahead. *Goddammit, go around!*

She pulled to the side of the road to let the impatient driver pass. Marie came up and pulled up to the curb ahead of her. She walked back and knocked on Claire's driver's-side window as the honking continued.

"Let go of the wheel," she said.

"What do you mean? I just want that woman to pass."

"Take your hands off the wheel."

Claire did. The honking stopped.

"My God, was that me blowing the horn?"

Marie smiled. "All the way up Monroe Street," her friend said. "Are you going to make it home all right?"

Claire did. She parked the station wagon beside her trailer and didn't touch it for a long time. She wanted to destroy it. She thought about taking it up the mountain and running it off the cliff. She thought about setting it on fire. She thought about all the ways she might make it disappear, but she never did.

A friend eventually straightened the damaged bumper for her, and a sympathetic insurance guy wrote her a check for the car's entire value. Even though it ran just fine and had no significant body damage, it was a total loss. He understood.

"Do I have to give you the car back?" Claire asked him.

"No, it's yours. You can do what you want with it. Spend the money on a vacation, or rebuild the car, or buy another one. Whatever you want to do. We don't care."

Claire thanked him. She felt he'd given her a gift.

"Or maybe you just want to drive it around a while and . . ." he said. "You know . . ."

He couldn't finish, but, yeah, she knew.

November 5, 1980, was Gerald and Alice's fourth wedding anniversary. Tradition dictated that they exchange gifts of delicate linen and lace, but the moment required something uglier.

It'd only been eight weeks since the disappearance, but Gerald felt the noose tightening. They found Virginia's car. Gerald had been arrested outside the laundry with a weapon. His various plots to neutralize Claire had failed. The cops were asking too many hard questions.

And hunting season was starting. It'd only take one curious or cold antelope hunter climbing down in that mine . . .

Oh, shit.

Gerald was on edge. Suddenly, his perfect hiding place wasn't so perfect. The murder weapon was mostly destroyed, and nobody knew the killing site. But the bodies were still findable. He needed to make sure they'd never be found.

That morning before work, he hitched his boat to the pickup. He loaded a couple old barrels—an empty fifty-five-gallon grease drum and a thirty-five-gallon galvanized trash barrel, both perforated by target practice—into the boat and went to work. After his shift, past midnight, he drove out to the Hidden Hand.

Gerald climbed back down in the mine with only a flashlight. He crawled into the stope that was Virginia and the boys' crypt, again face to face with their corpses.

Eight warm weeks had passed. They were flattened and rotting, crawling with maggots, and well gnawed by predators. Their eyeballs were pecked out, but he thought he could still recognize them. Maybe.

One by one, he stuffed them in black plastic trash bags and horsed them out to a spot where he could pluck them out of the hole with a rope connected to his truck bumper. Then he crammed Virginia's bulkier remains into the fifty-five-gallon drum and the two boys together into the smaller one. He wired the lids tight.

Their stink was on his hands, in his clothes, in his pores. But these three humans he'd once loved and who had once loved him weren't human to him anymore. *Isn't that what they say about the dead, that their souls are someplace better and this earthly flesh was just the useless shell?*

He strapped the barrels in his boat so they wouldn't tip over and spill their hideous contents on the long trip ahead.

Around three thirty in the morning, Gerald arrived at Fremont Lake, a cold, high-altitude lake in Sublette County, on the other side of the mountains and out of the local cops' jurisdiction. At more than six hundred feet and tucked in the high mountains where nobody would think to look, it would soon be ice locked.

Perfect, Gerald thought.

With only his dome light, Gerald cranked up his heater and made a 450-foot sounding line with a ten-pound steel bar and a nylon rope, then transferred the barrels into his boat.

He launched the Starcraft in the dark and motored out toward the center of the lake. He towed his makeshift sounding line behind the boat until he couldn't hear it dragging on the lake bottom any more. Deep enough.

Without a prayer or sentimental thought, Gerald rolled the two barrels into the black water under a waning sliver of moon. The near-freezing water rushed in through the bullet holes, and the barrels quickly sank.

When he was sure the scuttled barrels were well enough on their way to the bottom, Gerald returned to shore, hooked up the boat, and got the hell out of there. He arrived back at the Pavillion place just as the sun was coming up.

And Alice was waiting. He embraced her, but she quickly pushed him away.

"God, you smell like death warmed over," she said.

The slow-starting investigation into Virginia and the boys' disappearance began to heat up just as Wyoming's long, frigid winter set in.

The sheriff sent seventy-five volunteers and deputies up to Dickinson Park to search for any evidence on the ground around the spot where the car was found. Problem was, that area was a popular picnicking and hunting site for locals, who might drop or discard a lot of junk. It'd be hard to separate meaningful evidence and meaningless crap.

Nevertheless, Claire bought two shovels and joined the searchers. She'd offered to pay for any food or equipment the searchers needed, but the sheriff just waved her off. She wondered why the sheriff hadn't mobilized a month earlier, when the weather was nicer and the scene was fresher, but she'd given up expecting brilliant police work from him.

It certainly didn't improve her attitude when a volunteer asked to borrow a shovel. Or when she saw groups of searchers just standing around shooting the breeze for most of the morning. Not much actual searching seemed to be happening, Claire thought.

But somebody found a knife, some boys' underwear, a sock, a piece of brown carpet, an old car mat, a pocket comb, a pile of cigarette butts, a kid's left shoe, and an old brown furry coat. Every piece was catalogued, photographed, and stored.

Somebody showed the coat to Claire. It looked like one she'd bought and mailed to Virginia when she lived back East.

"Oh my God, that's Virginia's coat!" she said. "It's gotta be!"

She tried it on, and it was the right size and color. Its dark brown fake fur seemed right. She knew she'd bought a coat that buttoned up, and it had buttons. It seemed like the same coat, but she couldn't be absolutely certain.

It, too, was tagged and bagged.

It was time to have a heart-to-heart with the Udens. As the prime persons of interest, mainly because of the Mailgram and letters that seemed now to be deliberate red herrings, they had a lot to explain.

On November 14, Captain Larry Mathews called first Alice, then Gerald, to the sheriff's office for interviews.

Although she wasn't under arrest, Mathews read Alice her Miranda rights and had her sign a card that acknowledged she understood her rights. She didn't want an attorney, she said, because she didn't do anything.

The interview started at ten thirty that morning. The first questions were softballs and icebreakers, but Mathews quickly got to the meat of the matter.

"Did Virginia, at any time, indicate that she wanted more child support money?" he asked.

"No," said Alice.

"Why did you instruct your daughter to write bogus letters to Claire?"

"I thought Virginia and Claire were up to something," Alice repeated from her earlier confession, "and I wanted to see what it was."

"Why do you want to move to Oregon all of a sudden?"

"It's not sudden," she said defensively. "My mom doesn't like Wyoming and wants to live in Oregon, so we bought some land there. But my dad doesn't want to move to Oregon, so the idea is tabled for now. Someday, maybe. Not now."

"What was Gerald doing outside the laundry when he was arrested with a weapon?"

"Gerald is a different kinda guy. I don't know what he was doing."

"Tell me about the day Virginia and her boys disappeared."

"Gerald drove out to the corner and waited, but she didn't show up," Alice said. "So he came back in twenty or thirty minutes and started to work on our addition at the house. I went to town for groceries, and when I came back, it was still light out, but they still hadn't shown up."

Alice made a point of explaining that Gerald's red pickup was broken down that day, a bad oil pump. They only had her Pinto for transportation.

"Would you take a polygraph test? A lie detector?" Mathews offered.

Alice didn't think long. "No. It's just a matter of principle. Maybe I would if it was the last resort, but right now, no."

"What would that be, the 'last resort'?" Mathews asked.

Alice just shrugged.

"What do you think happened to Virginia and her sons?"

Alice shrugged again. "I have no idea," she said, then launched into a scathing description of Virginia as a welfare queen, conniving ex-wife, detached mother, and all-around horrible person.

Throughout the interview, Mathews asked her several times to take a polygraph test, and she always refused "on principle." On other questions, Alice would continually change the subject, rambling on about her two jackass ex-husbands, her kids, her many jobs, illnesses she'd had, places she'd lived, and other irrelevant topics.

Mathews, frustrated by Alice's verbal camouflage, tried a different tack.

"Well, you wanna know what I think?" he asked. "I think you didn't do anything but got caught up in the middle of things. You and Gerald knew you had to do something, so you took Virginia's body and stuffed it somewhere, and you took her car up on the mountain and tried to conceal it and had Thea write that telegram to throw us off. Sound about right?"

Alice looked as if she might cry, but stared teary-eyed into space. *She's thinking about how to word her confession*, Mathews thought.

"I understand why you'd think like that," she said, whimpering. "I know what you're saying, but . . ."

But? But what?

"But I didn't do anything," she said, wiping her eyes.

After four hours of questioning, Mathews had hit a brick wall. He might have better luck with Gerald.

At the bottom of his last page of notes, Mathews wrote: "It was apparent to me—but only my personal feelings—that she was very guilty & covering up the issue. Almost broke at one time."

So four days later, about three in the afternoon, Gerald sat down with Mathews in the sheriff's interrogation room, the "box." Again, Mathews read his Miranda rights, although he wasn't under arrest. And again, Gerald refused to have a lawyer present. Mathews was relieved.

Gerald was a talker, all right. He couldn't stop talking—about his job. Mathews let him talk for a while, then finally interrupted the meaningless blab.

"OK, Gerald, I brought you down here to talk about Virginia and the boys," Mathews said.

"I've already told you guys the truth," Gerald insisted. "I didn't do anything wrong."

As he'd done with Alice, Mathews laid out his theory: Gerald killed them all, hid them someplace, dumped the car, and tried to cover his tracks with bogus letters and Mailgrams from fake people.

Gerald hung his head and shuffled his feet. He crossed and uncrossed his lanky legs incessantly. He started shaking so badly he couldn't talk for a few minutes. He oozed guilt.

Mathews poured Gerald a cup of coffee, more to agitate than calm him. Gerald sipped it with both of his trembling hands.

When he finally regained some composure, he had a perfectly logical Nebraska farm boy's defense.

"You don't really have a case," he told Mathews, "because you don't have a body or a murder weapon. Even if I did it—and I didn't—you couldn't arrest me because you got no body."

As a legal scholar, Gerald was wrong. In 1960, the US Supreme Court ruled that a body (*corpus delecti*) wasn't always necessary to convict a murderer if circumstantial evidence was enough to exclude any other "reasonable hypothesis."

But as a country-boy lawyer, Gerald was right. A bloody murder scene, a motive, opportunity, and the victim's complete vanishing might sway a jury, but a skillful defense lawyer can easily cast reasonable doubt on any theory because without a body, the prosecution can't prove the victim is dead. So while no-body homicide prosecutions were legally permitted, they were few as a practicality.

Mathews knew he was in a pickle.

"You could still be indicted for murder or kidnapping, Gerald," Mathews said, but he knew it was a slim chance. "But if you're innocent like you say, just prove it to me."

"How?"

"Show me your innocence," Mathews told him. "I'd just as soon prove you innocent as guilty. But you know we have to get to the bottom of this. Tell me something."

Gerald said nothing.

"Do anything that proves you didn't do it," Mathews asked. It was starting to sound like begging. "Take a polygraph."

Gerald shook his head. "No polygraph. It's not about my guilt or innocence. It's just a matter of principle."

Mathews recognized that word "principle." It was Alice's argument against the polygraph. Gerald and Alice were getting their stories straight, even using the same words.

So Mathews moved on. He showed Gerald pictures of Virginia's abandoned car, and he studied them closely.

"I thought you said someone tried to burn it up?" Gerald asked.

"Yeah, it looked like that."

"That would have been a dumb thing to do."

"Why's that, Gerald?"

"By looking at those pictures, you could see town below, and people could have seen the fire."

Mathews glanced again at the crime scene photos.

"Gerald, you can't see any town in any of those pictures you just saw."

Gerald looked again. Sure enough, no town.

"Well, I heard it on the news," Gerald said defensively. "And I know where that's at and I know you can see town. I go up there a lot."

To Mathews' knowledge, nobody had ever told Gerald exactly where the car was found. Maybe he heard on the street . . . or maybe he slipped again.

Gerald began to ramble nervously. He talked about contemplating suicide once and how that might solve his problems now. He talked about not liking jails and how he couldn't possibly be confined in a small space for the rest of his life. He talked about how he tried to love Virginia, but she'd been bad to him. He talked about how much he loved those boys. He talked about how Alice hated Virginia, and vice versa.

Mathews let him run out of steam.

"Suppose you did kill Virginia and hid the boys somewhere," Mathews theorized. "You must know that they will be found sometime and that you can never have them and raise them."

Gerald seemed startled.

"Why can't I?" he asked.

"You'd be tied into this mess because the boys would know if Virginia met you out there that day—which you say she didn't."

Gerald face went blank. "Not if they didn't tell anyone . . . I never thought of it that way."

Ninety minutes after it began, the interview was over. Gerald left and Mathews added a familiar postscript to his notes:

"It is only my personal feeling, but I could see guilt all over him. I am convinced he is guilty & is covering up."

Gerald and Alice knew they were suspects. Alice was unperturbed, but it gnawed at Gerald.

He suspected the sheriff had set up a listening post in a neighbor's house, intercepting private conversations and phone calls to catch him talking about the case.

He also feared he was being followed. He saw strange cars in his rearview mirror every time he drove someplace. Once, he loaded his big Weatherby rifle and a .44-caliber pistol and deliberately drove to a secluded bend in a country road, where he pulled over and waited for his secret pursuer to come by. A few minutes later, a male driver in a sedan passed, and Gerald thought about shooting him. Only the fact that he'd bring more suspicion on himself stopped him.

Gerald worried obsessively that Claire Martin had hired a local Indian goon to "get revenge," maybe kill him. She hadn't—but, ironically, the thought had occurred to her.

Over the next two years, only Gerald and Alice looked like the killers, but Mathews couldn't connect the dots. This case had too many fingerprints from too many cops. Time passed too quickly. Early on, the sheriff had seen Claire as a pestering old lady and wasted precious time. Gerald and Alice hired a lawyer and suddenly went silent. Some other tantalizing leads came in over the transom during those first two years but were never the smoking guns Mathews needed.

For one, Alice's daughter Eliza politely warned her teacher that she might not be in class after Thanksgiving because her parents feared they'd be in jail. She further confided in the school nurse that she felt lonesome because her parents ignored her while discussing "things they were going to tell the sheriff."

One day in the nurse's office, Eliza drew a disturbing image of a person standing on a box, with her head in a noose and cocked at a dreadful angle. A cartoon bubble off to the side said, "Help me! Help me!" When asked about it, the seven-year-old said only that it "happened in the barn." The startled nurse gave the artwork to a social worker, but Alice shrugged it off.

Another time, Eliza told the nurse that she had a nightmare about two dead boys who were killed and the skin stripped from their bodies. Then they were wrapped in a blanket and buried in the desert.

Enraged, Alice stormed into the school and told the principal nobody was to speak to her daughter anymore. *Nobody. Period.*

"Are you sure, if there's some kind of accident, you don't want the school nurse to look at your daughter?" the incredulous principal asked.

"No, I don't care," Alice insisted. "If she gets hit by a truck, you call the ambulance. Don't let her talk to the nurse."

Another unconnected dot: no medical claims had been filed for the perpetually ill Richard or Reagan, no Social Security taxes paid for the perpetually broke Virginia, and no phone calls made to Claire from her devoted daughter since September 12, 1980. Two years.

Another: Gerald delivered to the sheriff an anonymous, threatening letter he'd received from an angry citizen ... and blurted out another strange statement, especially for a person of interest in a murder investigation.

"You don't have anything until you find a body," he reminded the sheriff in a casual conversation one month after he'd secretly dumped the bodies in Fremont Lake, "and you're not going to find one."

Another: a local hospital administrator told Mathews that Gerald had specifically come to the medical center seeking any medical records on Virginia, "you know, just in case they find a decomposed body and need to identify her."

If Gerald weren't such a clumsy galoot, Mathews thought, he might be taunting the cops. Maybe he was wrong about Gerald. Maybe Gerald was smarter than he looked. Or maybe Gerald was just covering his ass in his own awkward way.

Another: in June 1982, a maintenance man at Riverton's sewage treatment plant found a lower denture trapped in a filter pipe. Rather than take it to cops, he delivered it straight to Claire Martin, who delivered it straight to a New York private investigator she'd hired on her laundry manager's pay.

A local dentist said it matched the color and shade of the false teeth he'd made for Virginia, but it wasn't the same base. Virginia often complained about her lower denture's fit, he said, and she might have gotten another dentist to create a different base, but it wasn't the base he'd made. Was it Virginia's? Or did it belong to somebody else who probably barfed it up and flushed? Inconclusive.

Small-town cop shops, understaffed and undertrained, could be quickly overwhelmed. Rather than chasing leads, they sometimes just waited for leads to come to them. Without fresh leads, a case sat in a box. It wasn't exactly cold, but maybe only lukewarm.

Mathews really tried to keep Virginia's case on a front burner, but memories, excitement, and priorities fade after two years without an arrest. Locals came in with all kinds of weird tips, mostly unhelpful. Detectives moved on to more pressing crimes. Virginia's vanishing hadn't been forgotten, but without a lucky break—namely, a body, a murder weapon, or a confession—this case was dead in the water.

Literally.

In a legal Hail Mary on October 26, 1982—more than two years after Virginia's disappearance—Fremont County Attorney Arnold Tschirgi convened a rare grand jury to consider indictments against Gerald and Alice Uden.[2]

Unlike a preliminary hearing, which was by far more common in Wyoming, a grand jury meant there'd be no defense attorneys to present "the other side," no frustrating judges, no cross-examination, no exposure of the state's case, no public outcry. Grand juries are secret, and grand jurors absorb only what prosecutors want them to see and hear. Because the threshold for an indictment is lower and the final verdict needn't be unanimous, grand juries tend to be the best forum for prosecutors and cops with tenuous cases.

And the purely circumstantial case against the Udens was as tenuous as they come. In fact, prosecutors didn't really have a case; they merely hoped to rattle Gerald and Alice into a fatal mistake or confession.

But Tschirgi only needed to convince nine of the twelve jurors that Gerald and/or Alice "probably" committed a crime.

It was over in one day. Tschirgi's deputy prosecutors called Claire Martin, Larry Mathews, and a hunter who related in vivid detail how he saw some suspicious people in a red truck on Dickinson Park Road that day of the disappearance.

Prosecutors had subpoenaed Gerald and Alice, their daughter Eliza, and in-laws Sam and Vivian Barbier, but they might have saved themselves the trouble.

Eliza was "missing." In fact, she had been hidden out of state by Gerald and Alice.

Gerald's in-laws, Sam and Vivian Barbier, reluctantly appeared and danced around the questions. Ultimately, they either refused to answer questions or claimed they saw nothing, heard nothing, knew nothing. End of story.

On a lawyer's advice, Gerald and Alice both hid behind their Fifth Amendment protections ("No person . . . shall be compelled in any criminal case to be a witness against himself") and said nothing at all about the case. Gerald invoked the Fifth forty-nine times; Alice, ten times. They were further protected by the restrictions on spouses testifying against each other.

The cheerless prosecutors took it no further. Mathews knew the game: If they took a half-baked case to trial and lost, they'd piss away any chance of bringing Gerald and Alice to justice. His hands were tied with a Gordian knot: impatience might let at least one killer, maybe two, get away with murder, but at least one killer, maybe two, would definitely get away with murder while he was being patient.

"We're at a dead end," a deputy prosecutor told grand jurors at the end of that one long day.

"We presented testimony so that you would know what it is that we know about this case," he said, almost apologizing for wasting their time. "I feel probably without some kind of confession at this point, or discovering a body, or finding an eyewitness, that we're never gonna get anywhere with it.

"And while I'm convinced, and I think Captain Mathews is, that something happened, the feeling that something happened and being able to prove it beyond a reasonable doubt in a district court trial are two vastly different things.

"We're just trying to shake something loose."

But nothing shook loose.

The testimony had been so fruitless that prosecutors didn't even ask for an indictment. The grand jurors were thanked for their service and sent home without ever once voting their minds and hearts.

Cops, prosecutors, even Claire had always been one move behind Gerald and Alice, who'd stayed just one or two steps beyond their grasp for two years.

And now Gerald and Alice were about to make their next move, before their frustrated antagonists had even planned their own.

They planted a "For Sale" sign on the Pavillion place. They had bought a remote forty-acre farm near a wide spot called Eunice, Missouri, which they shared with dozens of free-range copperheads. But they were exactly where they wanted to be, far beyond the sight and reach of the flat-footed Wyoming authorities.

If connecting the dots was hard when they lived right there in Fremont County, it would be infinitely harder when there were a thousand miles between dots.

Before they left Wyoming, Gerald quit his maintenance job at US Steel, which itself was about to close forever. His medical insurance plan ended with his resignation. Although he'd been ordered by a judge to insure his adopted sons, Richard and Reagan, until adulthood, he never bought health coverage for them again.

He knew, better than anyone, the boys would never need it.

Chapter 4

. . . AND TOMORROW . . .

Just like that, Gerald and Alice were gone. As soon as the grand jury went home, they butchered all their farm animals, hitched their boat to a U-Haul truck, and blew town. They left nothing behind.

But Larry Mathews drove out anyway to the Pavillion place after they left. This awful story had gaping holes he could drive a snowplow through. He didn't know what he was looking for, or what he might find, or even why he went. Hell, the place had been searched before. He hoped, though, that maybe something just clicked out there this time.

Maybe it was more meditation than search.

Every patch of freshly turned earth, every glint of sunlight on something in the weeds, every color that didn't blend, they all caught his eye. None clicked.

Mathews inventoried what he had ... and what he didn't. Step after step, he pondered what he might have missed. His gut told him Gerald was involved in Virginia's disappearance, and Alice had blood on her hands too, if only as a silent partner. And they knew that he knew.

He picked up pieces of rusty metal and old wood. He squatted to see any shadow that might reveal a subtle variation in terrain. He inhaled the air, as if he might smell a clue, but only got a whiff of pigs, gone except for their stink.

Every careful stride, the unfinished puzzle frustrated him. The son of a small-town police chief, he knew he couldn't catch every bad guy every time. Still, it chapped his ass that Gerald and Alice could move around freely in this world while Virginia and her young sons could not.

He walked the fence line, the dirt road, the margins of this useless land. He studied every spot where Gerald had left his mark. He scanned the horizon beyond the fences as if the answers might be out there somewhere. *But which direction?* he thought.

Out there alone, Mathews smiled when he considered that maybe a chat with a couple local badasses might induce Gerald's spontaneous confession, but that wasn't his way. It wasn't his by-the-book father's way either, and that was even more important to him.

He found nothing that day. No physical evidence, no answers, no comfort.

He couldn't start over again. He couldn't rewrite the beginning of this vile story. Without something more, Mathews stood at the messy end of it. He had other, fresher cases, solvable. He had other victims he could champion. He could put away bad guys and do some good right now, in real time. He wouldn't put this one in a box or let it turn frosty cold, but he couldn't keep chasing ghosts.

He had to move on.

Gerald and Alice had certainly moved on. And life was good.

In Missouri, Alice quickly took a nursing job at a small-town hospital while Gerald became a househusband, cooking meals, caring for Eliza, keeping house, and posting a lot of "No Trespassing" signs on his farm's perimeter. Damn snoopers and cops.

But the homemaker's life soon grew old. A neighbor told Gerald about a truck-driving school in Florida where he could be trained as a long-haul trucker in just two months. Adopting the CB handle "Cowboy," he started driving big rigs for a living. By 1987, Alice had quit her nursing job and taken the course too so she and Gerald could hit the road together.

Gerald, who was already a pretty good guitar player, indulged another creative urge. Inspired by television painter Bob Ross, he attended landscape painting classes when he wasn't on the road. The proudest day of his life was when Ross himself visited Gerald's class and they posed for a picture together. Eventually, Gerald became a certified instructor in Ross's "wet-on-wet" style, although he never got the hang of the fuzzy-headed painting pitchman's chirpy patter. Gerald wasn't chirpy.

In 1986, Gerald and Alice sold the Eunice farm and moved to Springfield, Missouri. Their nomadic life on the road wasn't good for Eliza, whose life was turbulent enough without absentee parents.

It wasn't real good when they were home, either. Eliza was a sophomore in high school when she back-talked Gerald and he hit her. Children's Services took her away. She landed in the Presbyterian Home for Children, a historic orphanage that had more recently turned its attention to children with emotional and mental health issues. Gerald and Alice, who weren't in any hurry to get her back, took all her clothes to Goodwill. And when the state of Missouri inquired further about the case, Gerald responded, "You want her? You got her."

About that time, at the request of Captain Mathews in Riverton, two juvenile officers from Missouri interviewed Eliza about Virginia's disappearance. She revealed some shocking details that added tantalizing new vapors to the dark cloud hanging over Gerald and Alice.

She was eight years old on the day they vanished. Although she usually played with Richard and Reagan when they came over, her father had sent her on this day to the Barbiers' trailer. When she asked Alice why she couldn't play with the boys, her mom said she didn't want her around them.

Eliza confided to the juvie officers that she had never been told much about the case, so they let her read the police report. When she got to the part about the bogus letters to Claire, she blurted out that she recalled her mom typing a letter and discussing with Gerald how to sign Virginia's name.

Random memories then poured out. Eliza remembered Gerald removing pictures of the boys from a scrapbook after the disappearance and putting them in a drawer. She remembered being hidden from the grand jury. She remembered finding some old Wyoming license plates in the spare tire compartment of her mother's red Pinto and wanting to keep them because they had a bucking horse on them; Alice snatched them away and they vanished. And she remembered that the day after the disappearance, she went with her parents to nearby Ocean Lake, where Gerald went off by himself in his boat for a long time.

More unconnected dots.

Even if everyone else had moved on, Claire Martin could not.

She was still grasping at straws and getting nothing but older. The private investigator she hired was coming up empty. The sheriff was still stymied. The station wagon still sat, undriven, beside her trailer. And Virginia, Richard, and Reagan were still missing.

On April 30, 1984, NBC rebroadcast its movie *Adam*, about the 1981 kidnapping and murder of Adam Walsh. At the end, photos and descriptions of several missing children were shown, including Richard and Reagan Uden. It generated a few tips and raised Claire's hopes, but nothing came of it.

In 1986, she wrote to the Joint Chiefs of Staff, America's top military commanders, to inquire whether Richard—who would have been eighteen—had enlisted in the army, navy, or air force. He hadn't.

She sent similar letters to the Secretary of Health and Human Services and to the Social Security Administration, seeking any trace of Virginia or her sons. Nothing.

Two small life insurance policies on Virginia paid a few thousand dollars when she was declared officially dead in 1987. Claire spent all the money on her quest.

In her sixties now, she monitored missing persons networks, no small task before the internet. When boys popped up who might be Richard or Reagan, she called the sheriff because, well, such was her desperation that she believed a child who went missing once might go missing again.

Even more desperately, Claire sought the help of a psychic who ultimately had no answers in her crystal ball. She took deputies to several spots where she had "a feeling something bad may have happened." None were relevant.

But Claire remained upbeat and determined. She had many friends helping her, but none were as industrious as she was. She didn't have much money, but no expense stood in her way. What she had was a commitment to the task, and she spent every ounce, even though it was producing nothing but teasing tidbits.

On New Year's Day 1986, Claire typed a letter to her beloved grandsons, still lost after six years. Truth be told, she now believed that Virginia was dead, but she had not—and would never—give up her hope that the boys had been spared. She genuinely believed they were alive because *who could kill innocent little boys?*

But at sixty-six, Claire wasn't sure how long she had left. If the boys reemerged after she died, how would they know that she never gave up looking for them? How would they reconnect with who they really were? How would they know she loved them beyond words?

On this day of hope for the future, she poured her heart onto a blank page:

January 1, 1986

Dear Richard and Reagan:

I am writing this letter five years after your disappearance, September 12, 1980. I want you to know that your grandmother has not forgotten you for one minute and that I have been searching for you both and for your mother and praying for your safe return and will continue to do so until you do return or until my death. As long as I am mentally and physically able I will continue to search.

To this date I know nothing of what happened to you and your mother that Friday you left my home to meet your dad. So I am writing this letter so that if I have passed on before your return you will know who to go to for information.

I am leaving photo albums and family photos and information you will probably want and need with [names and numbers of friends]. They can tell you what has been happening for the past five years.

You are both very dear to me and I have missed you and your mother so much. It has been very lonely without you in these past five years. Be strong, do something good with your lives and if you have a dream, work toward it and always keep it before you. We all need a goal of some sort, something to aim our sites at, something to keep us striving toward that end. You are both intelligent and ambitious and remember that you can do anything you really set your mind to. I don't know how you both feel about religion but I would urge you to seek God's help in all things.

May God bless you both and give you happiness and His loving guidance to a good life ahead.

All my love to my dear grandsons,

Your Grandma

She folded it tenderly and slipped it into an envelope on which she'd written, "For Richard Loren & Reagan Cordell Uden—To be given to them should they be found or return after my death."

Tips had slowed to a trickle in the mid-1980s, but for ten years after Virginia and her boys were last seen, random bits of information about the case still fell into Mathews's lap.

In 1985, the bank foreclosed on some vacant land the Udens owned in Oregon, once thought to be a possible location of clandestine burials.

Every so often, Gerald's former coworkers would wander in to describe his odd behavior at work—"devious," "crazy," "weird," and "psychopathic spook" were some of the words they used—or vague recollections of him in places where he shouldn't be. Some even told stories about a shadowy hit man, another quirky coworker, Gerald might have hired to do the dirty deed; investigators followed up but never determined if the guy even existed. Another dead end.

Somebody recalled Gerald saying he had several good methods for disposing of bodies, including stuffing them in plastic bags with lime that would eat and dehydrate the flesh while smothering the stench. Not exactly lunchroom conversation.

Various rumors percolated about molestations within the Udens' fractured, dysfunctional family. Sometimes it was among siblings, others by the grandfather, but all were old and the statute of limitations had long ago expired.

In 1989, Alice sent an angry letter to sixteen-year-old Eliza at the orphanage, accusing her of colluding with the cops' "mind games" by simply talking to them.

Although the idea of collusion in mind games was preposterous, it was true that Eliza had shared memories with cops a few times. Most recently, she'd walked into Captain Mathews's office with her brother Ted to offer whatever help they could to find Virginia and the boys. The meeting wasn't long or very productive. Trying to be helpful about hiding places, Ted mentioned that his mother had an affection for the historic Remount Ranch near Cheyenne, an enormous horse-and-cattle operation where she'd once been a caretaker. In fact, he said there was an old gold mine on the place that'd make a perfect hiding spot.

After a few more fruitless questions, it was over. Alice's two grown children admitted their childhood memories were foggy and mostly not worth remembering. Then they left.

A few months later, under the lowering skies of an approaching blizzard, some helpful Laramie County deputies briefly searched parts of the ranch, including the uppermost chamber of a long-abandoned, caved-in mine, looking for Virginia and the boys. It might not even be the mine Ted described. So it was a long shot, they knew, but they found a few old bones, likely animal, that they shipped to the state crime lab, just to be sure. Yes, they were animal bones. End of search.

Change is inevitable, especially in modern-day sheriff's offices. Some sheriffs hang on until they're old and butt-sprung; others are removed quickly by voters for various crimes and misdemeanors—although not always *actual* crimes or misdemeanors. Many make enemies who run against them in election years. But they change, sometimes on a whim. And when administrations change, so do attitudes, pay grades, and people.

So, in time, Mathews was jobless when his sheriff was swept out of office and a new sheriff fired him for political reasons. New faces came aboard, and Virginia Uden's disappearance moved off the back burner to the fridge: not forgotten, but certainly not the personal quest it had been in Mathews's time.

Just cold.

But not frozen solid.

In fact, there was this twentysomething kid, a rookie working down in the jail on the graveyard shift.

Dave King grew up in Lander, Wyoming, the school superintendent's son. Back then, when he heard police or fire sirens, he'd jump on his bike and follow. He was intensely curious what was on the other end. Dad wanted him to be a teacher, but his heart wasn't in it.

He left the University of Wyoming married with a couple kids, got divorced, and then went to work for the railroad, where the money was good and the partying was better. Adult life was starting to be more serious than he imagined. Partying like a kid took the edge off.

When King came home to Lander for good, he took a grunt job at the local lumberyard and continued to party.

Then he heard about a guard opening at the jail. He got it, and Deputy Dave King got a crash course on what was at the other end of those sirens.

The overnights were long, and the occasionally bored King had access to the old files. He was fascinated with the old cases.

One in particular.

Something should be happening, he thought, *somebody should be running with this.*

He saw the lies in the letters. Even then, he considered Alice to be the loosest thread. She should be under a heat lamp, he believed. But having never investigated a case, much less closed one, what the hell did he know?

Over the next few years, under a couple different sheriffs, King moved from the jail to riding patrol in a remote corner of the county. It was quiet except for the occasional lost hiker or hunter.

In 1991, a single-engine plane carrying a pilot and two game wardens tracking radio-collared grizzlies went down in the rugged wilderness. King, now a sheriff's investigator in Lander, joined the biggest search-and-rescue mission in Wyoming's history, and not just because it was his job. One of the wardens on the flight was a dear friend.

He searched on horseback in the backcountry on weekends and vacations, camping up there when he couldn't get out by sunset. He flew thousands of hours in search planes for months afterward. He never found a clue, but he couldn't give up. The plane had been swallowed up by the hungry landscape.

Mostly, it just pissed him off. Death didn't play fair.

In late September 1995, four years later, an elk hunter found the wreckage, a rusty hulk barely recognizable as an aircraft. With only weeks before snow would shroud the spot again, King flew to the area by helicopter and hiked to the wreckage so he could recover the remains of his friend and the two men with whom he died.

The fire, weather, and predators didn't leave much of anything. The engine, with parts of it melted, lay at the front of the frame, where you would expect to find it. Most of the fuselage was melted, suggesting a fuel fire of more than two thousand degrees—just hot enough to cremate a human body. Fifty feet back along the plane's obvious path, he found the prop in one piece but with one tip bent grotesquely. The crash had been violent.

But King had a job to do, a job he'd already been working for the past four years.

There were few signs that this plane carried three men when it sliced through the trees, hit the ground, and burst into flames. Beneath the fuselage's bare frame, King collected a few bones, mostly small, and some teeth. He also found one warden's service pistol next to his seat. He found a piece of skull, likely the pilot's, a couple hundred feet away. He hadn't survived the crash but probably was ejected. Or a grizzly dragged his corpse away. There was no way to know now.

King placed the human remains in evidence bags, which he stuffed inside his backpack for the coroner. He'd spent four years looking for this mess from the air and horseback. At the moment, the only thing he could think to say was, "No more looking down."

That night, King went out and got half drunk, then crawled into bed and cried himself to sleep—not sad, just emotionally exhausted after four years. He'd hidden it from everyone.

Eventually, he comforted himself in knowing they died doing what they believed in. He sucked it up, went to three memorial services, and went back to work.

By that time, former jailhouse rookie Dave King had earned his gold shield as an investigator. Finding the plane brought closure to him and to the families he knew. It made touching the corpses worth the horror.

But it also illustrated graphically the value of persistence. He reckoned something inside every good cop motivated them beyond common sense.

King had shown he was game for any case that came his way, but he'd only asked for one: the 1982 disappearance of Virginia Uden and her two young sons, which was now more than ten years cold.

The real-life mystery preoccupied King, like the crash had preoccupied him. It too was personal. Here was an honest-to-God true puzzle involving real people in his hometown. The car on the mountain, the blood, the vanishing, the fake telegram and phony letters . . . and the two little boys. He knew somebody had done something rotten. He just didn't know who, what, when, where, why, or how. So many juicy tidbits about it stirred his search-and-rescue genes.

He decided his best strategy might be to start fresh. A blank slate.

His first task was to win back Claire Martin's confidence in law enforcement. He wanted to repair her attitude, find out what she knew, and get her trust back. A lot of the case pivoted on her, but when he envisioned the reason he wanted to solve it, he saw her face.

And King was confident he could solve the case. At the very least, he reckoned he'd see something that nobody else had. His fresh eyes could only help.

And his persistence.

Something else had changed since Virginia's case went cold.

Fueled by the popularity of television shows about real-life crime mysteries and stalled investigations—the hit *Unsolved Mysteries* debuted in 1987—cold cases captured the imagination of the American public and cops. Plus, advances in forensic science—such as the advent of DNA profiling in the mid-1980s—had given investigators new tools to solve cases in which no suspect had been identified any other way. The trend breathed life into Virginia's case too.

But Wyoming poses a unique challenge for cops in all missing persons cases, cold or not.

Anybody who's driven through Wyoming's boundless terrain has imagined how easy it would be to lose oneself in it.

And more than a few have fantasized about losing someone else out there.

The state's average population density of six people per square mile (in contrast, New Jersey has 1,200 people per square mile) is an unfair mathematical measure. In fact, the state encompasses thousands of square miles where nobody lives, nobody goes, and nobody ever will.

In other words, Wyoming—the least populous and most incomprehensible of the lower forty-eight states—is the baddest of badlands. There are more places to hide dead people than live people will ever find.

So Wyoming is a kind of coconspirator in foul play. Killers kill, and Wyoming hides their victims. Canyons, rivers, lakes, bear country, abandoned mines and caves, arroyos, roadless deserts, talus and scree, a million natural hidey-holes. Shallow graves or no graves at all. Hungry vermin and predators take care of the rest.

People have disappeared in this titanic wasteland since before humans contrived their puny laws, which haven't really helped much. Unsolved disappearances have piled up since Wyoming was a territory, more than 150 years.

In September 1934, a newlywed bride named Olga Mauger joined her husband Carl on an elk-hunting trip in the Dubois area. As they hiked the rugged mountains, Olga tired. She rested beside the trail while Carl went ahead. Twenty minutes later, when Carl came back to the spot where he left Olga, she was gone.

According to Carl, he yelled and searched for Olga in vain. He later joined a posse to look for her, but she was never found. Both had misgivings about their recent marriage, friends said. Carl might have killed Olga, or Olga might have simply run away into a new life, or a bear might have made a quick meal of her. Nobody knows.

If Carl did it, he never said a word. He later married an old girlfriend, and he died in 1978.

And Olga Mauger remains Wyoming's coldest missing persons case.

But she's certainly not the only one, nor even the most suspicious.

In the summer of 1974, four young girls went missing in Rawlins, a dog-eared prison town in Wyoming's southern desert. Two of the girls, Carlene Brown and Christy Gross, disappeared from a local rodeo and carnival. A month later, fifteen-year-old Deborah Rae Meyer left home to see a movie and was never seen again. Just three weeks after that, ten-year-old Jaylene Banker vanished from the county fairgrounds during a rodeo.

Nine years after the frightening disappearances chilled Rawlins to its core—the term "serial killer" had only been coined by the FBI around the time of the Rawlins disappearances—Christy Gross's skeleton was found in the desert six miles from town. She'd been bludgeoned to death and left for animals to eat. Her killer has never been caught, although local cops believed he was a midway worker who'd been working the summer carnivals.

The other three girls have never been found.

But one of Wyoming's most enduring disappearances has been even more frustrating, partly because it hasn't yet faded into history.

On July 24, 1997, a young long-distance runner named Amy Wroe Bechtel disappeared on an afternoon run in the Wind River Mountains near Lander. Just twenty-four, she dreamed of a spot on the US Olympic marathon team, but in the blink of an eye, she was gone.

At first, investigators from the Fremont County Sheriff's Office treated it as a missing persons case, but after three days, it was obviously something different. Suspicion first fell on Amy's rock climber husband, Steve, but—even while Virginia Uden's missing poster was still hanging on their bulletin boards—Fremont County investigators were unable to connect the dots in Amy's case. And there came to be plenty of reason to believe that there were no dots to be connected, that Steve was innocent.

Despite hundreds of searchers and hunters crisscrossing the area these past two decades, new high-tech forensic tools, thousands of calls to the sheriff's tip line, television reenactments, and hundreds of news articles and broadcasts, no shred of Amy Wroe Bechtel has turned up in more than a human generation.

In all these cases, and many more, Wyoming seemed almost to devour the missing, aiding and abetting whoever wanted them gone. They all seemingly got sucked down in the dirt.

Dust to dust.

Between Mathews and King, Virginia's case had been kept on life support by a good ol' boy detective named Jack Coppock. Ohio-born, ex-city cop

Coppock was well-liked, smart, fast driving, and an articulate smart-ass. Six foot two and white-haired at forty, he wasn't known for big cases, but he didn't let ego get in his way. Coppock knew his shit, and the rank and file respected him.

When King revived the case, Coppock had confidence in the young guy. He knew they had to rattle the bushes on a case nobody thought was solvable. Yeah, he knew the chances were slim. Wheels had slipped. But King was excited about it, and without some passionate effort, there'd be no results.

Although he was one of the caretakers of Virginia's memory, Coppock's main contribution was not standing in King's way. He didn't push the case forward very far by himself, except by accident. And it was accidental that in 1993, he was loosely acquainted with Alice Uden's grown son Ted. Coppock felt sorry for the kid, and he once told Ted to call him if he ever wanted to talk about anything, or nothing at all. His door was open.

That's why Ted went to Coppock's house one night, when he was going through a messy divorce. Ted was a troubled guy whose disarrayed memory had bubbled up a disturbing fragment about his mother. They sat on Coppock's couch and talked like a couple of old friends. Then Ted said he'd seen Richard and Reagan on a missing persons flyer and it stirred odd feelings. *Ghosts in the closet*, he said.

Ted told Coppock a strange, dislocated story. It was pieces and parts. Ted apologized up front, saying he'd blocked most of this bad stuff out for most of his life. It wasn't a suspicious "recovered" memory, but neither was it the kind of memory that might recalculate a lost detective's course. Nevertheless, it intrigued Coppock. It went something like this:

Ted had lived with his mom and stepfather, Don Prunty, at a historic spread near Cheyenne, the Remount Ranch, where they were caretakers, then up at a roadside rest stop, where they picked up trash for the state. Don died—*bad kidneys or liver failure or something*—and after that, Alice hauled her kids to several brief jobs she worked: barmaid, bus driver, roadside rest-stop janitor, maybe some others. *We moved around a lot.* When Ted was in junior high, it was his job to drive his mom to her waitressing job at a little bar in Buford, Wyoming, maybe twenty-five miles west of Laramie. *So we became drinking buddies,* and one night in a drunken haze—*yeah, maybe while driving and drinking a beer, when I was in junior high*—she told him how she'd shot her abusive, drug-addled asshole boyfriend—*I think his name was Ron*—in the head while he slept. She'd had enough of his cruelty. Some guy she met after Don Prunty died, early seventies. Ted met him once but couldn't describe him. He thought maybe they lived in Cheyenne, *probably a mobile home but I don't know where.* Ted had been farmed out to relatives back East by then. Alice told Ted she stuck Ron's body in her car, then dumped it in a hole someplace, maybe at the Remount Ranch, *maybe wrapped in bedsheets, I dunno, maybe crammed in a barrel.* Maybe she had help. He thought maybe Alice had already told his sisters, Eliza and Thea, but she commanded him to never tell anybody else. He never did . . . until now.

That was it. Ted didn't know what hole. He didn't know when or who or where. But he'd been thinking about the ranch. The Remount Ranch was a little boy's paradise, festooned with old bones, cool bugs, astonishing rocks that had never been picked up, humping cattle, and more chances to explore or frolic (or accidentally kill himself) than any city kid had. Ted loved it, like any little boy would.

And the Remount, he said, was full of holes.

Maybe, Ted surmised, *the dead guy is out there.*

Finally, some movement.

The next day, Coppock shared Ted's story with Dave King. Here, thirteen years later, Ted's disorderly, disturbing recollection seemed to offer investigators an indistinct trail of wind-scattered bread crumbs. He had suggested earlier that Virginia and the boys had been dumped on the Remount Ranch. Now this other guy? Where did these scattered, random thoughts lead, if anywhere? Nobody knew.

First, King needed to know if the guy's story about a killing in the late 1960s or early 1970s somewhere in Wyoming—maybe—was even true. If it was, who was the victim? Why would nobody miss him for damn near twenty years? And where was the hole his alleged corpse was supposedly dumped?

The hypothetical (for now) victim had a possible name—Ron—but what if Ted was misremembering that?

What if it's all a fever nightmare?

What if none of this crap is true?

What if it's just another of Alice's schemes to throw off cops?

Dave King and Jack Coppock had some bushes to rattle. They'd know soon enough.

Days later, Coppock flew to Illinois, where Ted's sister Thea confirmed that, indeed, Alice had told her the same disjointed story about killing an abusive guy, probably in Cheyenne, and hiding his body at least twenty years before. Alice had confessed to Thea *while she was sewing my prom dress, so back in the midseventies.* But now, Thea had no more specific details than her brother, except that she also recalled the dead man's name was Ron. *Last name? I dunno for sure. Maybe . . . Holt or Holtz?*

The missing persons case of Virginia Uden and her boys, which cops had treated as a benign miscommunication at first, suddenly metastasized.

The possibility—maybe likelihood—that Alice Uden had killed a troublesome mate added a whole new layer to this increasingly squalid tale. Confessing killers almost always told a good, defensible story, so King couldn't count on the hazy hearsay of Alice's children, who heard only what Alice wanted them to hear. What was the real story? King wondered. If she was a stone-cold killer, might she be more entangled in Virginia's vanishing than investigators ever presumed?

And if a man was dead, rotting in a dark hole someplace for the past twenty years, King had to know more. The alleged corpse was just a nameless ghost before, but now *Ron* was taking shape.

If a genuine marriage had happened, there'd be a record someplace. If he was young, it was a good chance there was a family who missed him. And a man might erase his future by changing his name and dematerializing—or by being murdered and thrown in a secret hole—but either way, he couldn't obliterate his past. Some trace of this Ron guy was out there, King knew.

Ron might have been a ghost, but his scent wasn't hard to pick up.

His name (or several variations of it) didn't pop up in any crime databases (nor did Alice's). He found no evidence of Alice's marriage to anybody named Ron in Wyoming. If they lived anywhere in Wyoming, there was no record of a job, utility bills, voter registration, taxes, even a phone number. He left no shadow.

Weeks passed without any hits . . . then a break. King had expanded his search to surrounding states, and Colorado had something.

On September 17, 1974, a marriage license had been issued to Ronald Lee Holtz and Alice Louise Prunty in Adams County, Colorado, which mainly encompassed Denver's northern suburbs. Around five o'clock that same day, Ron and Alice were married at 7680 Kearney Drive in Commerce City, a smelly, blue-collar refinery town on the outskirts of Denver. The ceremony was held in the private home of the pastor at Wallace Memorial Baptist Church—which was just a low-rent sanctuary in a clapboard house a few blocks over—Reverend Conway F. Holtz, the groom's father.

Ron Holtz was a Baptist preacher's kid.

By 1993, Ron Holtz's mother had died, and the good reverend Holtz was sixty-six years old. Also, a couple of younger sisters still lived in Colorado, with a handful of other relatives, so King made a long trip to Colorado to talk to the people who knew Ron Holtz best: his family.

They told a sad story.

His parents' second son, Ronnie was born August 30, 1950, in Colorado. His boyhood was typical, except for mental, emotional, and physical abuse, inflicted mostly by his tyrannical father. His chronically depressed mother wasn't really a factor, either way. But it was the 1950s, and the world was less sensitive to such things. Nevertheless, Ronnie grew up striving to please his unpleasable father.

They often fished together in the mountains. Silverton Lake was his father's favorite, and, maybe because he was at peace up there, there were no beatings, criticisms, or insults. Ronnie felt safest with his father when they were at the lake. It became the happiest place in his life.

Few pleasant memories about Ronnie surfaced. One sister recalled how their mother had "switched" her for some misbehavior and Ronnie intervened. The angry switching just shifted to him. She always believed he took the beating in her place. But that was about the nicest thing anyone had to say about Ronnie Holtz.

By sixteen, he'd been hospitalized at least once for behavioral problems and emotional instability. He'd run away from home and was eventually sent to reform school. On the outside, he was a handsome kid, well-built and well-groomed. On the inside, he was a hot mess.

Once Ronnie had the modest freedom that high school kids crave, his relationship with his exasperated family had worn thin. He found drugs. He also found girls, who supplied emotional succor he never knew. It was a different kind of drug that made him high, and maybe a little crazier than usual.

Funny, King thought, that nobody was sharing happier memories about Ronnie, as if he'd never smiled, never played, never did anything nice for his sisters.

At eighteen, as a draftee just home from army boot camp, his little sister introduced him to a fifteen-year-old friend, and they fell in lust. Both of them were aroused as much by rebellion against their families as the sex. Ronnie quickly proposed, and she quickly accepted before he shipped off to Vietnam. He mailed her engagement ring from Saigon.

If Ronnie Holtz was a little crazy before Vietnam, the war made him crazier.

As a door gunner on an attack chopper, he saw plenty of action. Maybe he saw worse. He'd certainly tell people he killed villagers, even babies. Maybe he did, and maybe he didn't. He had plenty of time to wrestle with his shadows in that wet, green hallucination called Vietnam. Back at the LZ, he smoked grass and dabbled in LSD, heroin, and other drugs common in Indian country. He scored some nasty tattoos. But after a couple scary freak-outs—he claimed it was all because his girlfriend seldom wrote to him—the army sent him home. Catch-22: Ronnie Holtz had to be crazy to fight this crazy war, but he was too crazy to fight this crazy war. His two-year hitch abruptly ended after only 478 days, not even a year and a half.

Stateside, it got no better. Ronnie was irreparably shattered.

He married his young sweetheart, and she was instantly pregnant. After only three weeks home, they got into an argument and Ronnie purposely overdosed on antihistamine caps, hoping to kill himself. He checked himself into Denver's VA hospital, claiming he was terribly depressed. They gave him Librium for anxiety and referred him to a mental health center. He never went.

Ronnie visited the VA hospital several more times in the next few months, always with similar complaints.

As a husband, he only wanted to party and get loaded. His immature wife never questioned him, and he never explained. She was timid, and he was violent. That was their wedded bliss.

Their baby, a girl they named Sharon, was born April 5, 1971. The new child was not a panacea for Ronnie's demons. In fact, in the waiting room after the birth, Ronnie punched his father-in-law and then prohibited his wife's parents from seeing their newborn grandchild for a week.

Ronnie didn't know how to be a man. He didn't know how to deal with problems. He didn't know the damage he did. He wasn't sly and sneaky, which would suggest he had a plan for the damage he did. He didn't. He just exploded.

It didn't require a degree in psychology to know why he developed an infatuation (bordering on a fetish) with a certain hit song, which he played over and over on a well-worn cassette or turned up loud when it came on the radio. "Father and Son" by Cat Stevens—an iconic song about a father and son who can't understand each other—became the soundtrack of Ronnie's life. In his restless mind, he was a lonely child seeking his own destiny, not a manic-depressive, abusive drug addict jonesing for a fix. His father, though, was never like that befuddled guy in the song, whose path was different and who simply had trouble letting go of a beloved son. That wasn't Conway, no way. Not in Ronnie's mind.

A little after noon on April 21, 1971, high on drugs and low with depression, Ronnie locked himself in his bathroom and slit his wrists. His wounds weren't deep enough to require stitches, but the military doctors wanted to commit him to the psych ward. He and his wife argued loudly against it, so he was released.

Three months later, orderlies from the VA's day hospital delivered Ronnie to the psych ward. He'd rampaged, shouting wild homicidal and suicidal threats to kill himself, his father-in-law, and police. He was out of work and out of money, and he spent his days mostly in trouble with authorities. He stayed only eleven minutes on the psych ward before he demanded to be released because his wife couldn't survive without him. When she wouldn't commit him, he walked away.

Again.

When he was home, Ronnie was as abusive as his father ever was. His temper had always been quick to flare, and he had been verbally cruel to his girlfriend. But after they married, the grace period was over. It turned physical, almost daily. She never called the cops for fear of another beating, maybe worse, when he bailed out. Every beating was followed swiftly by passionate apologies, but he never changed.

One time, he beat his wife savagely after an OB-GYN visit . . . because she'd allowed another man to touch her private parts.

Worst of all, the crying baby enraged him. Ronnie never touched little Sharon, but he flipped out every time the baby bawled for her mother.

In December 1971, Ronnie got into a violent ruckus with one of his sister's friends. Cops gave him a choice: go to jail or go to the psych ward. Ronnie chose the psych ward.

It was his young wife's chance. Ronnie was a mean son of a bitch who'd never change. Divorcing him and getting far away meant survival. She packed up everything and moved back to her parents' home. He saw his daughter once after that, and never again.

Six months after Sharon was born, her seventeen-year-old mother and twenty-year-old father divorced. They'd been married eighteen turbulent months.

Throughout 1972 and 1973, Ron Holtz was in and out of VA psych wards in Colorado, Nebraska, and Wyoming. He supported himself with menial, usually brief jobs as a janitor. His records followed him: clinical depression; uncontrollable anger; sociopathy; explosive personality disorder; impaired liver function; abuse of amphetamines, cocaine, heroin, and morphine; suicidal impulses; manic episodes; high blood pressure; and excessive smoking—and a reluctance to change any of it.

The government doctors always sent him away with scripts for powerful antipsychotic drugs.

In July 1974, Ronnie was busted with a few pills he shouldn't have had. His public defender made a deal: if Ronnie would plead guilty and seek psychiatric treatment, he could avoid jail. His fine and court fees were $65, payable to his Denver probation officer at $3 a week. Although he'd have to stay out of trouble for a whole year—something he'd never done in his adult life—he leaped at the deal.

The next month, the Denver veterans hospital transferred Ronald Lee Holtz to a small VA psychiatric ward in Sheridan, Wyoming. He landed on suicide watch a few times but got a custodial job at the local community college, along with the usual heavy dosages of antipsychotics.

The hospital wanted to help him, but it determined that he was his own worst enemy, an antiauthoritarian malcontent who constantly tried to outmaneuver the staff. He'd conflicted with so many staffers that he got only the bare minimum of attention from caregivers on his ward.

Except one.

A new nurse had taken a special interest in Ronnie Holtz. She spent more time with him, talking and smiling. He didn't treat her like he treated everyone else. The nurse, an LPN named Alice Prunty, was a fairly recent hire, but she seemed to have an obvious affection for her patients, especially Ronnie.

If they'd only known how special.

On September 4, 1974, twenty-four-year-old Ronnie Holtz checked himself out of the Wyoming psychiatric hospital, and thirty-five-year-old nurse Alice Prunty unexpectedly quit her job. It wasn't a coincidence.

Thirteen days later, they were married in Pastor Holtz's front room in Commerce City.

The newlyweds left immediately after being pronounced man and wife. They moved into a trailer in a crappy little trailer park somewhere in Cheyenne. Ronnie visited a few times after that, sometimes with Alice, but nobody expected it to last. One of his sisters recalled seeing a bruise on Alice's leg that Alice explained as an injury from a car wreck. The sister was suspicious, but she also thought Alice didn't seem like the type of woman who'd tolerate abuse from any man.

Ronnie's calls and visits stopped completely after Christmas 1974. His family wasn't surprised. None recalled seeing him after that December, but they didn't care much. Maybe he'd gone walkabout again, or OD'd on heroin, or finally pissed off somebody bigger and badder. Whatever bad thing might have happened to him, he probably deserved it, they all told King.

It didn't matter. They were so unconcerned about their son and brother, who'd been such an asshole all his life, that nobody even reported him missing.

King had struck the mother lode, although there was much more to be learned about Ronald Lee Holtz. It seemed like King knew a lot, but he'd barely scratched the surface. For one, he still had no idea what became of freakishly flawed Ronnie, who apparently knew he needed help but pushed it away, sometimes violently, every time.

What he heard from Ronnie's loved ones—although none seemed to love him much—painted him as a functionally insane and ferocious bully. Maybe Alice shot him to protect herself.

A battered-wife defense? Maybe. Ronnie Holtz was clearly a wife beater, but the accounts so far suggested Alice shot him while he was asleep, defenseless. The element of self-defense turned instantly murky when Alice chose not to flee her abuser, when she chose not to call the cops, and when she planned an elaborate cover-up that fooled cops for at least two decades. Maybe nobody would mourn for or miss Ronnie Holtz, but justice was (partially) blind to his personality flaws if he was cold-bloodedly murdered in his sleep by his wife.[1]

It wasn't King's job to decide when a murder was justified, and it would be wildly premature right now, at any rate. So he continued his search for facts.

Among the facts he found was that Ronnie had no activity on his Social Security record after 1974, even though he'd worked many jobs before that to support his various bad habits. Such a disappearance from federal watchdogs could only be explained if he'd changed his identity, died, or gone into witness protection, all still possible explanations.

Ronnie hadn't filed a tax return since 1974, either.

Weeks later, when King received the thick packet of Ron Holtz's VA medical records, he saw Ronnie's demons had been even worse than his family remembered. Multiple suicide attempts. Countless physical confrontations with orderlies, nurses, and doctors. Buckets of powerful meds. And always, quick exits. The last notation in his VA file, which was closed in December 1974 for lack of activity, detailed his last missed appointment. No VA doctor ever saw him again.

King also learned that at the time Ronnie disappeared, Alice drove a Pinto, a compact car.

Every stone investigator Dave King kicked, something poisonous slithered out. Almost nothing suggested this was a simple case of abandonment by a mentally unstable war veteran, drug user, violent sociopath, and wife batterer.

The search for answers had shifted to the Cheyenne area, so King enlisted the help of the Laramie County Sheriff's Office in Cheyenne, where they had a better idea of the local scene and knew all the right buttons to push to get hidden information without search warrants and official letterhead.

On a cold December morning in 1996, King spilled his entire case—at least, everything he knew—on Sergeant Terry Bohlig's desk in Cheyenne. He explained the frustratingly fragmentary Uden disappearance in Riverton and a possibly undetected Cheyenne homicide, separated by 270 miles and fifteen years.

Their only link? Gerald and Alice Uden.

Sergeant Bohlig's Cheyenne deputies soon added new flesh to the skeletal Holtz case: Within days of Christmas, Alice filed for a divorce from Ronnie, citing "intolerable indignities." A summons was sent to his father's Commerce City address, but the court received a letter from Reverend Conway Holtz stating that Ronnie had long ago moved without leaving a forwarding address. The law required Alice to seek Ronnie by placing a legal advertisement in a local paper, so she bought space in the tiny *Pine Bluffs Post*, the smallest paper in Laramie County and one of the smallest in Wyoming. Her ad listed Holtz's last known address as "unknown." Alice legally swore to the judge that she tried to contact her estranged husband but had no luck.

When Ronnie Holtz failed to respond to the divorce filing, a judge granted it on February 5, 1975, less than six weeks after Holtz was last seen. He also granted her request that her previous married name, Alice Louise Prunty, be restored. For all intents and purposes, it was as if she'd never met Ronald Lee Holtz.

On a different front, a little more research suggested that Alice had moved around with a new mobile home. She and her late husband, Don Prunty, had purchased it just a few weeks before he died in July 1973. A mortgage insurance policy paid it off completely; the widow Alice owned it free and clear. If Alice really killed Ron Holtz a year later in a Cheyenne trailer park, was it the murder scene?

One more tidbit: The toddler Eliza received monthly veterans benefits after her father, Don Prunty, who fought in WWII, died. No application was made for veterans benefits that might have been due to Holtz's survivors. But it didn't matter much: all of Eliza's benefits ended when Alice married Gerald.

Then there was this—not a clue, but still a telling detail, at least in King's mind: never in the past fifteen years, not once, did Gerald or Alice call to check on the progress of the search for Virginia and the two boys Gerald called his sons.

So now King had Ronnie Holtz's name and six entangled backstories. And he had reason to believe this was a more malignant case than anybody imagined.

But in Ronnie Holtz's case, he didn't have a body, a murder weapon, a crime scene, or a confession.

Again.

In September 1994, two state crime lab technicians, three Cheyenne deputies, and a federal mine inspector went back to the Remount Ranch, just to assess what challenges they'd face if they decided to dig deeper. The 1984 dig had literally only scratched the surface of the old shaft.

The McLaughlin gold mine claim was filed in 1896, almost a hundred years before. Nobody knows if gold was ever found there, but the hole was ninety feet deep, straight down, when they stopped looking. At that moment, the gold mine became a very deep trash dump where the carcasses of dead animals were tossed, just to keep the smell and carrion eaters away.

The four-thousand-acre ranch's real gold was in horses and cattle. It supplied "remount" horses to the US Cavalry during the Indian Wars and into the mid-twentieth century, thus its name.

The Remount's colorful history also included romantic connections to the infamous outlaw Tom Horn, but its true claim to fame was more bookish than bad guys. In 1930, the ranch was sold to Swedish immigrant Helge Sture-Vasa and his wife Mary, a Brooklyn girl who had always dreamed of owning a horse. While Helge did the dirty work of ranching, Mary, a former silent film scriptwriter, sat down at her Corona typewriter again and started a novel about a boy and his horse.

Eventually, Mary Sture-Vasa took the pen name Mary O'Hara, and her book *My Friend Flicka* became an instant classic when it was published in 1941. Wildly popular sequels followed, *Thunderhead* in 1943 and *Green Grass of Wyoming* in 1946. Hollywood made them all into movies starring a young Roddy McDowall, and even a 1950s television series.

Local lore claimed the carcass of the real-life Flicka (or her sire) had been dumped in the mine decades ago. Maybe it was true, maybe not. Indeed, the real-life horse upon which O'Hara based Flicka died of barbed-wire wounds at the Remount and might have been dropped in the hole, which O'Hara mentions a few times in her book as a kind of metaphoric hell:

> Gus tied a rope to the dead horse's head and fastened it to the back of the little Ford truck and hauled him away across the ranch to the shaft of the abandoned mine on the hillside, three hundred feet deep.[2]

Sometimes in the Old West, it's best not to try to disentangle myth from fact. Like stories about Billy the Kid or Butch Cassidy, some reality is so enmeshed in legend that it's damn near impossible to unravel it without losing something important to its appeal. So "facts" can exist in the American West's mythosphere as something more than truth, something less than fantasy, like affable ghosts who can never be freed from our attics.

But there are plenty of known facts about the historic ranch:

In 1946, the Remount—including a six-thousand-square-foot, cowboy-chic ranch house where O'Hara wrote her books—was sold again and became a dude ranch, popular with Hollywood celebrities of the day, such as Pat Boone, the McGuire Sisters, and Arthur Godfrey. It passed through many hands, including entrepreneur and politician John Ostlund, who bought the ranch in 1970. Early on, he hired Illinois grain seller Don Prunty and his wife, Alice, to run the place. In the mid-1990s, the Remount finally landed among the assets of Denver financial mogul Steve Bangert, who still raises Texas longhorns on the spread.

By 1994, the mine was nearly full of dead animals, loose dirt, debris, snow, and anything else that might fill an untended hole in Wyoming's rugged terrain. To be honest, when the deputies, mine inspector, and six crime scene techs arrived, they weren't even entirely sure it was the mine Ted had mentioned. Despite his offers to guide searchers to the exact spot, they'd never actually asked him to do it.

At the time, it didn't look like a ninety-foot shaft, more like an unimpressive manmade cavity—maybe only fifteen or twenty feet deep—in the slope of a nondescript hill, surrounded by ponderosa pines, lichen-encrusted pink granite, and range grass. A weathered barbed-wire fence surrounded the shallow mouth, but it was designed to be opened and closed for dumping.

The mine expert declared the walls solid enough for a couple diggers to work, but other safety issues made the threat of a cave-in very real. To excavate the mine properly, he said, would take weeks and a lot of arduous preparation to keep the walls from collapsing on searchers.

The deputies and crime scene techs counted their cards. Was it worth the risk to dig deeper into a hole that might be the wrong one, that might cave in and kill somebody who was looking for bodies that might not be there at all? Plus, these rutted ranch roads were hardly navigable with daylight and four-wheel drive, so it was hard to imagine a small car making it here at night in the dead of winter, possibly with snow on the ground. And would the driver—with a body in back—really take the chance that her headlights would be seen at the main house? And what about the two smaller, unexamined mines nearby?

The longer these cops lingered, the less appealing this mine looked as a crime scene. After less than an hour at the site, they left.

Jurisdictional issues were becoming a problem for King.

King's investigation crossed not only county lines but state lines. Different law enforcement agencies had different priorities; different prosecutors had different risk tolerance. At the moment, he couldn't prove he had a single murder, much less four. And he sure as hell couldn't pinpoint where any of these murders happened, if they did.

Forget where the bodies were buried. They could be anywhere. Murder weapons? Who knew? The prosecutors in the county where the original crime against Virginia and the boys happened couldn't get an indictment; he couldn't expect more from cops and prosecutors in distant jurisdictions. They had their own problems. They'd want more solid information before they wasted time and money on some other cop's cold case. And he had no smoking guns to offer.

They wouldn't blow him off, but he couldn't expect faraway cops to have the same passion he had. So far, he'd had excellent support from his colleagues in other departments, but he knew he couldn't go back to the same well every time with leads that didn't pan out.

The Remount gold mine was a lead that refused to pan out. Two cursory searches—"glances" might be a better word—had been disappointing.

Their reasons weren't nefarious, but nobody was in a hurry to open up that hole.

By 1996, the exploration of Alice's alleged spouse killing—even now, nobody could be absolutely sure it really happened—was at another standstill. Again, unconnected dots swarmed.

Larry Mathews, who had opened the Uden case in 1980 and followed it until his political firing by a new sheriff in 1991, came back as the new sheriff himself in 1995. Among his first official acts: he gave King his blessing on the Uden case.

But the line seemed to be crumbling on the Alice front. Just like the related Uden investigation, the lack of a body, a murder weapon, an eyewitness, or a confession left King without many options in the suspected Holtz murder.

So in early 1996, Mathews set aside the usual pride (and cockiness) of a small local law enforcement agency and asked for help from the closest thing Wyoming had to state cops, the Division of Criminal Investigation.

DCI had been created in 1973 over the aggressive objections of the state's sheriffs. At first, its jurisdiction was limited to drug cases that might cross county lines, but otherwise, DCI agents could only be involved if local cops or prosecutors invited them. They were restricted to the tasks that local cops couldn't do well or didn't want to do. Thus, DCI required local cops to recognize their shortcomings, which is hard to do in a culture that's competitive and proud, and often has political ramifications.

In those early days, DCI agents had a reputation as *Starsky and Hutch* types, driving muscle cars, growing their hair long, wearing flashy duds . . . and playing hard after hours. They really played by their own rules, and they didn't have much time for the Barney Fifes in local law enforcement. They didn't answer outsiders' questions, and they stayed aloof. All that was true, but early DCI agents were also all type A people doing difficult, dangerous things.

But that image—cowboys working and playing hard at "retail drug enforcement," hanging out in bars and parties, busting mostly low-level dealers—made it hard for county sheriffs to ask for their help. Sheriffs had to worry about reelection, and they didn't want voters to think they weren't in perfect control of their counties' crime problems. Even small things got big traction in some of Wyoming's little counties, where there might be more cattle than people.

By 1996, DCI had sobered up. Some high-profile cases had both exposed the agency's weaknesses and proved its value. Changes were made, and DCI was evolving. It harvested some of the state's best investigative talent, improved its crime lab, and became a serious resource for understaffed, underfunded local cops.

So Mathews swallowed his pride and asked for DCI's help. The agency's deeper pockets added free resources that he couldn't afford. But he also couldn't afford to let big cases go unsolved.

King was glad for the help, but he still felt possessive of the Uden case. He'd invested a lot of blood, sweat, and shoe leather in it. He wanted the extra eyes, but he feared the state investigators might come crashing in, bigfooting the little guys out in the boonies.

He couldn't have been more wrong.

DCI assigned a soft-spoken, petite, and sharp detective who happened to be its first female agent, Lynne Callaghan. She had broken the gender barrier, but she wasn't a rule breaker or even a rule bender—a perfect agent for the maturing DCI.

At five foot two and 105 pounds, Callaghan had long ago learned to turn her size to her advantage. The daughter of teachers, she grew up wanting to be a lawyer, but the shades of gray troubled her. Instead, she went into law enforcement, where right and wrong, good and evil were not such ambiguous questions.

Callaghan's superpower was interrogation. She might not be able to wrestle a burly perp to the ground, but she could read him like a comic book. Her interview skills got her a few big confessions . . . and a job offer from Wyoming's DCI.

Just a few weeks after the Fremont County sheriff joined forces with DCI, Dave King and Lynne Callaghan invited Alice's son Ted into the SO's basement interrogation room for another fresh start. They'd learned a lot about Alice and Ron Holtz in the couple years since Ted first unburdened himself to Jack Coppock. Now they hoped to flush some new dirty memory from his mind and give new life to their investigation.

The interview started about seven o'clock that cold February night.[3] Near six feet tall, Ted had a working man's build, strong and muscular. He wore jeans and a crooked, dirty smile, exaggerating his own jovial presence. He tended to cover some of the serious stuff with little giggles and a trace of belligerence. And although he'd had some minor beefs around town with drugs and booze, he was reasonably sober, as far as King could tell.

In fact, he appeared to be eager to tell his story again. Maybe it comforted him to get it off his chest someplace other than a barstool, King thought.

Callaghan asked most of the questions, starting easy and working her way up to the tougher stuff; guiding the uneasy Ted through his itinerant childhood; putting him at ease with her casual, nonthreatening style; and occasionally giggling with him about funny things he said.

Her simple questions led him up to his life at the Remount Ranch as she sidled up to the sweet spot, subtly nudging his foggy memory.

"And Don [Prunty] died," she said. "What did you and your mom do then?"

"At that point we moved into a trailer right next to the school I went to," Ted recalled, "and she drove a bus for the school system there."

"All right, and then from there, where'd you guys move to?"

"That's when we lived at the Lincoln Memorial [by the rest stop], at whatever that pass is, um, the summit. Yeah, she was the caretaker there then. Basically, we cleaned the bathrooms and did the trash, little stuff like that. It was somewhere in that time period that she also bartended at Buford."

The itinerary got tangled after that. First, they moved to an apartment in Laramie, Ted said, then he was shipped around between the midwestern homes of his biological father, grandparents, and adult sister and his nomadic Wyoming mom again.

"Can I ask why you moved so many times?" Callaghan inquired.

"I missed my dad and I wanted to move back with him," Ted said. "I guess things didn't work out there. I really missed Mom more than Dad, and I moved back. I don't remember why I lived with—Oh yeah, my mother got tangled up with her third husband."

"Do you know his name?"

Ted paused a moment.

"Ron. I met him one time."

"How do you remember meeting him? That's what I need to figure out."

"Um, that's all pretty vague to me, but the only time was at my grandparents' house. I really didn't interact with him or anything. Just another boyfriend in my mom's life."

"OK, good," Callaghan said, but pressed on. "So you just remember he was there? Do you have any impression of the man at all?"

"I really don't remember hardly anything of him. I didn't really have much impression of this guy one way or another. I know later down the road my mom told me that he beat her a lot, and he wrecked her car one time, he was real into drugs and alcohol and..." Ted sighed deeply. "I really don't remember much of him."

Ted recounted more moves: his mother working at the VA hospital in Sheridan, his time pumping gas at the Buford store while Alice tended bar there, chauffeuring a drunken Alice around, her confession about killing that asshole Ron—all either repeating his earlier memories or corroborating what the investigation had already uncovered.

"Tell me how your mother came to explain it to you," Callaghan said. "Where were you, how old were you, how did it come about?"

"Well, we still lived in Laramie, and she was bartending at Buford. I must have been twelve or thirteen. I'd drive her back and forth from Laramie. She got me to be her drinking buddy. It was in one of those times that she told me."

"Driving?"

"Yeah, it was one of the times we was both kinda drunk. Just us by ourselves, and she was quite drunk and broke down. She had this terrible burden on her shoulders and I guess she just had to get it out. I didn't really say nothing. I didn't know what to say."

"What did she say to you?"

"She just told me that this Ron guy was very abusive, beat her, wrecked her car, did this and that, and then one night she'd had enough of it. She went to his bed while he was sleeping and shot him in the head with a .22. She told me she wrapped him up in the sheets that was on the bed, and got him out to the trunk of the car . . ."

"All by herself?"

"Yes."

"Was he a very big person, or is your mom pretty sturdy?"

"I remember Ron as being kind of a big person, but the way she explained it, she was all by herself. That's when she loaded him up, I don't know if a car, or truck, or what, not sure about that . . . but she drove him to Buford and got with Kay Florita."

A new name. Dave King scribbled the name *Kay Florita* in his notes.

"That's when she got a little help," Ted continued. "And it seems to me like she told me they put him in some kind of a packing drum of some sort."

"Kay helped her do it?"

"That's what she told me."

"And then what did they do?"

"They drove to the ranch, the Remount Ranch, which is probably only ten miles from there. They put him in an old gold mine, like a two-hundred- or three-hundred-foot shaft. While we was living on the ranch, if a cow or a dog or a horse died, it went in there." Suddenly Ted brightened. A new memory. "Actually, that's where Flicka or Flicka's dad is at," he said, delighted by his odd brush with a celebrity, as grim as it was. "You know, *My Friend Flicka*?"

"In the gold mine?"

"Yeah. We'd drag a dead cow or horse up there with a truck, and just drag it in. I remember the ranch dog, a German Shepherd that got killed by a bull and we put him down there. His name was Jefe. . . . I'd drive you guys right to it. That's why I'm here, to be whatever help I can . . . to get this situation resolved."

Dave King clicked his pen and wrote *Jefe* in his notebook.

"Did you ever look down in there?"

"All you can see is darkness. Deep, ya know? You could throw rocks down in there. Just a big hole."

"When it comes time, I might need you to come show me."

"Call me, I'll take you right down there. . . . I'll crawl down the goddang shaft myself."

"Well, I think because there's other holes out there, no one calls anything a gold mine. I just don't want a bunch of folks trying to find something that's the wrong place. But if you know what your mom referred to as 'the gold mine' as a specific place . . .'"

"I could take you right to it."

"After your mom told you what she and Kay did, did she say what they did next?"

"No. After it got to that point, I felt that her conscience was relieved a little. She never mentioned it afterwards, and I never brought it up afterwards. . . . It was something she put on a kid's shoulders, and I buried it. I really did."

"What'd you do when you heard it?"

"Try to console my mother. She was so upset, and I was the man in her life at that time, you know, taking care of stuff. And the actual thing didn't faze me at that time. It was more to console my crying mother. I just kinda buried it after that. It was a secret that I just want to forget."

"Who else have you talked with?"

"I've talked to my sister Thea about it. Quite a few years later, we were sitting around drinking one day, and just kinda having a heart-to-heart, and this just kinda come up. I told her this is something that has been bothering me, and she told me that Mom had told her this story also."

Callaghan abruptly changed the subject, from one suspected murder to another.

"So what do you think of your mother and Gerald Uden as related to the missing Uden family?"

Ted pulled no punches for his stepfather . . . or his mother.

"In my own heart, I think Gerald did it," he said. "And I think my mother knows something, if she didn't help him. I do remember at that time they was going through a battle with those kids' mother, Virginia Uden. They was tired of paying child support. Virginia was very dead set against Gerald seeing 'em. So he figured, well, if he couldn't get visitation he wouldn't have to pay child support."

Ted didn't stop there.

"The whole thing was Mom and Gerald didn't wanna pay any more child support. So, they was figuring up schemes of ways to get out of paying child support. There was no love between Gerald and his two adopted children, I know that."

"Do you ever think about what might have happened?"

"I thought of a lot of different things," Ted said. "Gerald worked at the mine up there. There'd be all kinds of places to get rid of a body. He knew these mountains very well. We lived right next to Ocean Lake. What would it take to tie a couple of bricks on the kids and throw them in the lake? As for what really happened, I don't know. Knowing Gerald, who knows? Gerald was very cunning."

"Is your mother cunning?"

"In her own way, yes. I don't believe like killer-cunning. And with this other guy, I think it was more she'd been beaten, pushed, and everything else so long that she just blew a fuse. She's not cunning in the way Gerald is, but she loved Gerald enough that I think that she would go right along with everything Gerald did."

"So this has got to be bad for her to have to live with too . . ."

"It's got to eat on her," Ted said. "Maybe this will set her free one way or another. Maybe it's not what she wants, but, god-dangit, the truth needs to come out and it needs to be put in the past, no matter what happened. It just needs to be done. I would like to see something good come out of this. If nothing else, I'd like to see that grandmother in Riverton know where her kids are at."

"Did you know the little kids involved?"

"I never met 'em, never did. I think Virginia's mother is the one that kinda keeps pushing this a lot. You see the little flyers for the missing kids. I guess she's still alive."

"Have you talked with your mother about it since it happened?"

"I've never sat down and asked her if they did it, or what happened, or anything. It was basically one of those subjects that was just never brought up."

"How come?"

Ted sighed again before answering.

"I don't know. I guess it's kinda human nature. If you have your eyes closed, there's no ghosts out there."

"Are you afraid to ask your mom?"

"Kind of, yeah. After I talked with Jack Coppock, I called her on the phone. We had a pretty good relationship up to then, but I said, 'Mom, you know I really feel in my heart that you and Gerald had something to do with this. I talked to the sheriff.' I told her with the Ron deal, I'd like to see her come forward on her own, but if not, I was gonna go talk to 'em."

"What did she say to you?"

"She said, 'Fine. I guess I have nothing else to say to you,'" Ted said. "And I have not talked to her, or Eliza, or my little brother since then. They just kinda threw me out the door. Which I can't blame them."

"Do you think you did the right thing?"

"In my own heart, yes. If Gerald did it, the way those two got along, she knew everything that happened, I can tell you that."

"Did your mom dislike Virginia?"

"They both hated her," Ted said without hesitating. "No, they didn't just hate her. They both *hated* her."

"Did Eliza get along with Gerald?"

"Not real well. I didn't know anybody who got along with Gerald."

"Why not?"

"I know nobody that spent a day with Gerald and didn't come away saying, 'That guy's strange.' He's just a spooky kinda strange."

"Tell me what you mean."

"Like when he first met my mother," Ted recalled. "Me and Thea ate dinner over there, and we both come away like, *This guy is really weird.* Not like a child molester weird or anything, just spooky weird . . . just spooky."

"Was it like he doesn't have feelings, or . . . ?"

"Yeah, like he has no feeling. You're exactly right."

"But he likes your mom."

"As far as I know, as far as I seen, he always treated my mother really well."

"What are your personal reasons for talking to us, Ted?"

"To have a good clean name in this community. I plan on spending the rest of my life here, my kids probably the same. I want to be a pillar of the community, you know. I don't want nothing like this behind me. It's something that needs to be cleared up."

The interview was almost done. Ted had amplified his earlier interview with Coppock, but King didn't think he was exaggerating as much as he was exorcising certain demons.

"How will you feel about it if your mom is involved?" Callaghan asked in her last question.

"If she is, she is," Ted said. "I broke my ties with my mother when I talked with Jack Coppock. And if she's guilty, I guess she needs to pay the price."

Kay Florita, sixty-six, now lived alone on a modest ranch across the highway from her old store and bar at Buford (pop. 1). A few weeks after

Ted dropped her name in his interview, King and Callaghan paid her a visit. They were curious if she played any role in Alice's alleged disposal of Ron Holtz's corpse back in 1973.

Perched eight thousand feet in the Wyoming Rockies, Buford was established in 1866 as the highest railroad stop on the Transcontinental Railroad, which was still under construction. It was named for Major General John Buford, a heroic Union cavalry officer whose defense of the high ground at Gettysburg was the key to the Yankee victory. Unfortunately, it cost Buford his life, and he died in the arms of his aide, Captain Myles Keogh, who himself died with Custer at the Little Bighorn in 1876. Three years later, the railroad barons named this little spot for Buford. Alas, the memory of the great hero, like the town itself, barely survived in the late twentieth century.

A little store and post office were built there in 1939, mostly for a dozen ranching families that lived in the windswept area.

Since long before settlers came here, it wasn't unusual to have three-day blizzards with forty-mile-per-hour winds and forty-below temperatures. It was a place where the weather could ice up chimneys and extinguish winter fires, or unzip electrical lines like a loose thread on a sweater, or drift snow so deep your house disappeared. You didn't call a handyman. You fixed it yourself and survived, you moved to the city, or you died.

That's why nobody lived there.

Kay and Mateo Florita bought the store, bar, and gas pumps in 1968 (and when they divorced seven years later, Kay got the whole town).

At the time, the "interstate" highway outside was just a divided, two-lane blacktop, not the superslab it'd become later. Back then, it was more dangerous and less traveled. In some spots, the median just disappeared completely into deep caverns, so if plunging off the road didn't kill you, the hurricane-force winds, black ice, or whiteouts might.

And you couldn't holler for help. The nearest town was thirty miles away.

Buford demanded hardy, unconformed souls. And Kay Florita, barely five foot four and 130 pounds if she was packing, was one. She didn't waste her time hoping for better seasons that wouldn't come. She ran a bar in the middle of Nowhere, Wyoming, so she could take care of herself.

Her little mercantile stocked boxed donuts, soda, bread, jerky, motor oil, air fresheners, the usual c-store stuff. College kids from Laramie often asked for "cigarette" papers, but Kay always refused. The highway patrol usually dropped off lead-footed drivers to buy traveler's checks or money orders to pay speeding tickets, so for many years the Buford post office led Wyoming in sales of money orders.

A cozy little bar in back was frequented mostly by railroad section crews after work. Two Conoco pumps served travelers. The post office was a countertop. The pay phone outside was useless in the wind.

But nobody complained. Kay didn't take shit from anybody, although she was generous when people needed it. She was raised Catholic but never went to church. She hated fancy stuff. She lived in a wasteland where death was ordinary, but she refused to look at her late friends in their caskets. She didn't put on airs, although she colored her hair reddish auburn.

She didn't seem nervous at all when two cops came calling. She liked cops.

Yeah, I knew Alice.

Yeah, Alice knew Remount Ranch like the back of her hand.

Yeah, I've seen that guy with her at the bar, always drunk or high.

Yeah, I heard he was in a mental asylum.

No, I never saw him hit her or be mean.

Yeah, Alice worked at the bar once, but I fired her for sleeping with all the Navajo railroaders who drank there. She'd live with one, date another. It was a problem.

No, my dogs didn't like her. And neither did I, but help is hard to find around here.

Yeah, she told me she killed a guy.

No, she never asked me to help her get rid of him. I couldn't do that.

No, the highway patrol guys come by here every day, so why would I risk everything for her?

No, I wouldn't help my best friend get rid of a body. Why would I do it for somebody I didn't like that much?

Yeah, it pisses me off that she'd say I had any part of it.

Even after looking her in the eye, Dave King didn't know if Kay Florita had helped dump Ronnie Holtz's body or not—if there was a body. Her words, demeanor, and body language all signaled she hadn't, but why would Alice implicate a friend so casually if it wasn't true? Alice's kids might have made wrong assumptions or misremembered.

There was a fellow Buford barfly who was closer to Alice and lived nearby, but she couldn't be found. She, not Kay, might have helped Alice and in many ways was a likelier suspect.

But until she turned up, wherever and whenever that might be, King couldn't be sure anyone helped Alice dispose of Ronnie's corpse. Or that it even happened at all.

By the late 1990s, Claire Martin's resolve hadn't waned, although her scars made her tougher. Even in her seventies, she continued to search for her grandsons, whom she still believed had been spared but were secreted away, brainwashed, or simply restrained from their old lives.

Claire had no money, except what little came from her government pension. Nevertheless, she posted a reward for any information that led to Richard and Reagan's safe return.

They'd be in their twenties now. Claire knew because she had celebrated every birthday since they went missing. They could have their own children, and if they did, Claire hoped they protected them better than she had. But wherever they were, they were young men who knew . . . who just knew.

If Virginia survived—and in her heart, Claire believed she hadn't—she'd be around fifty, maybe a grandmother herself. If she lived, maybe she understood Claire loved her with all her heart. If only . . .

Yes, she had regrets, things she should have done differently, things she should have said or not said. But she was trying to make it all up to them by devoting every moment, every last bit of energy, to finding them. She truly thought the search kept her alive.

Claire was still angry at what she believed had been a bungled investigation early on. Her anger, though, was giving way to a persistent sadness. She believed she was the last person who should give up hope—but now, she was the last person who hoped.

For almost ten years, Dave King had tried to make things right with Claire. He spent time with her, spoke honestly, had ideas about what she might do next. He wanted to repair her relationship with the sheriff's office, to soothe her resentment, but it ran too deep and too hot for him to touch.

Claire's face and demeanor were hard, King thought. Her expression rarely changed. He never saw her smile. He heard anger and hurt in her voice; her words were rough but calculated. With him, she was always cautious, although he certainly understood why.

He regularly updated her. The news always buoyed her at first. Then the updates all started feeling the same. Lots of movement, no action. No smoking guns, no bodies. But in the dark, she also imagined that if nobody found bodies, the boys, maybe even Virginia, might still be alive. Every little clue had a flip side, and it made her a little crazy.

She wanted to hear only one thing: They'd all been found. Dead or alive.

By then, Claire had retired from the Riverton laundry and moved into a cabin in Dubois, a tiny town high up in the shadow of the Wind River Range, near the Continental Divide. Still the independent woman who had ridden motorcycles during WWII, when she was a real-life Rosie the Riveter in Pennsylvania factories, Claire found solace in open spaces. She rowed her scull on mountain lakes, cavorted with her dogs, camped alone when she could, tended a high-mountain garden, and sought an uneasy peace in the outdoors. She saw them there. Their names were written in starlight, their innocent little faces sketched in moving water. Out there, she felt closer to them. Or maybe out there, the outside emptiness balanced her inside emptiness.

Sometimes after they all went away, Claire went up in Sinks Canyon. It was an exquisite gash down the eastern slope of the Wind Rivers, where the middle fork of the Popo Agie River disappears, or "sinks," into underground caverns. When the river was running in spring, Claire would lie down amid the wildflowers and close her eyes, just listening to the river. She could exhale there. She found peace.

She awoke every morning with a thought that today was the day something wonderful would happen, that an answer would arrive, or that Richard and Reagan would appear at her door. Nearly twenty years on, it hadn't happened yet, but such was the nature of faith and dreams.

And every day, she looked at that forlorn old station wagon in her driveway. She didn't like to drive it, but she couldn't sell it either. It ran well enough, and she traveled a lot in it, but she imagined that someday, somebody might be able to find new clues hidden inside. It was a sickening artifact of a bad memory she just couldn't shake.

Claire didn't know how much longer she had. She pushed back with all her might against her age. She wanted desperately to keep living, although she couldn't truly live until the boys were home where they belonged. Some days, though, she felt like she hung by the thinnest of threads.

She hadn't felt whole in a long time. It wasn't much of a choice: living without them or dying without them.

Time had caught up to Claire, and days weighed more heavily on her since they left. Maybe it was the weight of hope.

Or maybe it was the weight of blood.

The last few years of the 1990s, the end of the century, were tumultuous for Dave King and his search for four missing people in two different but related cases.

He'd hung his Stetson on Ronnie Holtz as the backdoor solution to Virginia and the boys' disappearance, but all the leads stopped at a hole into which nobody wanted to peer. And the Uden side of the case had long ago petered out.

His friend Jack Coppock retired. Sheriff Mathews tried to demote King to a patrol job, but public pressure helped him remain a detective. After a stint at the FBI Academy in 1997, and still smarting from his attempted benching, King started to think he might like to run for sheriff himself.

Other big cases came along in those years, too, stealing whatever oxygen the plodding Uden case was consuming.

On Thanksgiving Day in 1994, in a wretched ditch camp outside of Crowheart, Wyoming, a village on the Wind River Indian Reservation, a drunken and belligerent Steven Swallow slaughtered his wife, two brothers, and a friend with a hunting rifle while their turkey roasted in the oven. Although it was a federal case because it happened on the "rez," King was up to his bloody elbows in the investigation. A judge eventually sentenced Swallow to four life terms plus sixty-five years in federal prison.

In July 1997, when Amy Wroe Bechtel went missing in the mountains outside of Lander, King was on a wilderness pack trip. He joined the investigation a few days later, but it had already gone south. The "crime" scene was hopelessly tainted, and at first, nobody considered the possibility of murder; it was merely a missing persons case. When King began to dig deeper, he got a strange feeling that Bechtel's husband might be involved. But the husband lawyered up when the deputies and FBI agents tried to interview him. The incriminating silence focused them even more on the husband, away from potentially better suspects and theories.

King worked dawn to dusk on Bechtel. He spent too much time at the office and drank too much afterward. It made him even more resentful of his boss, Larry Mathews, so he drank some more. It all took him away from the Uden case, in which he at least had some good suspects. Ironically, the twentieth century would end, too, without a trace of Amy Bechtel and with no suspects—and another future cold case was born.

So Dave King ran for Fremont County sheriff in 1998, and won. Suddenly, he was an administrator, not an investigator. The thrill of the hunt went missing. His days were spent playing politics, worrying about budgets, and extinguishing little brushfires. He had fewer real friends, more phony ones.

About the same time, Lynne Callaghan resigned from the DCI to become—finally—the lawyer she once dreamed of being. She put her Uden notes in the bureau's cold-case binder, turned in her keys and badge, and left.

Then Jack Coppock died, a personal pain for his protégé Dave King. Bechtel was unsolved, Uden was unsolved . . . King suddenly felt like the wheels were coming off. So he drank some more. Sometimes, he used harder stuff, too, to hide his depression and anxiety.

When he needed more than he could get at the saloon, he went to the evidence locker, which was full of illicit comfort. He stole a large amount of cocaine that was used to train drug dogs, because it was the likeliest to be overlooked if stolen.

The sheriff had enough for a damn good four-day bender—which nearly killed him. He landed in the local hospital with a shunt in his jugular and hooked up to a dialysis machine to help clean his blood. His kidney and liver problems were touch and go for a day.

When he recovered, curious cops wanted to know how the county sheriff got so loaded on coke that he almost died. At first, he claimed he must have been dosed, but King failed his polygraph. A day later, he resigned and was no longer the Fremont County sheriff.

That day in 2001, Dave King stepped over some imaginary line into another life, leaving behind the two biggest cases of his career, both unsolved.

And for the third time in the past twenty years, the disappearance of Virginia, Richard, and Reagan Uden was without a champion. Ron Holtz, if he was indeed dead, was just a name in a folder someplace, still a ghost. And nobody stepped up.

Their cases were officially cold. Nobody was looking for their killers anymore.

Whoever was responsible had gotten away with murder.

Chapter 5

. . . AND TOMORROW

Lonnie TeBeest missed the street.

He'd been a cop in the "big city" of Casper for twenty years before he was hired as a special agent at Wyoming's Division of Criminal Investigation. In Casper, he'd bounced around between patrol, undercover narcotics, and investigations, not knowing what strangeness he'd encounter in his little corner of humanity. He loved it, especially when it involved death, white-collar crime, and ordinary mystery.

TeBeest was a small-town South Dakota kid. Mostly, he grew up in Iroquois, a barely noticeable eastern South Dakota village (pop. 350) on roads nobody traveled. It was the kind of burg where everybody listened for the six o'clock whistle, and all the kids were forbidden from skinny-dipping in ponds at the edge of town, so they did. That was usually the worst crime that occurred in Iroquois.

Lonnie descended from hardworking Dutch and Norwegian stock who settled in the ice latitudes of America's upper high plains. He didn't like a lot of drama, but he needed to feel busy. His father was one of those denizens of the Depression who always had at least one job, often more. Allergies made farming and grain elevator jobs impossible, so the elder TeBeest sorted mail on a South Dakota mail train, drove a postal route, sold headstones in Watertown, cleaned septic tanks as a "honey dipper," walked door to door selling Fuller Brush products and greeting cards, resold old mantel clocks from a dog-eared storefront in Iroquois . . . whatever kept food on the table for his wife and four kids. Lonnie was the youngest.

And Lonnie inherited his father's work ethic. An average student, he dreamed of a college football career—maybe more—until a back injury permanently sidelined him. When he graduated with his forty-seven classmates, some went to college, and some went back to the farm. Lonnie went to work in a lumberyard, then buried telephone lines and tended bar, where he saw a lot of his neighbors spending money they probably didn't have.

One day, for no special reason, he decided to study criminal justice at the tiny Huron College, eighteen miles down the road. He didn't have any particular ambition to be a cop but needed a good job. If anything, he was resigned to living the rest of his life in Iroquois as a carpenter who'd always have a job or two in his back pocket.

Studying was tough because Lonnie exerted only as much effort as he needed to pass. He earned his associate's degree in five semesters—and went back to the lumberyard, according to plan.

Then a friend saw a classified ad in the newspaper. Casper, a small city ten hours west, was looking for cops to keep a lid on the oil field roughnecks and the related chaos of its 1970s oil boom. A written test, an interview, a lie detector, and a physical, all in one day. No problem. Lonnie thought, *Why not?*

Lonnie showed up for the big day wearing long hair and a hippie flowered shirt. Oddly, he passed every step except the oral interview. Afterward, the police chief took him aside and recommended that he read *Dress for Success.*

He didn't get the job or the book, but he got the message.

Lonnie showed up two months later with short hair, a white shirt, and a black tie. He passed. The chief said his main quality was that he'd played football and wasn't afraid to "mix it up." He decided to give TeBeest a chance, even though he didn't expect the kid to survive his probation. It was 1978, and the job paid $958 a month. For the rest of his time on the force, the chief called him "Mark."

His first week was the week of the rowdy county fair, when Casper's usual hell-raising turned big league. Training back then was a flexible concept, not especially rigorous in the small force. It was more sink or swim. Six weeks after the kid turned cop, TeBeest was patrolling the city alone.

His pragmatic, country-boy approach served him well, even if he was occasionally surprised by what city folks did to each other. It wasn't long before he stopped being surprised. In time, he'd be able to see right through people.

At first, he shared a mobile home on the edge of town with another rookie cop, but he'd reconnected with a girl from his high school days, Sandra Baird, one of five state-champion baton-twirling sisters. She was a farm girl, and he was a town boy. She knew he'd worked as a bartender, so she assumed he was a drunk. On their first date, he took her to a cop movie, *The Choirboys*. He drove ten hours home to Iroquois whenever he could, and he dialed a lot of long-distance calls for the next eighteen months, until a fateful day when Sandra was visiting his trailer in Casper. He proposed, and she accepted.

Then he tossed a local department store's catalog in her lap.

"I'm going to work," he said without a hint of romance. "Pick out a ring."

They had three kids over the next seven years, while Lonnie was working his way up to investigations, back to patrol, up to sergeant, back to investigations, then back to patrol. He had a tendency to speak his mind in a blunt, pragmatic, Scandinavian farm-boy way. He was a good cop—one of the best—but he didn't always toe the company line, especially when it didn't necessarily make anyone safer. He was still a country kid who knew that seasons, crops, rainstorms, and church days had a certain order. He didn't make enemies, per se, but he sometimes made his bosses shift uncomfortably in their chairs. And when they didn't care, it was worse.

By the autumn of 1998, it was time for a change.

DCI was a big step up for TeBeest, but the agency itself was a bureaucratic beast whose only connective tissue was red tape. It got blown around in the state capital's hurricane-force political tempests like a fart in a windstorm. In those days, its bosses were still more politician than police.

But DCI's only jurisdiction was narcotics, illegal gambling, and gangs. If a local police chief or sheriff asked for help, which was rare, DCI agents might be farmed out on an interesting case. But they always played second fiddle. For an old street cop—although TeBeest was only forty-four when he joined DCI—the work was monotonous. Chasing drug dealers, gamblers, and gangbangers just didn't crank his engine.

Some days were downright boring.

It was one of those tedious days in 2001 when Special Agent Lonnie TeBeest, the gruff old beat cop, pulled his chair up to the Wyoming Attorney General's computerized database of older, unsolved crimes, looking for something, *anything*, to bust up the fluorescent dreariness of a state detective's drab day.

When he first got interested in cold cases, TeBeest had no experience. He attended a couple conferences, just to learn. They all talked about how expensive the investigations were, warned that it might be hard to find money. They suggested prioritizing cases by their solvability—pick the "low-hanging fruit" first to show results that might make money flow later.

A couple of cases caught his eye. He pulled the archived reports. One was the vicious 1982 rape and fatal beating of an elderly woman in her own home up north, in Sheridan. It was purely a DNA case, but Sheridan cops hadn't asked for DCI's help. That was an insurmountable boundary for TeBeest.

The other looked juicier. A DCI agent had already done a little work on it but hit a wall. Twenty years cold. Four missing people, including two kids, probably dead. A husband and wife who looked guilty as hell. A grieving, activist grandmother seeking answers. No DNA, no bodies, no weapons, no crime scenes, no confessions ... and not a single damn reason to bring the prime suspects in.

Yeah, this was something TeBeest could sink his teeth into. Sure, he'd need his bosses' approval and maybe some travel money, and it'd be purely an after-hours, part-time labor of love. A hobby project, really. But this case reached out to him.

Maybe because he was a sucker for a cold case, and he was bored silly.

Maybe because Richard and Reagan Uden were near his two young sons' ages.

Or maybe because back in Iroquois, the TeBeests said grace at every meal, the Lutheran pastor sometimes came to dinner, and (despite the occasional skinny-dip) there was no doubt about right and wrong.

And this was wrong.

Next, DCI Special Agent Lonnie TeBeest did what any good detective would do.

He started all over again.

First, he needed the new Fremont County sheriff to reinvite DCI to the Uden case, which had been on a back burner for a few years. There was literally a new sheriff in town, and without his blessing, TeBeest was hamstrung. Fortunately, Sheriff Roger Milward welcomed renewed interest and promised to make his staff available for anything TeBeest needed.

What he needed were twenty years and several cardboard boxes full of reports, interviews, video and audio recordings, photos, and physical evidence that had drifted up like dirty snow in Fremont County's vault. From the original missing persons teletype to be on the lookout for Virginia Uden and her two boys, to old reel-to-reel recordings of witness interviews, to ex-sheriff Dave King's notes about his last chat with Kay Florita, TeBeest copied what he could and took all the tapes to be duplicated and transcribed by DCI experts. The physical evidence—some relevant and some not—was collected for the technicians at the state crime lab.

He stayed up late most nights reading everything, looking at the photos, trying to see a new path to the answers. TeBeest didn't need personal proof that Virginia and her boys were dead. He knew they were, but he needed to be able to prove it to a jury.

The Social Security Administration confirmed that there'd been no activity on Virginia's account after 1980, even though Virginia had previously worked consistently for various employers. And Ronald Holtz's account had no activity, either, after 1974. In the tortured vernacular of government bureaucracies, the SSA basically said the accounts were deemed "stale" and "suspicion of death was probable."

Gerald's former health insurer similarly reported no claims after September 1980, even though there had been eleven pages of claims for Virginia and her boys up to that moment.

He followed up on a few leads, not promising but also not ignorable. A former babysitter recalled rope burns on Richard and Reagan's necks and said that they'd told her their father had tried to strangle them. Claire's private investigator said she had evidence that two boys matching Richard and Reagan's description had enrolled in a Canadian school. A $1,000 life insurance claim was paid to Virginia's estranged father, now dead, seven years after her disappearance. Virginia's last lawyer had no record of her case.

When he knew everything that inanimate police reports and sketchy witnesses could tell him, TeBeest sought the living and breathing human who knew and cared more than anyone else: Claire Martin.

They connected by accident. When TeBeest dialed an old phone number in the case file, he expected the nursing home's front desk, who could tell him if she was still alive. After all, it had been several years since a DCI agent had talked to her.

To his surprise, Claire herself answered the phone, and they arranged to meet face-to-face soon.

Claire was eighty years old now, her hair turned white as snow. Her face was drawn. Insomnia sucked her dry.

Frail and resigned, she lived alone in a subsidized apartment at Push-root Village, an assisted living facility in Lander. She had a few friends who looked in on her occasionally, but no family. She had her monthly Social Security checks and a little money she'd saved over the years, some clothes and pictures, not much else ... except a slightly dented 1973 Country Squire station wagon parked at a friend's house in the country. He'd wanted to soup it up for the demolition derby, but she refused. It had finally died completely a few years before, but she kept it anyway. It still might have a purpose.

She couldn't drive, anyhow. She took the bus where she needed to go.

TeBeest arrived that morning around nine. They sat in Claire's spartan living room. She owned a little mutt poodle she called Babe, and the place stank.

He looked around the room and saw some family pictures, a few photos of her in the old days when she rode motorcycles and sculled, and a few pretty pages she tore from old calendars and framed, but no shrines to Virginia or her grandsons, and no religious items. Claire's faith was a funny thing: she'd once argued with her mother about theology and stopped going to church, but she prayed and studied the Bible anyway.

She'd been disappointed in God for a long time. She wanted to forgive somebody for this evil, but only because she thought God might trade her mercy for some good news that hadn't yet come. So it was an article of her personal faith, too, that she still believed the boys might be alive somewhere.

Before she moved in, Claire's furniture was always secondhand, rickety. She never owned anything brand-new. The only thing she could salvage in her last move was an old bed frame. Her treasures were just paper and tin; her memories were sturdier stuff. Among her few personal possessions were an 1800s antique doll with real human hair, and the gun she bought after Virginia vanished. And the station wagon.

She moved much slower now, but Claire repeated her sad story for the thousandth time, still as clearly as if it had happened yesterday, not twenty years before. She forgot nothing.

For two hours, TeBeest asked a lot of questions, showed a lot of evidence pictures. He also saw, all at once, this cold case in human form. He instantly felt Claire's pain and heard two decades of sadness in her soft, sweet little voice. He always wanted to solve crimes so bad guys got what they deserved, but Claire deserved something too: answers. He hoped he had time to give her answers.

For her part, Claire still harbored suspicions about cops. She was apprehensive about TeBeest too. She'd written a lot of letters, telephoned every new detective. None of them wanted to disappoint her, but they always ended up disappointing her.

"We've never had a case like this," one of them told her once. "We just don't have the skills."

"Well, get them," Claire had demanded.

She had resigned herself to thinking nothing would happen. She liked to talk about the case but had stopped getting her hopes up—or letting other people get her hopes up.

So some of the fire had gone out, but not all. It showed when Claire told TeBeest about how she'd tried in vain to push the prosecutor into action, about how she'd dug holes in the earth looking for personal things where the car was found, about all the stories she'd heard from well-meaning people who thought they might have seen something . . . but didn't.

TeBeest listened, making notes. She'd begun to talk about Virginia and the boys in the past tense. Maybe she didn't trust him either, but he wanted to try to soothe her. He wanted to solve this case for her.

When they were done talking, TeBeest drove Claire to the Lander Valley Hospital, where her blood was drawn for any future DNA comparisons that might be needed. Then he dropped her back in her dowdy little apartment.

"I will never give up," he promised her, "even if it takes ten years."

"I don't know if I'll live that long," Claire told him.

TeBeest smiled. "You have to."

Over the coming year, TeBeest amassed a trove of evidence. He interviewed everybody and anybody who'd ever had contact with Virginia or Gerald, including coworkers who uniformly thought Gerald was devious and odd.

He collected medical records for Virginia, her boys, Ron Holtz, even Don Prunty.

He tracked down Gerald's 1968 Ford pickup, which Gerald had sold in Missouri in 1987. It had been resold three or four times since then and now sat forlorn, somebody's farm truck. TeBeest and Missouri agents sprayed the truck's cab with Luminol to see any blood evidence, then cut four swatches of fabric from the seats for the crime lab. Ultimately, they showed nothing.

He tried to track down a shadowy person named "Tim Priest," who'd been mentioned by Gerald as somebody who might have harmed Virginia. The mine was long closed, but its parent company said nobody by that name had ever worked there.

TeBeest interviewed Alice's troubled son, Ted, again. It wasn't friendly. Ted resented being asked all these questions again, and he didn't like TeBeest's manner, but he recounted it all. Gerald and Alice were always scheming, he said, to get out of the child support payments. This time, Ted added a new story about Gerald's "gunfight" with a neighbor over a boundary issue—which turned out to be a simple argument about a fence in which Gerald had apparently brandished a gun. Nobody called the cops.

TeBeest also visited Claire several more times. Once, he drove her out to the former Uden place in Pavillion, now vacant land, where she described where the house and outbuildings stood. She gave him all the Christmas cards Virginia had sent, and pictures of the boys. She told him more touching personal stories. He felt her pain. It only made him more determined to solve this case soon.

Every so often, he received letters from Claire about missing children in far-flung states. She always saw Richard and Reagan in their faces, and TeBeest always checked them out . . . and they were always fruitless.

He'd spent three or four years on this case already. It was no longer just a few unconnected dots. The dots had multiplied exponentially, spilled out of their bucket, and splattered in every direction.

Right now, every new document, interview, or search warrant—every single moment TeBeest spent on the cold Uden case, not to mention the even colder Holtz case—was squeezed between his more pressing daily investigations of fresh crimes that happened yesterday and could be solved today.

At first, TeBeest's bosses supported his investigation, but state government is like a flowing river. It changes constantly. TeBeest had already worked for two directors—both good ones—when in 2006, former Uinta County sheriff Forrest Bright became the new director. From day one, insiders were leery that an ex-sheriff from a county roughly the size of Delaware with only twenty thousand citizens could handle the high-fliers, higher politics, and highest expectations of the Attorney General's most important law enforcement agency.

Soon enough, TeBeest's bosses started to grumble. They weren't real high on TeBeest anyway because he tended to speak his mind, a liability in government jobs, even state police. The more intimate he got with the entangled Uden and Holtz cases—the more he cared—the more leverage the director; his obedient deputy director, Kebin Haller; and their overly influential crime lab chief, Steve Holloway had over TeBeest.

He turned angry about it. Not the obvious loss, really, but how the politics at DCI had cost Claire Martin valuable time she didn't have to waste.

He called Claire on her birthday—Christmas Day—every year, maybe Easter, when resurrection was on his mind. He'd send the kind of gifts a crusty cop might send, maybe a Hickory Farms box every so often, or a card. She didn't have anybody else.

And around September 12 every year, TeBeest called her, just to talk. They both came to expect it. One year, he was a couple days late, and she remarked that she'd been expecting his call. He felt bad.

He needed help if he was going to close the Uden case fast, under the radar and without neglecting live cases. He looked around DCI's field offices for a partner who, on his own free time and under his own power, could bring the same expertise and vigor to the investigation. He liked a young agent up in the Powell office, Tom Wachsmuth. He was a former Minnesota cop who specialized in "people crimes" like murder and rape. He liked Wachsmuth, who saw things the way TeBeest saw them. They'd talked casually about the Uden case, and Wachsmuth had eagerly offered his help if TeBeest ever needed it.

Now he needed it.

If the political bosses weren't happy about TeBeest's attention to it, they wouldn't be thrilled about *two* agents wasting time on a case that was too old and too cold. Big drug interdictions and high-profile perp walks made better headlines and bigger budgets. They had to fly under the radar.

But it never occurred to TeBeest or Wachsmuth that the Uden case might be "too" cold. Not with the prime suspects alive—and seeming to thumb their noses at cops. Not with at least one survivor who cared deeply about the victims. Not with four bodies that never received a respectful burial.

Yeah, he had bad guys he could put away today. Yeah, he had victims and survivors he could help today. Yeah, putting a young killer in prison for the rest of his life is more satisfying than locking up an old one whose life is almost over. Yeah, justice could be swifter with warmer cases.

But Ron Holtz, Virginia, Richard, and Reagan still deserved justice too.

Claire, bless her, still deserved answers.

And TeBeest still had plenty of questions for Gerald and Alice.

By 2005, the search for Richard and Reagan Uden had evolved well beyond Claire Martin's photocopied flyers tacked to telephone poles. In

1980, Claire's reach was as limited as her budget. In the years after her grandsons' disappearance, she'd pay for slick mailings to be printed and mailed locally whenever she had some extra cash.

Then came personal computers, followed soon by a revolutionary government information network eventually known simply as the internet. The organized hunt for missing kids eventually went from milk cartons and power poles to a web of nonprofits, amateur sleuths, chat rooms, websites, electronic bulletin boards, Amber Alerts, and social media. In time, everybody was part of the hunt for every missing child, including Richard and Reagan.

Of course, interlinked police databases spread Richard and Reagan's story almost as soon as they were truly deemed missing, but the information reached only law enforcement officers, who were deluged every day with missing person reports—and BOLOs for killers, rapists, escapees, stolen cars, and a thousand other urgencies they couldn't possibly commit to memory.

The National Center for Missing and Exploited Children, founded in 1984, first posted photos and descriptions of the boys for the public. Over the years, others helped spread the word, through both old-fashioned means and cyberspace. The occasional newspaper, television reporter, or true crime show told their story, sometimes with national heft.

In 2005, the Rocky Mountain Information Network, part of a police information-sharing cooperative, published an article about the Uden case at TeBeest's request, specifically focusing on the two child victims.

In theory, tens of millions of North Americans were on the lookout for two innocent boys—one with a scar on his eyelid and a gap between his front teeth, the other with surgical scars on his neck and nose. If they were out there, they'd have been grown men by the time the internet took up the hunt, in their midthirties when Lonnie TeBeest became their champion.

Various wacky reports trickled in after every article or television episode, and some web sleuths contemplated the case from the comfort of their own basements, but the fact remained that not a single person ever saw Richard and Reagan Uden after September 12, 1980.

Over the next couple years, Lonnie TeBeest and Tom Wachsmuth interviewed an array of supporting characters in the Udens' prolonged drama.

First, they talked to all the cops who'd ever touched this case file. It was a bad memory for all of them.

Then they talked to as many of Gerald and Alice's shirttail relatives as they could find. All were estranged in some way, but they all told vaguely troubling stories about nasty family secrets, whispers of bad behavior, Alice's manipulative nature, and Gerald's odd demeanor.

They found one of Ron Holtz's sisters in Colorado and arranged to meet, but when the time came, she stood them up and refused to give a blood sample that could be used for DNA comparison in case they ever found Ronnie's body. She was too busy, she said, and she didn't want to talk about her brother ever again because it brought back too many bad memories.

Another Holtz sister gave them blood but not much else. She didn't remember much about Ronnie except that he was mentally ill, addicted to drugs, and inclined to run away from home after frequent physical fights with their dad. She had vague recollections of a wife named Alice, and she babysat Alice's kid a couple times. She presumed her brother was dead, or he would have called. He had no other friends.

Then they talked to Alice's first husband, Jerald Scott, a retired state cop who'd kicked her out after thirteen years of marriage when she lost interest in being his wife or a mother to their four kids. He'd recently received some legal papers from Alice, asking him to grant an annulment of their marriage, which she claimed was sanctioned by the Catholic Church. In fact, they were married by a justice of the peace when Alice was only sixteen. For reasons he didn't understand, she signed the request with her maiden name, Alice Barbier. He was simply flummoxed why a sixtysomething woman he hadn't seen in twenty years and who'd married four men would suddenly want to annul a marriage that no church had anything to do with.

He didn't sign the papers.

They also talked to Virginia's first husband, Mirt Beard, definitely the father of Richard but probably not Reagan. He didn't remember much about her. He'd been a horny young lumberjack and she was a doable barmaid in Jackson when they hooked up. Virginia got pregnant, and Mirt quickly felt trapped. Their misbegotten marriage lasted only a few months. A judge granted Virginia $150 in alimony and child support for Richard, which Beard paid faithfully. On this day, Beard didn't know anybody named Gerald Uden, and he didn't know about Virginia's disappearance until the late 1990s. He gave TeBeest some blood for future DNA uses and offered to identify the bodies if cops ever found them.

They talked to Alice's other kids and heard all the various old horror stories they'd told previous investigators. Thea recounted how she'd been tricked into sending the bogus telegram to Claire Martin in 1980. She still held it against Alice, whom she hadn't seen in years.

Eliza, then a thirtysomething employee at a Missouri trucking company, was surprisingly candid about some weird things. Eliza remembered Alice claiming she had taken control of her husband Don Prunty's alcoholism by secretly "putting something in his drinks" that would make him stop drinking. Anti-alcohol medicine, or something more evil? It sounded so ominous that Eliza offered to let TeBeest exhume her dad's corpse to determine if he was poisoned.

Eliza then told TeBeest a story he'd already heard: Alice had confessed Ron Holtz's murder and disposal to her a few years ago. She hadn't said anything until now because, well, "she's my mother." TeBeest wondered why she was coming forward now.

"And Mom said she'd die in jail for what she did," she recalled.

Stranger still, Eliza told another story that sent a chill through TeBeest.

Back around 2000, a few years after Eliza lost custody of her children in a messy divorce, she plotted to murder her ex-husband as a way to regain her kids. She knew Gerald's entanglement in Virginia and her boys' disappearance, so she sought his fatherly advice about how she might best kill her children's dad.

They talked about shooting and poison, but Gerald raised an important issue: if she killed the guy, how did she plan to get rid of the body?

Eliza shrugged.

"You can't just dump it," he said. "And you don't have pigs."

Pigs?

"Or you could cut up the bodies in small pieces and throw them in the Mississippi."

Wait . . . pigs?

Gerald told her that pigs would eat human flesh and bone, digest most of it, then shit it out in unrecognizable plops—except for the teeth. "You'd have to collect the teeth and get rid of them," he advised helpfully.

Eliza remembered they had several pigs on the Pavillion place when the Virginia mess was happening. She pressed Gerald further about Virginia and the boys, but he waved her off.

"You were in school that day," he said. "You don't know anything."

She begged for the truth.

"I'm really sorry," he told her. "There's nothing I can do. There's just nothing I can do."

Their tender father-daughter moment ended right there.

God works in mysterious ways.

Gerald Uden's family had only bumped against the stained glass windows of religion, like passionless Protestant moths. Their church attendance could be described as "drive-by." Like many shirtsleeve Christians, they invoked the Bible only to make whatever points suited them at the moment. The church didn't play much of a role in his young life. Later, he'd go to church only when Alice made him go.

Alice Barbier had been raised Catholic by her adoptive parents, although she floated in and out of the Church—mostly out—all her life. She had sinned, to be sure, but she was confident all would be forgiven eventually. She had enrolled Eliza in a Catholic school, dragged Gerald to Mass occasionally, and had a Bible somewhere, all for good measure. But just in case forgiveness wasn't in her cards, Alice found a back door.

Alice chose confession. Not to the cops or her kids again, but to a priest. Nobody knows what she told the good father, if anything, but she emerged from the sacred confessional in 2005—not long after being interviewed by the DCI agents—straight into the loving embrace of the Carmelite sisters. Not as a full-fledged nun, but as a sort of nun lite. As a lay Carmelite in training, she made "promises"—not vows, which are more consequential in the Church's carefully parsed vernacular—to be faithful to Mother Mary, to attend Mass and take communion as often as possible (preferably daily), to serve the needy, and to spend at least a half hour in intense prayer every day.

She also donned the Carmelites' distinctive brown scapular, two small pieces of blessed cloth, paper, or wood that hang on long shoulder straps over the chest and back, like an old-fashioned sandwich board. In Carmelite lore dating to the Middle Ages, Mother Mary promised, "Whosoever dies in this garment shall not suffer eternal fire," so it is worn day and night by the devout. In return for the special protection, Alice promised to be as chaste as an elderly married woman could be, recite a special prayer every day, forgo meat on Wednesdays and Saturdays . . . or get a priest's permission to do something entirely different. She had options.

She didn't waste much time on ministering to the needy. Communion and Mass were infrequent. And although the sex had trailed off naturally in her post-Midol years, Alice was nothing if not a carnivore.

The spiritually half-awakened Alice intermittently wrote in a journal, which was mostly empty. On one page around this time, she listed the flaws and sins she wished to confess to her priest. They included being easily distracted from her daily prayers; a tendency to lose her temper; lust for recognition; irritability and impatience; proud thoughts and vanity; "curiosity of the eyes," a Catholic idiom for an unwholesome love of material things; uncharitable feelings and comments; unseemly jealousy; a penchant to judge other people harshly, yet to defend herself against every perceived slight; a propensity to criticize others; "discouragement" because of unspecified difficulties; and spiritual inertia.

No mention of murder.

Gerald and Eliza called her a nun, although she really wasn't. Lay Carmelites were something more than ordinary Sunday Catholics, something less than monks, nuns, and priests. To her family—and maybe to her—that was a distinction without a difference. Others might say Alice still had a few bugs to work out in her make-believe monastic life.

For some, religion is justification; for others, purification. For Alice, it might have been a genuine effort for absolution from her serious sins, or just a pious disguise. She regularly caught religion and lost it at opportune times. Her scapular might have been a lot like her white nursing uniform, a symbol of purity that was simultaneously a sucker punch to the rest of the world's kidneys.

No matter. Suffice it to say, Alice had her own reasons for finding (and proudly displaying) religion late in life.

Alice works in mysterious ways.

By 2005, the time had come to hear what Gerald and Alice had to say.

TeBeest and Wachsmuth had reached a point in their investigation where they had nothing to lose. They didn't really have any realistic hope of a dramatic confession, but they'd been around long enough to know a lie is sometimes just as valuable as a confession. Confessions save time, but lies can be tracked down and revealed. Sometimes a lie tells a cop everything he needs to know.

Neither Gerald nor Alice had spoken to police for more than twenty years, since the grand jury in Wyoming, when they hardly spoke at all. Since then, they'd lived mostly under the radar in rural Missouri and had plenty of time to get their stories straight.

Back then, they'd put distance between themselves and cops on purpose. They knew the case hadn't gone away, but they were confident it also wasn't moving forward, even with Ted's blabbing, which they believed had been so vague and incoherent that investigators had dismissed it. For sure, nobody had found Ron Holtz in the past ten years and probably never would.

But every action has an equal and opposite reaction. If distant detectives couldn't keep tabs on Gerald and Alice, then Gerald and Alice couldn't keep tabs on the distant detectives either.

So Alice certainly wasn't expecting DCI Special Agents TeBeest and Wachsmuth and two Missouri Highway Patrol sergeants on her doorstep on a frosty January Tuesday in 2005.

Maybe that's why this pale, wizened grandmother with thinning hair answered her door wearing only a bra and panties. Or maybe she had other ideas.

Either way, she casually invited the two veteran detectives—who'd previously thought they'd seen everything—into her living room before she slipped into a bedroom to drape herself loosely in a ratty housecoat. Gerald was on the road, she said, but he'd be home tomorrow.

For the moment, Alice had the upper hand. TeBeest and Wachsmuth were already off their game as they explained to Alice that they had some questions about the disappearance of Virginia, Richard, and Reagan Uden. She wasn't under arrest, they told her, and she didn't have to talk to them at all. They could talk there or go to the Christian County Sheriff's Office in nearby Ozark, her choice.

Alice chose the sheriff's office. While TeBeest and Wachsmuth waited, she changed into street clothes. She followed them in her own car to Ozark. On the way to town, the investigators changed their strategy: go soft on Alice or risk scaring Gerald off... and Gerald was the weak link.

In the sheriff's interview room, they courteously repeated she wasn't being arrested, wasn't being forced to talk, and could leave anytime she wished. Soft-spoken Alice, smiling like a sweet little lunch lady, told them she had nothing to hide.

At two o'clock, she started her long, exceptionally detailed biography at the beginning, from her unwanted birth to an unwed teenager in 1939 to her life riding shotgun with her truck-driving husband, Gerald. She recalled where she went to school. She remembered the exact dates of her three marriages—to Jerald Scott, Donald Prunty, and Gerald Uden—and the birthdays of her five children. She recited all her nursing jobs—Jacksonville and Sterling, Illinois; Riverton, Lander, and Laramie, Wyoming. She even remembered that she and Gerald paid $79,000 for their new 110-acre farm in Chadwick, which she proudly announced was worth at least twice as much now.

Gerald had been married three times before her, she recalled, but she said she'd never known any of his ex-wives. There should be no relationship with ex-spouses, she emphasized.

Alice claimed she'd been molested by her adoptive father as a child, and that he had continued molesting her own daughters.

With the help of the internet, she'd found her biological family in 2003, although her birth mother had died. When she flew from Missouri to Wyoming to meet her aging uncles, aunts, and cousins, they gave her a letter her mother had written to the daughter she gave up, she said, but she didn't have it anymore.

Throughout the long interview, the detectives served Alice several sodas, offered many bathroom breaks, and suggested time to collect herself. She declined it all.

She'd never met or talked to Virginia, she told them. Didn't even know what she looked like until the paper ran a photo of her later. But she had welcomed Virginia's sons, Richard and Reagan, into her home two or three times. Good boys, they were. They always stayed in the house, never caused any problems, and never required discipline, she said.

Yes, she and Gerald had exchanged cordial letters with Virginia about custody, but none were threatening or nasty in any way, Alice said. And they never discussed child support money, she added. In fact, Virginia had never asked for more, and Gerald was happy paying it.

After first refusing any visitation, Alice said, Virginia "wrote a letter to Gerald and let him see the boys."

On the day of the disappearance, she had no idea about the outing Gerald and Virginia had planned. Gerald was his own man and went his own way. She repeated the story: He'd gone to meet his ex-wife and sons at the crossroads, they didn't show, and he came home within the hour. He'd worked the night before, so he went straight to bed until later that night, when he discovered in a call to Claire Martin that Virginia hadn't come home. Then he helped search for her because he was a nice man.

They later learned from the newspaper that Virginia and the boys were seriously missing. That's when they started receiving threatening anonymous letters, few of which were reported to police.

She recalled Gerald's arrest with a weapon outside Claire's laundry, but he was only watching and protecting her from mysterious under-world people.

Believing the disappearance was all a scam by Virginia, Alice admitted she'd arranged for her daughter Thea to send the bogus telegram and had signed Virginia's name to a fake letter "only to see how Claire would react" and to smoke out the scheming Virginia. She was sorry now for the bogus correspondence that seemed like a good idea at the time but now looked mean. TeBeest noted that Alice had never before acknowledged writing and mailing that letter.

If anybody asked—and TeBeest and Wachsmuth did—Alice would gladly offer her theory: Virginia had an evil plan to disappear, possibly to collect insurance money on her boys and start a new life.

Alice had collected a lot of paperwork from that awful time, she said. She happily offered to give it to the DCI agents the next day, and they accepted.

TeBeest asked if she'd take a polygraph test, but Alice refused adamantly. She and Gerald had researched lie detectors, she said, and they were notoriously unreliable. But she voluntarily gave her fingerprints, blood, and handwriting samples before the two-hour interview ended.

A few hours later, Alice's daughter Eliza called TeBeest to ask if DCI had reopened its investigation because of a tip from her ex-husband. Alice, he reckoned, was gauging the seriousness of these new questions by sending her own daughter on a fishing expedition.

The next morning, Gerald voluntarily drove to the Christian County Sheriff's Office. No doubt he came prepared by Alice for the same questions, TeBeest imagined.

Almost from the start, Gerald exuded his aw-shucks resistance to their questioning. He advised TeBeest and Wachsmuth up front that he'd won a Top Secret clearance in the US Navy by successfully keeping his secrets during waterboarding and other simulated torture. Now he had the further protection of the Fifth Amendment, and he wasn't likely to give up any secrets to a couple cops.

Who said anything about secrets? TeBeest was puzzled. He assured Gerald he wasn't under arrest, could refuse to answer questions, was free to walk out at any time, and wouldn't be tortured.

But Gerald had questions of his own. He wondered why nobody had ever asked about his fingerprints on the car, then volunteered that he'd been in the car the day before the disappearance, fetching something for Virginia while visiting Richard in the hospital. Nobody had asked for a fingerprint alibi, TeBeest thought, but he gave one anyway.

When the talk turned to Virginia, Gerald just shrugged. He didn't know where "the shrew" Virginia went in 1980, and he didn't know where she was today. He figured she and the boys were dead or they would have turned up. She liked to pick up hitchhikers, he said, and maybe she finally picked up the wrong one.

Gerald nervously explained that he'd read a lot of true crime books.

"There are many ways to kill a person," he said. "From a simple hand-kerchief to a pen."

That struck TeBeest and Wachsmuth as an odd thing to say. Nobody had asked him about books or causes of death.

Everything between him and Virginia had been mellow. She never asked for more child support, he happily provided health insurance for the boys, and minor visitation disputes had cleared up when she moved back to Wyoming. All good.

He hadn't seriously searched for Virginia after that first night, he said, because police didn't want any help. Nor did he call for updates about the boys because, well, the cops suspected him. Now, right here before cops and God, he generously offered to let the National Center for Missing and Exploited Children get involved.

Like Alice, he refused a polygraph, and he also refused to give blood, fingerprints, or handwriting. With that, TeBeest produced a search warrant signed by a judge that allowed investigators to take those things without Gerald's consent. He complied without resistance.

Conveniently, Gerald had no recollection of talking to Eliza a few years before about murder or pigs. Toward the end of the three-hour interview, Gerald cloaked himself in religion, which he wore awkwardly. He opposed the death penalty, he said, because the Bible says, "Thou shalt not kill." And whoever killed Virginia and the boys should be forgiven, he said, because the Bible says people should not judge.

Does he hear himself? TeBeest wondered.

"Saint Peter will decide," Gerald continued. "I will confess what I've done to Saint Peter. If you guys charge me with something I can't get out of, I will go peacefully. It will be up to a judge and jury."

"Are you saying you will never confess here on Earth, to anyone, before you die, what you have done?" Wachsmuth asked.

Gerald was ambiguous. Again.

"This is all I have to hang on to," he said.

After Gerald left, Alice showed up as promised with a folder of two dozen documents, including some letters, clippings, and legal papers. Among them were Gerald and Virginia's original divorce decree and Virginia's many letters to Alice from New Jersey. The sheaf also contained two curious lists in Gerald's handwriting: one with ten reasons why prosecutors believed he and Alice were involved in Virginia's murder, and the other with nineteen reasons his defense lawyer could use to prove he'd been framed.

TeBeest and Wachsmuth led her back to the interview room and reminded her she wasn't under arrest and could leave anytime. Alice sat at the long table, her big purse held snugly in her lap. *Her shield*, TeBeest thought to himself.

TeBeest, sitting beside Alice, dispensed with pleasantries.

"Alice, you left out a few things yesterday," he said. "You didn't tell us the truth."

Alice looked startled, hurt.

"I did," she said.

"We know you didn't."

"I did," she repeated.

TeBeest leaned so uncomfortably close to her he could smell her.

"Ron Holtz."

Alice recoiled as if he'd hit her with a hammer. She pulled her purse close, but her shield had failed her. Wachsmuth, sitting across the table, watched her eyes glaze over. Her face showed real fear.

Suddenly, Alice keeled to her left, literally falling out of her chair. She thunked against the wall behind her, catching herself with her left arm and hitting the floor with her left knee. Bracing herself, she clambered clumsily back into her chair and stammered, not knowing what to say next. In hundreds of interviews, Wachsmuth had never seen anything like it. She must have momentarily lost consciousness, he thought.

"My kids told you," were the first words out of her mouth when her wits returned.

"It's just funny you never mentioned him yesterday," TeBeest bored in, relentless. "You never mentioned being a nurse in Sheridan in 1974, either. You didn't mention meeting Ron Holtz in the VA psych ward, or marrying him in Colorado on September 17, 1974, or your divorce in 1975. All the other husbands and jobs, you mentioned. We know all of that, but you never mentioned any of this. Why?"

Alice was stupefied and evasive. At that moment, she could have walked out, but she didn't.

She didn't like talking about Holtz, she said, because she was embarrassed by the whole thing. As a nurse, it was unprofessional. As a woman, it was stupid.

But Holtz was her only untruth, she swore. She promised she hadn't lied about anything else. She remembered almost nothing about Virginia and her boys' disappearance because she "didn't like to think about them" (although she recalled vividly, when asked next, about the day of John F. Kennedy's assassination).

TeBeest deliberately let Alice wonder if he had Ron Holtz's body, and he didn't let up.

He pointed out several creepy similarities between Ron Holtz's and Virginia's disappearances, mainly that two people Alice disliked had vanished completely from the face of the Earth.

Alice said nothing, just sat there silent.

TeBeest stood up and shoved his finger in her face. "Stop! You know, Alice, you insult me by lying," he said, throwing up his hands. "You lied. If you're gonna lie, just don't say anything."

Alice took the cue. She told Wachsmuth she'd answer nothing more because TeBeest had instructed her to stop answering his questions.

The short but definitely unsweet interview was over.

That night, just a few hours later, Eliza again called TeBeest's machine and asked him to call her back. The number she left was Gerald and Alice's home phone.

When he called back, she reiterated that she had no memory of that tragic day. She said she couldn't imagine her mother was involved, but said nothing good about Gerald. She talked about all her personal problems and a life that had gone south. And she asked a lot of questions about what would happen next in his investigation.

Alice had sent her again, TeBeest understood, to scout what he really knew.

And what he knew, beyond any reasonable doubt, was that Gerald and Alice were involved in the disappearances, probably deaths, of four people. But he still didn't have a body, a weapon, or a confession.

And he didn't know it at the moment, but he also didn't have a legal recording of the telling interviews with Gerald and Alice. It would be crucial to bringing any charges, especially in a no-body case like this one, but a Missouri deputy had forgotten to turn on the tape recorder.

Back home in Fremont County, where any charges in Virginia's disappearance would be filed, a district judge—finally frustrated by a flood of defense motions about one particular polygrapher who never recorded his interviews—had recently issued a blanket order that all interviews must be recorded. Without tapes, no trials.

TeBeest and Wachsmuth were back where they started.

Over the next couple years, between their current investigations, obstructive bosses, and a hundred dead-end leads (or no leads at all), they had to live with the knowledge that while they knew Gerald was a killer (and probably Alice too), they just couldn't prove it in court beyond a reasonable doubt.

In 2007, ten years after long-distance jogger Amy Bechtel vanished in the Wyoming mountains, nobody had a clue what might have befallen her. A frustrated local detective who'd inherited the case grasped at straws. His bafflement led him on a peculiar quest, like a hayseed flatlander seeking a wise man on a mountaintop. In this case, his mountain was a Civil War–era brick-and-brownstone, vaguely Gothic building on Philadelphia's Broad Street. And his guru was, well, plural.

The Vidocq Society is a famous network of forensic specialists—FBI profilers, prosecutors, homicide detectives, medical examiners, anthropologists, scientists, psychologists, crime scene techs, government spooks, and authorities on everything from DNA to cults—who meet on the third Thursday of every month in Philadelphia over lunch and cold-case murders. One colorful description: "It's like seating Sherlock Holmes, Hercule Poirot, Miss Marple, Inspector Morse, Jessica Fletcher, Kurt Wallander, and Kojak in front of a sumptuous meal, presenting them with a cold case that needs an injection of new thinking, and watching the sparks fly."[1]

Convened within the mahogany walls, polished marble, and aromatic leather of Union Hall, the eighty-two members of the Vidocq Society (eighty-two because that's the age at which their celebrated namesake, pioneering nineteenth-century criminalist Eugène François Vidocq, died) choose a case from America's hundred thousand unsolved murders. Then they fly the lead detective to Philadelphia for a briefing on the case and cross-examine him or her over cordon bleu cuisine. After dessert, they suggest clues that might have been missed, thoughts that never occurred.

The society was founded in 1990 by three criminology superstars: Richard Walter, William Fleisher, and Frank Bender. The burly Fleisher was a polygraph expert and former FBI agent. Bender, a wiry, tattooed ex-boxer, was a renowned forensic artist who reconstructed the faces of victims and suspects to help identify them.

And Walter was one of the world's most distinguished forensic psychologists, a skilled excavator of the criminal mind.

Raw-boned and melancholy, Hollywood might cast Walter as an uncannily brilliant coroner. He resembled the actor Basil Rathbone, the most famous portrayer of Sherlock Holmes, but if anyone said that out loud, Walter would look as if they'd just farted. He was glimpsed less flatulently in *The Murder Room*, a 2011 book by journalist Michael Capuzzo about the Vidocq Society: "Walter was the coolest eye on murder in the world. Tall and acerbic, he spoke with a clipped propriety that had earned him the moniker 'The Englishman' from certain criminal elements. Walter had spent twenty years treating the most violent psychopaths in the state of Michigan at the largest walled penitentiary in the world. . . . Walter was unsurpassed in his understanding of the darkest regions of the heart."[2]

Together, they dreamed up a social club of diverse experts who could engage each other in a kind of nuclear chain reaction that ordinary police bureaucracies couldn't or wouldn't pay for. Not a shadowy cabal in a star chamber, they approached crime solving with a degree of fun. The total paycheck for this lunchtime crowd of crackerjack criminologists would exceed the annual budgets of most American police departments, yet here their expertise was offered quite generously for free, with a four-star lunch to boot.

What they do isn't profiling. Profilers speculate about the criminal's psychology, while the Vidocq Society focuses on the crime. Its crime assessment process analyzes the presence—or absence—of direct and circumstantial evidence, which is then reconciled with known crime patterns and psychology. Put more simply, they examine real clues and behaviors that happen before, during, and after the crime to paint a portrait of what happened and why.

In other words, a profiler would look at Gerald and Alice first; the Vidocq Society looks at the crime first.

(Vidocq has no animus toward profiling: the society not only counts several eminent profilers in its membership, Walter himself was among the tiny group of American criminologists who invented modern profiling in the 1970s as a way to anticipate serial killers' next moves. Vidocq simply considers its process to be more fact based; less vulnerable to intuition, prejudice, and gut feelings; more defensible in court. Science, Walter believed, could educate, inform, and correct the muddled story line of any crime.)

The Bechtel detective's eyes were opened by the crime masters, and he returned home as a Vidocq evangelist. One of his converts was SA Lonnie TeBeest, who wasted no time calling to request his own audience with the gurus of Philadelphia.

But the entangled Uden and Holtz cases were too complicated for Vidocq's customary murder matinee, which normally consumed only a couple of hours. Without a body, a crime scene, or significant physical evidence, it would require deeper attention for a longer time. And Richard Walter already knew from his conversations with TeBeest that he wasn't seeing this case clearly.

Walter knew he could fix that.

So Walter extended an unusual offer: He would personally devote a week to disentangling TeBeest's long-unsolved crimes, if TeBeest didn't mind spreading out for a few days in Walter's new, mostly unfurnished bachelor bungalow in the Philadelphia suburb of Montrose. He'd adhere to Vidocq's strict rules of evidence, but without the benefit of Vidocq's collected expertise (or crème brûlée for dessert).

Naturally, TeBeest quickly accepted the help.

He and Wachsmuth arrived in Philadelphia on October 13, 2007—a Saturday—schlepping boxes full of evidence, transcripts, timelines, notes, and photos.

Walter's ranch-style cottage, in the old colonial heart-earth, amid stone walls and country lanes, couldn't have been further from hard, wind-scraped Wyoming for the two midwestern-born cops. But they weren't tourists.

At his little house the next day, a Sunday, Walter wasted no time. He'd already hauled tables and chairs into an empty room, where the detectives unboxed their material into neat piles.

Lacking a squad room's "murder board," Walter designated one empty wall to display "pre-crime behavior," another for "post-crime behavior," and a third for the crime itself.

"Now, show me what you have," Walter said.

TeBeest and Wachsmuth weren't exactly sure how to start.

As Walter suspected, they didn't know their story line. Good cops were fueled by a mixture of evidence, intuition, experience, intelligence, and guesswork. Both were good cops. But they needed to know *why* they knew what they knew. TeBeest's gut wasn't enough. A timeworn legal aphorism applied: there's what you know, what you think you know, and what you can prove in court. Opinion wasn't important; facts were.

So Walter assigned TeBeest and Wachsmuth little tasks, mainly organizing the mess of paperwork before them and putting their fingers on real answers to his questions.

Then he began his four-day quiz as he scurried around the room, tacking papers and Post-it notes and taping photos and scribbling on walls, peppering them with more questions. It was a mess, but an organized mess. Walter's madness had purpose.

In the first day, with Walter's prompting, they synopsized Alice's biography in excruciating detail, filling in gaps between the high points: Unwanted newborn. Adopted by childless couple. Molested by father. Married a cop. Had four kids. Got kicked out. Menial work until she got a nursing degree. Nomadic worker. Met alcoholic Don Prunty, a war vet thirteen years older than her, in a hospital and married him. Had a fifth child. Prunty died. Met crazy Vietnam vet Ron Holtz in hospital and married him. He disappeared. Later told kids she killed him. Met Gerald Uden, another military vet, and married him. Increasingly uncomfortable with Gerald's ex-wife and adopted sons. Ex-wife and sons soon disappeared. Fled to rural Missouri when suspicion fell on her and Gerald.

They did the same for Gerald: Nebraska farm boy. Navy veteran. Moved to Wyoming. Took glorified janitorial job at a mine. Met a local girl and married her. She left him. Met another local girl and married her. She left him. Met a third local girl and married her. Adopted her two sons. She left him. Boys required $150 a month in child support. Met Alice in local trailer park and married her as soon as his last divorce was final. Alice's discomfort with ex-wives and ex-families caused strife. Ex-wife and sons disappeared. Fled to rural Missouri when suspicion fell on him and Alice.

Then they fleshed out Gerald and Alice's alleged crimes, rambling across the six years between the murky disappearance and supposed murder of Ronnie Holtz and the equally murky disappearance and supposed murder of Virginia, Richard, and Reagan Uden. They hit especially hard on Alice's escalating agitation about Virginia's activities just before she vanished forever.

Walter zeroed in on Richard and Reagan's so-called swimming lesson just weeks before they disappeared. It was likely an aborted murder attempt, he said, intended to look like the accidental drowning of two little boys in a cold, deep lake. But Alice, not Gerald, determined that the circumstances weren't right, Walter noted, and Gerald always did as he was told.

The two detectives weren't unquestioning rubes. They sometimes bridled. After all, Walter occupied a world of theory, while theirs was a world of bloody reality. Thought versus action. Hypothesis versus messiness.

Their conversation occasionally strayed off the path . . . but maybe not. One day, Walter and Wachsmuth engaged in a vigorous debate about who really controls the situation in domestic abuse. Wachsmuth, who'd seen the blood and bruises on too many powerless women, argued that the abusers hold all the power. Walter, in his profane and incisive way, took the counterintuitive, contrarian, politically incorrect position: The abused, not the abusers, often wield power by pushing all the buttons and determining all the action by threatening to expose a beast to the world. Worth a beating? No, but worth the psychological control they ultimately win.

Clearly, Walter was talking about Alice. Gerald saw himself as a macho, John Wayne–type protector, an identity Alice gave him. In fact, he was the stoolie, Walter believed, not the director of the action. Alice played him for a fool, including inspiring (or conspiring with) him to kill his own kids. If he didn't play along, she would get rid of him, one way or another.

In the last couple days, the detectives brought Gerald and Alice's sinister story forward twenty-seven years, through a thousand promising leads that stopped just short of closing the case for good. Through investigators who worked their asses off but fell short. Through the doors left open by the suspects themselves, and the doors slammed shut by politics, budgets, civil liberties, and the rest of the damn universe.

Walter had come to know Wachsmuth and TeBeest pretty well—maybe better than they imagined—and now he heard their barely contained frustration with the investigation since 1980.

Post-crime behavior was especially telling, Walter believed, even if it was often overlooked. In natural, accidental, or suicide deaths, survivors have little to gain, so life continues without much of an agenda or suspicious behavior.

But homicides are different. Although the body is dead, killers will almost always unwittingly identify themselves to the keenest observers by their actions and agenda.

As a psychologist, Walter knew the crime wasn't over until the perpetrator stopped deriving satisfaction from it. In Gerald and Alice's case, Walter saw plenty of evidence that they still took pleasure from their crimes. And Alice's agenda, before, during, and after her crimes, was control.

He recapped it for TeBeest and Wachsmuth.

Take Alice's confessions to her children about Ronnie Holtz's murder. It wasn't guilt that motivated her, Walter said. To her sadistic way of thinking, her crime didn't count unless somebody knew about it.

Alice's confession about putting "something" in Don Prunty's drinks to make him stop drinking sounded ominous to Walter. Maybe salt or some other common substance that would aggravate his high blood pressure or diabetes?

Think about the bogus letters that Alice wrote, and how she enlisted her daughter's help to throw off cops. If she didn't know what really happened to Virginia, how could she possibly have known Virginia wasn't already communicating with Claire Martin?

Or consider how Alice took Eliza out of school for talking to teachers and the nurse. To Walter, the highly organized Alice was exerting complete control of her own narrative.

Gerald took all his cues from Alice.

As a suspect, Gerald had made several odd statements, maybe not entirely accidentally, to investigators over the years.

Claire was the last to see Virginia alive—before anybody presumed Virginia was dead.

You can't arrest me because you don't have a body.

You can see town from the abandoned car—when he hadn't been told where the car was found.

He added another during his 2005 interview with TeBeest and Wachsmuth in Missouri.

Destroying a body with pigs? Walter knew that not everybody would know pigs eat people, and damn few of them would know that the teeth were undigestible. Gerald knew. *Did he have experience?* Walter wondered.

When TeBeest and Wachsmuth had disgorged everything they knew so far in great, chaotic gusts of reports, photos, and memory, Walter put it in composed, scientific order for them.

After being dumped by her first husband, Alice had chosen her husbands carefully for their flaws, which made them easier to control. When they outlasted their usefulness to her, she took control of the relationship's ending, either secretly "fixing" Don Prunty's alcoholism or murdering Ronnie Holtz while he slept. When Virginia became an intolerable problem, Alice either actively inspired or conspired in her disappearance. Afterward, she controlled the narrative.

Walter did the math. *Before* the crime, Alice exhibited eight behaviors related to financial issues, thirteen about control. *After* the crime, she demonstrated only four related to money but twenty-two about control. It meant that before the murders—Walter and everybody else knew that's what happened—Alice was obsessed with both money and with controlling the victim; afterward, she still had some concern about money but was more focused on controlling the stories she and Gerald told.

Eager to please his manipulative wife, Gerald matched her almost perfectly, behavior for behavior. Before the crime, he exhibited six money concerns and eleven efforts to control the victims; afterward, three money issues and twenty-nine instances where he tried to control the narrative.

The four presumed deaths—Ronnie Holtz and Virginia, Richard, and Reagan Uden—had all been committed by power assertive killers with nonsexual motives. Alice, in particular, was also sadistic, using all available means to gain control over anyone she touched by spawning dependency, dread, and degradation.

Gerald, however, had a power reassurance personality. He wanted to be John Wayne, but he wasn't smart or skilled enough, so he lived in a fantasy world that could be easily controlled by someone else.

In other words, Alice was an aggressive leader in need of a submissive follower, and Gerald was a cowardly follower who needed a bold leader.

Walter took Alice at her word: Ronnie Holtz's corpse was likely to be found in a great hole, shot in the head. Without bodies or other evidence, he was left to guess what happened to Virginia and her poor boys; he leaned toward a theory that they'd been fed to Gerald's hogs, their teeth scattered. They'd never be found.

The suspicious psychologist also raised a different homicidal specter. The manner of death for Don Prunty—Alice's abusive, alcoholic second husband who died young and left her a brand-new, paid-up trailer plus some monthly veterans benefits—might not be natural at all.

Walter summarized his five-page, single-spaced analysis of the Uden case in a single paragraph of legalese:

> The subsequent admission by Alice Uden [to her children, about killing Ron Holtz] speaks for itself. As for the murders of Virginia, Richard, and Reagan Uden, the pre-crime, crime, and post-crime evidence indicates that Alice and Gerald Uden acted in a conspiracy that caused the victims to be dead by malice of forethought and premeditation. The confidence level of this opinion exceeds the 95th percentile.

The letter's legal language softened what Walter's heart shrieked to him: Gerald and Alice deliberately chose to be evil, degrading, and exploitive. And Alice was by far the more sinister and coldly ruthless. Like a scorpion, she'd willingly kill anyone who challenged her control and power. On the other hand, Gerald was a spineless, feckless sponge without decency. For God's sake, he killed his own children simply because Alice told him to do it.

Walter, one of the best detective brains in America, knew who did it and why, even if he didn't know exactly when, where, or how. He had shown the detectives where Gerald and Alice had been stupid and made mistakes. It comforted TeBeest to know he was on the right track.

But even if the entire world appointed itself the grandest jury and voted unanimously that Gerald and Alice were guilty as hell, the law couldn't touch two cold-blooded killers because of those goddamned unconnected dots. TeBeest grappled with the same frustration Mathews, King, Callaghan, and every other cop who touched this case felt.

No bodies.

No murder weapons.

No crime scenes.

No confessions.

But now he had a solid story line. Walter had taught TeBeest how to look at his case. The inarticulable gut feelings, the frustrating gaps in the evidence, the incalculable evils, the barely imaginable motives, even the inexplicable taunting . . . it all lined up. More work awaited—and a little more luck wouldn't hurt—but now some of the clouds had lifted.

TeBeest had this. And he knew exactly what he needed to do next. Dig.

DCI Special Agent Lonnie TeBeest flew home to Cheyenne reinvigorated. He knew what must happen next in this macabre story.

By Christmas, he presented his "new" narrative to Fremont County Attorney Ed Newell. TeBeest believed Newell was a cop-friendly risk-taker who might see that he had a strong circumstantial case against Gerald and Alice, even without a body.

But no-body cases had a significant risk: If a jury acquitted an accused killer because a death hadn't been proven beyond a reasonable doubt—a far greater likelihood than in cases with a tangible victim—there could be no retrial if a corpse surfaced later. Double jeopardy.

TeBeest laid it out just as Walter had shown him, and his story flowed smoothly. Although he wasn't completely convinced Gerald had chopped up his ex-wife and adopted sons for pig food, he pushed Walter's hideous theory that the Udens' hogs had thoroughly digested the corpses (except the teeth, apparently).

Newell took his job seriously. He supported cops, but he made them follow the rules and do their jobs right. He was also an avid outdoorsman and hunter, and he knew what beastly meat eaters could do.

He knew about human predators too. At the moment, Newell and Wachsmuth were hip-deep in a different, stomach-churning cold case. Jerry Joe Bradish was the prime suspect in the rape and strangling of his thirteen-year-old daughter on a back road near Lander in 1985, but cops could never nail him.

That is, until twenty-two years later, when DNA from a discarded work glove in the curbside trash matched semen found in the young girl.

TeBeest and Wachsmuth were part of the team that sought help from the FBI's Behavioral Analysis Unit to strategize how to elicit a confession from Bradish. Without it, Newell might not have gone to court.

When it was time to fly to Texas to confront Bradish, Newell sent DCI's Wachsmuth, the best interrogator he knew. But Newell went along too. Wachsmuth always thought the prosecutor should have been a cop because he loved the chase so much.

In a couple quick hours, the easy-going Wachsmuth cajoled a confession from Bradish, who vividly described screwing his teenage daughter, choking her to death, and leaving her body for coyotes for a mere $10,000 in life insurance money.

Within days, the prosecutor would be extraditing Bradish, who'd eventually pleaded guilty to the rape and murder "of Biblical proportions" to avoid a death sentence.

Now Newell pondered TeBeest's equally gruesome story line. The Uden case was a rare whodunit, and the photos of Richard and Reagan had haunted him for a long time. He relished another chase.

"If that's your theory," he said, "then you need to excavate the pigpen."

The clarity Walter had imposed on the Uden storyline was already paying off, and suddenly, a new goose chase was on. TeBeest just hoped it wasn't too wild.

When spring finally arrived, as soon as the ground thawed, they'd be digging.

Other goose chases—marathons, really—picked up steam too.

A month after Philadelphia, SA Tom Wachsmuth arranged to meet Alice's son Ted at Remount Ranch, near Cheyenne. Since 1993, Ted had been offering to lead investigators to the abandoned gold mine where his mother had claimed she dumped Ronnie Holtz's dead body. Fourteen years later, somebody was finally taking him up on it.

To be fair, Ted had become a feisty, sometimes reluctant witness over the years. Six months earlier, faced with questions about inconsistencies in some of his earlier statements about his navy service, he clammed up and became uncooperative. He was often drunk or high when Wachsmuth called, but he finally agreed to meet the persistent DCI agent and take him to the mine where he'd often played as a child.

On a chilly Tuesday morning in mid-November 2007, the two of them bumped along the ranch's rutted dirt roads for a while as Ted pointed the way through the fog of his damaged memory. It was on a hillside . . . but which hill? It was in a wooded area . . . but which trees? They backed up and circled around. They bumped over rough two-tracks that only led nowhere. Ted was certain they were in the right area of the mammoth ranch, but not quite certain enough. They wandered like that, lost, for a couple hours.

Wachsmuth, who'd picked up a lot of his people skills as a street cop, kept the conversation light to keep a mildly hostile Ted calm. Ted especially hated TeBeest, who'd questioned him for the umpteenth time about this painful crap, and he generally mistrusted cops. Hell, he mistrusted most of humanity.

It wasn't Ted's fault. Wachsmuth genuinely felt sorry for the guy, as prickly and defective as he was. Ted seemed embarrassed, haunted by the dark shadow that had been cast across his life.

So Wachsmuth was the "good cop." He worked hard to gain Ted's fragile trust. The veteran cop patiently reassured him that he had no other place to be, and he asked a lot of nonthreatening questions about Ted—cars, sports teams, the weather, his family—as if they were just buds sharing a beer on the back patio instead of a cop and a witness searching for a missing corpse in a clandestine grave.

"We can do this," Wachsmuth said. "We got it."

While they searched, Ted loosened up a little. He retold the story of his mom's confession about shooting Holtz, cramming his naked body in a barrel, driving out here, and getting help from Kay Florita—although he couldn't remember her name at the time—to drop Holtz into the godforsaken hole, which had been filling with other dead carcasses for decades.

But Wachsmuth came to find the hole, and it wasn't happening.

Finally, he drove back to the ranch house, where he found the manager, who guided them to a wooded hillside in the same area where they'd been circling for hours. It turned out Ted hadn't been completely lost.

Ted instantly recognized the hole, encircled as it was by a rickety barbed-wire fence that was barely standing. "This is it," he said.

Wachsmuth looked around, then recorded the mine's GPS coordinates and elevation. Two smaller, shallower holes lay nearby, likely would-be mines that were started and stopped by a disconsolate prospector who saw no reason to continue. But Ted was absolutely sure this was the spot his mother described—a deep, dark shaft where he'd played, where the ranch's dead animals had been dumped for a hundred years, that two previous teams of investigators had declared not worth exploring.

Three days later, SA Lonnie TeBeest hauled five of Wyoming's top abandoned-mine authorities out to the Remount's remote site. If the state's chief mine inspector, two of his deputies, and two officials from the Wyoming Abandoned Mine Land Division couldn't tell him what it would take to excavate this morbid hole, nobody could.

They confirmed it was a claim known as the McLaughlin Shaft, a nineteenth-century pit reportedly ninety feet deep. But the mining experts could tell at a glance that the material around its edge didn't look like eighty feet worth of tailings. Maybe the mine had collapsed in on itself, or some of the tailings and loose dirt had eroded back into the mine, filling the empty space not taken up with dead cattle, horses, and pets and ordinary trash. If they drilled down to the bedrock bottom, they'd know for sure how deep the original shaft went, but on this particular day in late 2007, they measured the gaping maw and found it to be only twenty-three feet deep.

TeBeest's bigger question hung in the crisp high plains air. What would it take to safely dig down, maybe all the way to the bottom, hunting as many as four human bodies among the rotted animal flesh and bones down there?

The experts agreed: he'd need heavy equipment and a skilled operator, poised just so at the edge of the mine, painstakingly scraping a little fill at a time and hoping the decaying walls didn't cave in. That didn't take into account whatever health or environmental issues lurked among the concentrated putrefaction of decades and God knows how many dead creatures. It'd be madness to send people down there, for sure.

To TeBeest, they were suggesting more of a hard-rock mining operation than a delicate forensic archaeological excavation, a hulking earthmover when they needed little trowels and brushes. Who knows what trace evidence could be destroyed by a ponderous bucket loader?

Spring finally came.

In May 2008—because May is usually the only reliable start of spring in Wyoming—Lonnie TeBeest and Dr. Rick Weathermon, who oversaw the University of Wyoming's Human Remains Repository and was DCI's go-to guy for forensic archaeology, went to Pavillion to look for human bones on the Udens' old homestead, especially around the abandoned pigpen.

Weathermon was a fifth-generation native who knew the landscape, and an eager forensic digger who knew what lay beneath it. He'd written extensively about pioneer burial practices in frontier days and analyzed the bones of cavalry soldiers killed in Indian skirmishes, among others. His university bio included "an interest in antique weaponry, and documenting saber-toothed rodents of unusual size in Black Hills field camps."[3] This earth wasn't just his job; it was his history.

But more important, he could spot better than most a shard of human bone at a glance.

The adult human body contains 206 individual bones, more in children, whose skeletons are still fusing together in some places. If Gerald and Alice disposed of Virginia and her boys, their grisly trail might be marked by more than seven hundred bones. Could those pigs have turned every particle of their bodies into unrecognizable crap?

Four cadaver dogs sniffed every inch of the place. They all alerted at a few random spots, but they went mad around the old pigpen. Weathermon gridded it out, and the next day, a small cadre of grad students and county coroner employees started to dig.

Over several days, interrupted only by a spring storm and its mud, they found and catalogued a small landfill's worth of material that looked out of place. They collected remnants of old duct tape, thinking it might have been used to bind and gag victims. In the end, though, only seven items—six small bones and a possible toenail—got any real attention as possible human remains.

Dr. Weathermon took them back to his university lab in Laramie. He determined the bones were all nonhuman. The toenail might have come from a man, as it was the right size and shape, but without samples to compare, Weathermon called it inconclusive.

The other odd spots where cadaver dogs alerted were excavated, but nothing was found.

If Gerald and Alice fed their victims to the pigs twenty-eight years before, nothing of them remained. Not even their teeth.

On their own, TeBeest and Wachsmuth doggedly returned to the place a few days after the kids and coroners left. With ordinary shovels, they dug a few holes and collected a lot of bones, clumps of hair, a possible tooth, miscellaneous shell casings, cloth scraps, buttons, and eyeglass and jewelry parts. Alas, all the biological material proved to be nonhuman, and the rest of the rubbish had no obvious connection to Virginia and her boys. Another dead end.

But one more excavation awaited.

Richard and Reagan attended the 1974 wedding of their mom, Virginia, to Gerald Uden, who would soon adopt them. *Photo courtesy of Tracy Morrin.*

Home again in Wyoming, Claire Martin snapped this photo of Virginia Uden just before she disappeared in September 1980. *Photo courtesy of Tracy Morrin.*

Gerald Uden and Alice Prunty wed on November 5, 1976, after a whirlwind courtship. *Photo courtesy of Gerald Uden.*

Virginia, Richard, and Reagan in 1971.
Photo courtesy of Tracy Morrin.

SING BOYS MAY HAVE SEEN MOM MURDERED

is appealing desperately to GLOBE readers to
missing grandsons so she can rest at night.
he missing boys, Richard and Reagan Uden, hold
that not only involves abduction, but possibly the
her, Vir-
d.
tain my
killed,''
verton,
LOBE.
grand-
can find
y about
lved.''
is the
ramatic
of the
d chil-
each

agan
1980,
d 11.
ed the

emar-

HAVE YOU SPOTTED THEM?

MARTIN with photos of
Richard (left) and Reagan: "I
believe they are alive"

briefly to live in another | said they had not showed up. | of my daughter or the boys."

Claire Martin's hunt for her missing daughter and grandsons was a tabloid story. *Photo from the Wyoming Division of Criminal Investigation.*

Claire's missing station wagon was found lodged on a rock in the nearby mountains three weeks after the disappearance. At first, there was no sign of Virginia and the boys. *Photo from the Wyoming Division of Criminal Investigation.*

Reagan, Richard, and Virginia Uden. *Photos from the Wyoming Division of Criminal Investigation.*

Gerald and Alice lived happily secluded lives in Missouri after leaving Wyoming in 1982. In this 1986 family photo, Eliza was thirteen. *Photo courtesy of Gerald Uden.*

Gerald and Alice in 2004. *Photo courtesy of Gerald Uden.*

Teenage Ron Holtz in his Colorado high school photo. *Photo from the Wyoming Division of Criminal Investigation.*

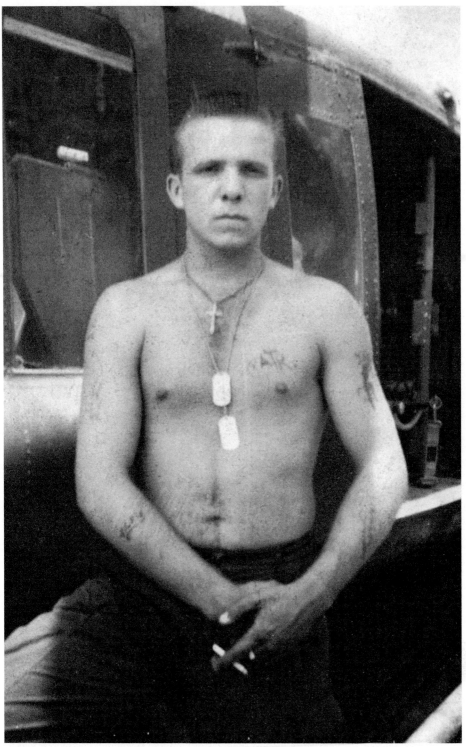

If Ron Holtz was crazy before Vietnam, being a door gunner on a chopper made him even crazier. *Photo courtesy of Sharon Mack.*

Alice's second husband, Don Prunty, with his son Joe in 1969. *Photo courtesy of Joe Prunty.*

DONALD J. PRUNTY
OCTOBER 8 1926
JULY 23 1973

Don Prunty was only forty-six when he died suddenly in Laramie, Wyoming. *Photo by the author.*

The mouth of the Hidden Hand Mine near South Pass City, Wyoming. *Photo by the author.*

The McLaughlin Shaft on the Remount Ranch is believed to be ninety feet deep. *Top photo by the author; bottom photo from the Wyoming Division of Criminal Investigation.*

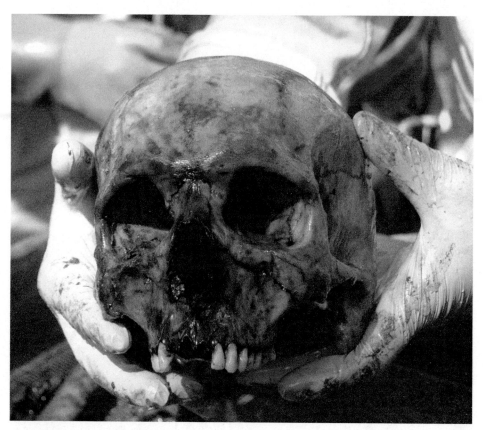

On August 27, 2013, diggers at the Remount Ranch's abandoned mine found what had long eluded them: Ron Holtz's skull. *Photo from the Wyoming Division of Criminal Investigation.*

Even after almost forty years buried in an abandoned mine, the bullet hole in Ron Holtz's skull was clear. *Photo from the Wyoming Division of Criminal Investigation.*

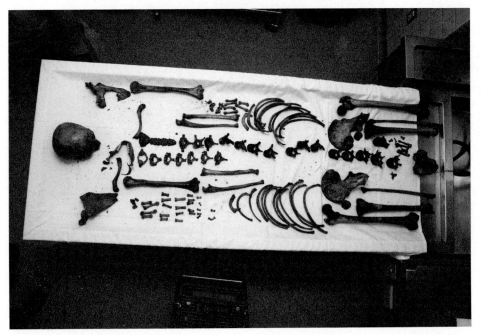

Every bone in Ron Holtz's body was found forty feet deep in the McLaughlin Shaft. *Photo from the Wyoming Division of Criminal Investigation.*

The lonely spot where Gerald Uden said he killed Virginia, Richard, and Reagan. *Photo by the author.*

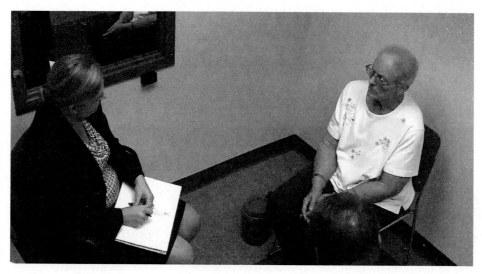

SA Tina Trimble (left) confronts Alice Uden, 74, just before her arrest in 2013. *Photo from the Wyoming Division of Criminal Investigation.*

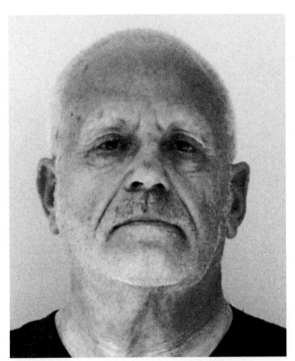

Gerald Uden's prison mug shot. *Photo from the Wyoming Department of Corrections.*

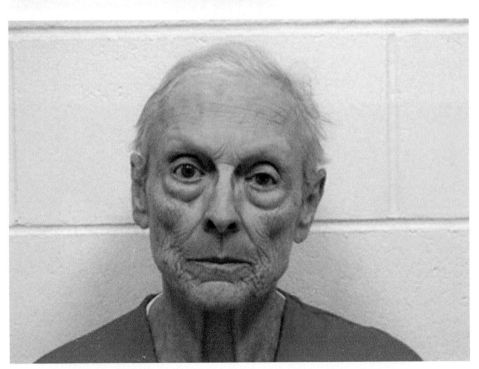

Alice Uden's prison mug shot. *Photo from the Wyoming Department of Corrections.*

Tip Top Search and Rescue's sonar and ROV boat, just one of the craft that searched Fremont Lake for Virginia and her boys several times over two years. *Photo courtesy of John Linn / TTSAR.*

Tom Crossman operates one of the ROV units that were used in the Fremont Lake searches. *Photo courtesy of John Linn / TTSAR.*

Gerald and Alice, living the good life in Missouri around 1999. *Photo courtesy of Gerald Uden.*

Chapter 6

UNDER THE WIND

By 2009, the Uden and Holtz cases had blended into one big case without a case.

SA Lonnie TeBeest still worked it between his other cases, on evenings and weekends as he could. He continued to harvest tidbits of information about Gerald and Alice, Virginia and her boys, and Ronnie Holtz—little pieces that added color to their edges without completing the whole puzzle—but he focused on the Remount Ranch's old gold mine. He made a hundred phone calls to cover all his bases, from landowner agreements to heavy equipment rentals to forensic archaeologists. He even studied whether a county bridge between Cheyenne and the ranch would be strong enough for heavy equipment.

His gut couldn't tell him for sure, and he wasn't clairvoyant, but thirty years of rabbit trails all led to one spot. Anybody with a lick of sense—an academy recruit, a dropout from any Law Enforcement 101 class, even a serious viewer of crime dramas—knew it. It was imperative to explore that abandoned gold mine for the single piece of evidence he needed to break this bewildering puzzle wide open: Ronnie Holtz.

And he couldn't be sure that he wouldn't find Virginia, Richard, and Reagan down there too. Was it beyond the realm of possibility that Gerald would repeat Alice's "perfect" crime? Why mess with his beloved wife's macabre success? It was certainly possible that Alice had dictated to her pliant husband exactly how to do it.

TeBeest had all the permissions he needed to excavate on the ranch ... except his own bosses'. To him, they resisted every big idea. The more TeBeest protested, the more they seemed to dig in. It was starting to feel personal.

But every Wyoming winter has its thaw. Spring finally came, and the DCI bosses gave their tepid approval to explore the Remount mine. Not a full-on excavation—there was no money in the budget for a $50,000 fishing expedition, no desire to indulge a bellyaching agent, and no trust of TeBeest's gut—but they approved a couple shovels and a little travel money. *Yeah, that might shut him up.* One catch: TeBeest wouldn't lead the team. The director himself would be there to supervise, but his crime lab chief, Steve Holloway, would be in charge.

In exchange for their help (or protection), some of TeBeest's fellow agents made him promise to be good and not say or do anything that might hurt himself... or their bosses. He agreed.

So in late May 2009, with the consent of the weather and the ranch owners, DCI's three top administrators led a team of twelve agents, seven top-notch crime lab technicians, Dr. Rick Weathermon, and a couple of his UW grad students to find what might have been hidden under a secluded hillside in Wyoming's high plains.

In fact, they were about to burrow into three distinct holes—three different aborted nineteenth-century pits of varying depths—that lay very close to each other on the same hill. Two of them were just modest indentations where some long-dead prospector scooped some dirt and rocks but quickly abandoned them for more promising pay dirt. The bigger, deeper McLaughlin Shaft was the centerpiece, but the diggers couldn't ignore the two shallower depressions that might be deep enough to be Ronnie Holtz's grave.

The motley team split up. The crime lab specialists and the DCI executives focused on the main shaft, while most of their agents scratched and scraped in the smaller depressions.

The shallower holes, which had apparently also been used as the ranch's trash dumps over the years, yielded the first booty when an agent found a discarded earring. A young DCI agent named Tina Trimble, one of the few female agents since Lynne Callaghan broke the gender barrier almost twenty years before, found a few clothing scraps, including a zipper and two clothing snaps that might have been from a Western shirt. Over the next few hours, the team sifted a ton of Wyoming dirt through Weathermon's special screens and found other garbage: various cartridge casings, a metal watchband, some old bottles, a belt buckle, a scrap of a sock, and older artifacts that couldn't possibly be related to this case.

Down about six feet into one hole, the agents found some Depression-era car parts, distinctive bottles, and other items that suggested they had hit a layer of junk that had been discarded long before any mid-1970s murder victim. He wasn't there.

The other hole was even more trivial, and it was also abandoned after lunch when they found artifacts in a junk layer dating to 1964. Ronnie Holtz wasn't there either.

Ah, but the big hole, already about twenty-five feet deep, was different. It was corked like a wine bottle with four or five feet of snow, which acted as natural refrigeration for whatever lay below. It wouldn't thaw on its own until July, when the sun rose higher in the sky, but they couldn't wait. They'd have to dig it out before they could see what was down there.

TeBeest didn't know exactly what they'd find, but the McLaughlin Shaft held a lot of hope and promise . . . and more ghosts than he imagined.

TeBeest was told it might also contain the remains of a filly named Misty, great-grandfoal of the horse that supposedly inspired author Mary O'Hara's famous Flicka. The colt died around the time of Ronnie Holtz's disappearance and was chucked in the hole with other dead livestock.

Then there was Jefe, a pet German shepherd/husky mix that Ted recalled tossing in the mine in the early 1970s. Jefe had tangled with a wild coyote in broad daylight while Alice and toddler Ted watched from the porch. The coyote was killed and hauled away. Fearing the odd-acting coyote might be rabid, Don Prunty shot the dog and dumped him in the mine. The county's veterinarian later determined the coyote had a brain tumor, not rabies. The protective Jefe died for nothing.

But if the diggers found the bones of a good-sized dog and a colt close together, they might find Holtz nearby.

One agent started digging, inches at a time. First snow, then dirt. Only it wasn't so much dirt as hard-packed carrion, decay, and death dreck.

Every bone—and there were plenty—was closely inspected by Weathermon. A small herd of animal carcasses had been dropped to rot in that morbid maw. *Here* was a small white box containing a pet's cremains that the ranch manager identified as a favorite dog that had died only eight years before, in 2001. *Here* was a plastic bag full of fermented animal guts that almost made everybody vomit when it suddenly burst and spilled rotten slop on the ground. *Here* was a dead calf's white plastic ear tag that identified it as the offspring of a prize cow named Mistiq; it had been dead about twelve years. *Here* were bowling-ball-sized clumps of adipocere, a greasy-gooey soap known as "grave wax" that sometimes congeals like putrid cottage cheese from a decomposing body's soft tissues—all probably from fairly recently dead animals.

Up on the lip, Weathermon—who really wanted desperately to be down in that prodigious hole, digging—soon amassed the biggest collection of cow bones he'd ever seen.

But it wasn't without risk. Once the snow had been removed, the walls of the shaft tapered inward, cramping the digging area. It was a crisp forty degrees deep inside; the surface temperature was more than twenty degrees higher. An agent questioned whether the rancid air down there might carry poisonous chemicals or bacteria. Worse, somebody worried aloud that the diggers might be standing on a false floor of frozen carcasses; if they punched through, anybody in the hole might plunge sixty feet to the black, frozen bottom.

They'd scraped down only about two feet when the digging was abruptly halted.

In midafternoon, Holloway, an ex-cop who had experience in technical rock climbing and mountain rescues, declared the risk of a cave-in greater than the chances of finding any murder victims. He closed down the whole dirty business and told everybody to load up.

Game over.

They hadn't gone deep at all, but in all that disgusting muck, no sign of Ronnie Holtz. Nor the famous Flicka's great-grandfoal or heroic Jefe, for that matter. They found nothing important, then stopped looking.

Weathermon, the sidelined bone collector, was disgusted. TeBeest could barely contain his rage. They came to dig. *We barely started and now we're done?* He suspected that the hasty shutdown had more to do with stink than safety. They were nowhere near deep enough to find Ron Holtz, much less their own asses. The director and his two jackass toadies didn't want to solve this case, he thought, they only wanted to appear to care. Or maybe they just wanted to stick it to him. This wasn't cop work. It was just bullshit political theater.

On the long drive home, TeBeest felt it again, that nagging sensation that another chance to close this case had been squandered.

And he thought about how he'd tell Claire that smaller hearts and minds had failed her again.

For some, that was the end of it, but TeBeest didn't stand down. He wasn't going to let a beef with his bosses stop him.

He kept seeking witnesses, talking to anybody who'd ever known the key players, suggesting to his bosses new ways to get into that awful hole, to rethink the case . . . anything. His team leader, Tim Hill, was in his corner and tried to keep him calm (and employed), but it wasn't Lonnie TeBeest's nature to just shut the hell up when he knew something was wrong.

And he always tried to keep the Uden cold case from freezing solid.

TeBeest interviewed a Cheyenne realtor named Joe Prunty, the son of Alice's second husband, Don Prunty. Joe told a sordid story.

Don Prunty had grown up poor in a small Illinois farm town and married before he went off to war as an army quartermaster during the Second World War. He came home to his authoritarian schoolteacher wife and new son to run his family's Illinois grain elevator. Farmers liked

Don because he was one of them, and he was a smart businessman. But he also had a weakness for women and booze.

Most mornings started with a highball at the County Seat Tavern or the VFW. He drank all day, although he seldom appeared drunk.

Don's first wife divorced him when she caught him with his secretary, literally with his pants down. She kept the grain elevator and sent him packing. To his credit, he married the secretary and bought a new grain elevator, but when he took ill suddenly and went to the hospital, she sold all his grain and money, then took off. He declared bankruptcy.

It was all too much for Don Prunty. He'd lost everything, including his sanity. In 1970, he had a mental breakdown and committed himself to a psychiatric hospital for electroshock therapy. One of his nurses was a big-bosomed, raven-haired, recently divorced gal named Alice Scott. Apparently his mental collapse hadn't affected his wandering eye or his libido. They quickly fell into bed.

They were married less than a year later.

Son Joe remembered Alice as a controlling woman, always looking for something to own or take advantage of.

On their honeymoon in Wyoming—the farm boy Don Prunty was obsessed with the romance of the West—they saw a classified ad in the *Cheyenne Tribune*. The absentee owners of the Remount Ranch, a historic horse and cattle spread between Cheyenne and Laramie, were looking for a caretaker. Without a moment's hesitation, Don applied.

John Ostlund, a politically connected businessman from Wyoming's coal country, interviewed Don for the job and liked him a lot. Don was friendly, outgoing, pleasant, and eventually proved honest, to boot. The caretaker search ended almost before it began.

In October 1971, Don and a pregnant Alice loaded up a U-Haul—including, inexplicably, a live pony—and drove cross-country with three of her kids to the sprawling Remount Ranch on Wyoming's windswept High Plains, their new home.

Don and Alice lived in an old bunkhouse. The work wasn't backbreaking. In summer, the Pruntys kept an eye on a few dozen steers whose job was mainly to keep the grass down before they were sold in the fall. Otherwise, Don and Alice only mowed lawns around the main house, fixed fences, maintained the outbuildings, cleared the roads, and tidied up after the Ostlunds' frequent weekend visits.

Four months after they arrived, Eliza was born. In the depths of a howling Wyoming winter, with a new baby, snow blindness, and suffocating cabin fever, Don sunk even deeper into his cups. Worse, Don became abusive when he drank, and he sloughed off his ranch work.

Spring and summer came. Life returned to something that passed for normal, but nothing was really normal out there. The Pruntys never socialized much with the Ostlunds, mostly because Alice felt like "the hired help." Don was getting worse, the work began to slip, and then they were fired in the depths of the next winter.

Alice and Don quickly found work as caretakers of the Lincoln Summit turnout on Interstate 80, shoveling snow, picking up litter, cleaning public bathrooms, and answering tourists' questions. Don moonlighted as a school bus driver so they could afford a brand-new mobile home, which they parked in the rest area.

But Don was suddenly in bad physical shape. He was only forty-six, but his chronic alcoholism and high blood pressure were taking a rapid and vicious toll on his body. Within a few weeks of moving off the Remount Ranch, he became lethargic, increasingly confused, and physically weak. By the time Alice rushed him to the hospital in Laramie—where she had recently gotten a nursing job—his heart and kidneys were failing, his normally high blood pressure had skyrocketed, and his brain functioned only foggily. His electrolytes were way out of whack, and he was showing signs of kidney failure. He grew less and less responsive.

Once he was admitted, Laramie doctors controlled his blood pressure, but he remained seriously confused.

Two days later, on July 23, 1973, a relatively young Don Prunty died, and Alice prepared for a funeral.

He'd been a good man whose demons ultimately killed him. The Albany County coroner ruled the cause of his death to be natural. His malfunctioning brain had been damaged by excessively high blood pressure, while other alcoholic symptoms had banjaxed his heart, kidneys, and eyesight. No autopsy was done.

When Alice discovered Don's $5,000 life insurance policy was paid to his son Joe and Joe's sister, she was furious. But Don had also bought mortgage insurance on his brand-new trailer, so Alice inherited the shiny mobile home free and clear. It was the only sure thing in her life.

Donald Prunty came to a cheap ending.

His half-hour funeral was in the mortuary's little chapel. Mourners were few: his brother, two sisters, his first wife, and his daughter Rachel traveled from the East; Joe and his family drove over from Cheyenne; and Alice brought Eliza and two of her other kids.

Don wasn't big on church, so the prayers by an on-call pastor were perfunctory.

Just a week or so before he died unexpectedly, Rachel rode the train from Illinois to see her dad, not knowing it'd be the last time. They talked about a lot of things, including his wish—should anything ever happen to him—to be buried with his first wife's family in the small township of St. Mary's, Illinois.

Alice had other plans.

Nobody said goodbye at the graveside. A few days after he died at Laramie's Ivinson Memorial Hospital, Don Prunty was lowered into a bargain-basement eighteen-gauge steel casket and vault near the back fence of Laramie's Greenhill Cemetery, forever a part of the Old West landscape he romanticized. Only the gravedigger attended.

Don's plot was in a row of "singles," where lone graves were dug as needed, because Alice never expected to be buried with him. Alice spent nothing on the whole funeral. Don's brother paid for most of it, and military burial benefits paid a little. Much later, when Joe discovered Alice hadn't even bought a headstone, he ordered one.

Joe Prunty recalled an especially ugly argument with Alice during a low-rent trailer-house wake on the day of his father's funeral. Alice offered him Don's wallet as a memento. Joe responded that he wanted the wallet *plus* a shotgun Don had owned all his life *plus* a hunting rifle that Joe had given his dad at the Remount Ranch. Alice refused, saying she needed all those things. Joe told Alice to kiss his ass and stormed out. They never talked again.

That was about all Joe could tell TeBeest for sure. Over the years, he'd lost track of Eliza. She'd only called once, to ask him for money.

TeBeest had been nursing a nagging feeling about Prunty for a couple years, but he felt there were more immediate incriminating, haunting questions to be answered. And his bosses were clearly not eager to spend money on wild hairs. But . . . *might Alice have murdered Don Prunty too?*

At TeBeest's request, an independent Casper doctor evaluated the county coroner's causes of Don Prunty's death. Most of the symptoms, he said, suggested a possibility that he'd died of complications from diabetes, but one thing bothered him. Encephalopathy, or brain dysfunction, rarely caused death on its own. Prunty's medical records, which had never been shared outside of DCI, might reveal more, the doctor said.

In October 2009, just a few months after the aborted dig at the Remount mine, crime lab director Steve Holloway claimed he'd contacted a private group of trained forensic volunteers, the Colorado-based NecroSearch International. NecroSearch specialized in helping cops find clandestine graves with a wide variety of modern forensic sciences, from ground-penetrating radar, cadaver dogs, and old-fashioned human tracking to sophisticated geophysics, entomology, and computerized analysis of the search area. And they'd do it for free.

But bad weather set in, and the safety of the old mine was still an open question. The NecroSearch visit was canceled. Holloway told TeBeest it would be rescheduled, but somehow it fell through the cracks. It never happened, and TeBeest wondered if it was ever arranged at all.

Around this time, Deputy Director Kebin Haller took a close look at TeBeest's caseload and ruled that it was far too light. He was wasting too much time on the Uden case. The deputy director issued an official reprimand. TeBeest accepted his scolding but responded with an ill-advised email . . . which earned him a second reprimand for insubordination.

Yeah, I probably was insubordinate, TeBeest had to admit. It made him smile.

Two formal rebukes were the price of his principles. Maybe he could have been more measured in his words, but he didn't play games. *Their* games.

In cop work, every problem had a solution. But every time TeBeest proposed a solution, his bosses only saw problems . . . the biggest of which became TeBeest himself. They turned down almost every request, sometimes not for defensible reasons but just because they wanted TeBeest to quit. They disliked him and his attitude. They didn't think he was a team player.

Then, just before Thanksgiving, TeBeest and his team leader, Tim Hill, were summoned to a high-level meeting at DCI's Cheyenne headquarters. The three top administrators—including the crime lab's Holloway, who wasn't in TeBeest's chain of command—were there, looking stern. They'd determined that a serious excavation at the Remount mine would cost as much as $50,000. DCI's budget didn't have it. In a budget-cutting administration, they could "guarantee" neither the governor nor the attorney general would find the money for them. This case simply wasn't worth the political capital it would cost.

But the real reason they wanted to sit down with TeBeest was his bad attitude. They didn't like the way he talked to them. He was bad at communicating, and he had the temperament of a junkyard dog. He knew that they'd rather be done with him.

Hill asked Lonnie to leave the room briefly so Hill could talk to their bosses privately and frankly. Once they were alone, he spoke bluntly about the appearance that TeBeest was being unfairly targeted for vague reasons. If the Gang of Three had been contemplating a suspension or a firing, they backed off. In state government, no rhetorical skill spoke like the threat of a scandal, as minor as it might be. Hill might have saved TeBeest's ass, and the old agent knew it.

But the day still ended at an impasse. The director and his top lieutenants had to reblock this drama, and TeBeest had to collect his wits and refocus on his work.

A month later, the director raised the scant chance of a grant from an outside confederation of police agencies, maybe five thousand bucks, to pay somebody else to excavate the mine. TeBeest's hopes were raised, even though the amount was a fraction of the estimated cost. He just sensed that there could finally be movement if the director was seeking solutions too.

But TeBeest never heard another word about it. Communication wasn't his bosses' strong suit either.

TeBeest was tired of being jacked around. He hated especially that they were keeping two killers on the street and doing nothing to get justice for four Wyoming citizens who desperately needed it—and an old grandmother who just wanted answers before she died. It didn't take a good detective to know they didn't think much of him.

To be fair, TeBeest didn't think much of them either. He was tired of their bullshit, tired of bashing his head against a brick wall, tired of caring more about Claire Martin than anybody else did, tired of dead ends . . . just tired.

He'd become cynical. He thought about the South Dakota kid who first put on a cop's uniform in a small town in Wyoming, and he knew he'd changed. He still wanted to solve crimes and give people justice, but the uphill fight against bad guys—some of whom were supposed to be good guys—had taken its toll.

Two months later, SA Lonnie TeBeest put in his retirement paperwork. He was fifty-five years old—ancient for a cop. His hearing was deteriorating from three decades on police shooting ranges (where sometimes his only protection had been empty shell casings he used as earplugs). He'd been bumping up against bad guys on both sides of the thin blue line for more than thirty years, too. The Uden case itself had consumed him for almost ten years—on slow days, weekends, vacations, sleepless nights—and the only argument against his retirement was staying long enough to close it.

But while his retirement paperwork worked its painfully slow way through the state of Wyoming's bureaucratic bowels, he continued to work the case.

A state forensic analyst reported the scraps of duct tape found in the pigpen area couldn't possibly be from a roll of tape found in Virginia's car back in 1980. Dead end.

Another technician reported the hairs found by TeBeest and Wachsmuth in Pavillion were animal, not human. Another dead end.

Nothing else panned out. Over the years, multiple investigators had collected almost everything they could ... except bodies, weapons, and confessions. The investigations hadn't been perfect, but they hadn't been awful either. Now, other current cases needed attention. TeBeest was preparing to hand thirty years of investigation over to another agent—although nobody had yet been assigned by the bosses—and he worried that nobody was left to care about solving it. Or about Claire, who was almost ninety years old and had outlasted all of them.

On the last page of the Uden case file—now a couple inches thick, at more than 250 pages—TeBeest noted that he had gone back to Fremont County, where it all began, to return copies of all the reports, transcripts, tapes, and photos to the sheriff's department there. The originals and all the physical evidence were stored safely in DCI's Cheyenne vaults. He knew it'd be assigned to a new caretaker, but it'd probably get lost in the day-to-day shuffle and the bosses' political machinations.

In the "Status" box at the bottom of the page, he typed one final word that felt more to him like surrender than a status report.

"Open."

A year after he put in his papers, SA Lonnie TeBeest was a civilian again. It didn't mean he didn't care about the Uden case anymore. It just meant he couldn't do much about it any longer.

Just before he left for good, he checked his personnel file. His letters of reprimand were missing. In fact, they'd never been filed at all. He was told there had been procedural errors in the whole mess, but he didn't care to pursue it further. He'd be going out clean.

Even though he was no longer an agent, he still telephoned Claire Martin occasionally, but he had fallen out of the loop. At first, he'd hear tidbits about the investigation, maybe get a couple calls every so often, but it trailed off after a while. He heard the expectation in Claire's voice when he called, and it broke his heart that he never had any good news to share.

Claire was failing. The outsized hope that kept her alive was flagging. Her profound light was going out, and it saddened Lonnie that he couldn't give her the comfort of knowing how the story ended. He blamed himself, nobody else. He never lied to her, although he never interrupted her prayers either. She believed the boys were alive, and Lonnie knew they weren't. She liked Gerald and couldn't fathom that he might be involved, while Lonnie hated him for doing what everybody but Claire knew he'd done.

For her, Special Agent Lonnie TeBeest (retired) had put his full heart into his part-time case but did little more than add a thousand extra dots that he couldn't connect. In the end, he came up empty.

He reckoned the key—a skeleton key—was very likely lying in that noxious prairie hole that would probably never be excavated. He couldn't be sure, of course, but he knew the Remount mine was the next best place to look for clues. They had to find the bottom or find a body, but they had to dig. He even thought about paying for an excavation himself, but he didn't have that kind of cash. It pissed him off to suspect where the smoking gun was hidden but be utterly powerless to grab it.

He never knew that someone else had been watching him the whole time, taking notes.

Directors of the Wyoming DCI were like county sheriffs: they came and went with the wind.

Less than two years after Lonnie TeBeest retired, Director Forrest Bright took a new job on the Wyoming governor's security detail. In a state once described as a small town with very long streets, almost everybody felt they really knew the governor by his first name, his poker tells, and how he took his steaks, and when the governor ceased being everyone's buddy, he didn't last long. That made his security detail, a cowboy version of the Secret Service, either the hardest or the easiest cop job in Cheyenne.

Either way, there was a new sheriff in town.

Steve Woodson was an investigator's investigator. A personable, small-town Missouri kid with more than thirty years' experience, he knew his way around casework.

In fact, there was never a time in his life when he wanted to be anything else but a cop. His mother told anybody who'd listen that a five-year-old Stevie once wrote a letter to the colonel of the Missouri state police to find out if he might already qualify for the force.

When he graduated from high school, this ambitious son of a trucker and a homemaker would have gone straight to police work—except he wasn't yet twenty-one. So his mother convinced him to take some college classes in law enforcement, and he chose Central Missouri State University in Warrensburg for its police program.

In college, he became "Woody." His dad had been known as Woody when Steve was growing up, so he especially liked it. It was friendly and unpretentious, like him. Titles could be barriers, and he always felt a little uncomfortable being called "officer," "detective," "agent," or (eventually) "director." Woody was just easier. It became so natural that it stood out when anybody called him Steve.

As soon as he was old enough, Woody was hired by the Warrensburg Police Department as a patrol officer, even though he was still a college student. He went to class during the day, protected and served at night. He loved it.

And from the start, his favorite part of the job was going after people who didn't think they could be caught.

The Warrensburg PD only had one detective, so it occasionally assigned uniformed beat cops to investigations, everything from gas drive-offs to the rare homicide. Woodson distinguished himself as a perceptive, diligent sleuth. His college graduation gift was a promotion to the Major Case Squad, a kind of multijurisdictional task force, when a lot of young cops were still rookies on probation.

Then a chance to join a big-time force came along. After a six-year stint at Wyoming's DCI doing mostly drug cases, Woodson got his shot at the big league, the federal Drug Enforcement Agency. The DEA had only two agents in Wyoming, so they worked closely with the state agents at DCI, which occupied the same office, just to keep their heads above water.

That's where he met SA Lonnie TeBeest, worked with him, and first learned the good, bad, and ugly about the Uden case. He'd hear about it in the joint Monday briefings, and he sometimes asked TeBeest the latest developments at the watercooler. Once, when TeBeest had spread his case on a not-big-enough conference room table, Woodson came in to ask about it. Secretly, that stuck in TeBeest's impression of the guy.

And what stuck with Woodson was TeBeest's passion for that old case and his commitment to Claire Martin. TeBeest was old-school, not the kind who'd ever sit down with anybody, much less a cop from an outside agency, to bitch about the internecine political problems. But, frankly, nobody in the squad room needed big ears to hear TeBeest's frequent frustrations with the bosses in Cheyenne.

In 2012, when the governor asked Forrest Bright to turn in his keys, Woodson was the guy they recruited to replace him. He jumped at the chance because he knew DCI agents were some of the best.

But he'd leave no doubt who was the boss. It wasn't megalomania; it was efficiency and protection. One guy would decide, one guy would take the heat, one guy would be fired when the governor finally got pissed: Steve Woodson. Nobody had to guess who was in charge.

Woodson moved into the DCI director's office on September 4, 2012, with a few boxes and a new way of doing things. This was the Division of Criminal *Investigation,* and that's exactly where the emphasis was now going to be. Every case was going to get their best damn effort, even the cold ones.

Woodson knew well how cops had long passed their dirty bucks: an outgoing investigator handed his cold-case folders to the new guy, who would often hold them until the next new guy.

He also knew internal politics caused internal strife. He didn't want or need the drama. And it should never interfere with catching bad guys. *No more. Not in this house.*

With all the twenty-first century's new investigative tools that never existed when most of these unsolved mysteries happened, Woodson believed it would be a sin—maybe even a firing offense—if DCI agents didn't take an honest, fresh look at all of them.

With the first stroke of his pen, Woodson created DCI's first Cold Case Team, comprising ten agents from the intelligence unit, the crime lab, investigations, and the FBI—some of the best investigative minds in Cheyenne.

Up until now, cold cases were make-work. DCI agents worked them only when they had a special interest and when time allowed (which was practically never). Now, Woodson made them a higher priority—not more important than the new cases that happened every day, or than ongoing investigations, but certainly not less important when justice might still be served.

He handed it all to a hardworking, enterprising agent named Tina Trimble. A month later, before he'd even gotten comfortable in his new chair, he gathered them in one room with a single purpose: *Look at every unsolved case and start solving them.*

Now.

Claire Martin died on a Thursday, when spring repaid years of her faithfulness with a warm day, clear skies, and a gentle goodbye kiss of breeze.

On April 4, 2013, the number of Claire's days was 33,703—ninety-two years, three months, and ten days. One of those days, an awful one, had posed a question she spent the rest of her days trying to answer. She never did, but maybe wanting to know kept her alive longer.

Claire's overtaxed heart had been giving out long before her death. She was angry that she had been taken out of her apartment and moved into a nursing home where people fussed over her. Her Social Security check was now mailed directly to the main office, so she had no control over her money anymore. On her best days, she couldn't understand why; on her worst days, it just confused her, if she remembered at all.

A few months before she died, she signed over the title of her old 1973 Country Squire station wagon to the Fremont County Sheriff's Office. Over the years, she'd borrowed a few thousand dollars against it to pay for her search. Now, she reckoned that as-yet-unimagined future science might reveal untold clues. But even if it didn't, she couldn't bring herself to junk the car. Better that it sit forever in the sheriff's impound lot than be scrapped.

Toward the end, Claire still showed love for her friends and their children, but every now and then, a shadow fell over her, as if a dark cloud were passing. She struggled to see good in people, but her demons were bigger. Her world had shattered in a million tiny pieces years before, and she never really had any hope of putting it back together.

In her last weeks, she broke her hip in a fall. She was not robust enough to survive a surgical repair and couldn't take painkillers, so she suffered a constant ache. It shriveled her physically and emotionally. Bedridden in her sterile hospital room, away from her few treasures, she hated when visitors left. She resented the decisions being made for her at the end, and she just wanted to be in her own home, living her own life.

When she stopped eating altogether, her doctors moved her to the county's hospice in Riverton.

She couldn't speak at the end, either. A few close friends like Marie Roskowske visited her, but Claire was already empty. No words, no energy, no tears ... no more of the hope that had once filled her. Her hope was broken. At the end, Claire had made a silent peace with the likelihood Virginia, Richard, and Reagan had all been dead since the day they vanished.

Tracy Morrin, a poor thirtysomething mom when she met Claire just after the disappearance, spent as much time at the hospice as she could in those last days. For years, they'd hiked together, shared long road trips, talked late into the night. In other circumstances, Morrin might have become a surrogate daughter to Claire, but they were close friends, that's all. As a friend, Morrin never walked on eggshells and escaped being judged and guided.

She knew this day would come, but it didn't make it easier to say goodbye.

Now, she spoke to Claire quietly as she hovered near death, awake but failing. Morrin reassured Claire that soon she'd see Virginia, Richard, and Reagan, and she'd learn the answers that had eluded her here.

Claire's face was thin and her mouth was slightly open, but her eyes seemed to brighten through her tears. She squeezed Morrin's hand feebly.

"Claire, it's OK to go," Morrin whispered before she left. "I love you so much. Go be with Virginia. Go be with Richard and Reagan. It's OK."

Claire died the next morning. The hospice nurse had called Morrin and told her that death was at hand, but Claire was gone before Morrin arrived. Her old friend's passing was peaceful, although her face had frozen in a gasping, pained look. When Morrin looked down upon Claire just minutes after her death, she imagined it wasn't a willing passing but somebody still trying to hold on.

According to her wishes, Claire was cremated, although she had long ago spent some insurance money to buy cemetery plots in Glendo—where she raised Virginia in a little cabin, with an outhouse—for her daughter and grandsons if their bodies were ever found.

The local paper's obituary noted she was born on Christmas Day in 1920. It recorded her time as a Rosie the Riveter–type factory worker during World War II and her cross-country move to Wyoming as a single, divorced mother in 1962. It listed her many menial jobs and forgettable towns. The requisite list of her joys—the outdoors, gardening, hiking, pets, camping, sculling on mountain lakes, motorcycles, and long road trips—was far longer than the list of her survivors. And, of course, it described the moment when her life changed forever.

But the obituary didn't say she'd once been happy and funny. That she yearned to sleep through the night just once. That she believed in the healing power of stars and moving water. That God never answered her. That at the end, all she had were memories, and they weren't enough.

Morrin organized a low-key memorial service for Claire ten days later in the community room at Claire's assisted living complex. Maybe forty people came to say a last goodbye. Most knew her story and the empty space it left in her. The beloved antique doll with a friend's real hair was there with a couple of pictures and finger food. A few words were said, prayers were offered, and Morrin read a poignant poem she'd written for Claire.

After a few weeks, Morrin took her last walk with Claire. She hiked up the switchbacks on a stone path to an old fire lookout tower on Blue Ridge in the Wind River Mountains above Lander. Claire always liked the long view. There, she scattered some of the ashes.

But Morrin kept some of Claire's ashes so they could be buried with

Virginia and the boys someday. For all the natural beauty that lay before her now and forever, that's where Claire truly wanted to be.

If there was anything Claire had taught her friend over the years, it was that life goes on, even in the face of very bad stuff. She never said it out loud that way, but she lived it out loud.

All part of the journey, she would have said. *None of us gets out alive.*

By the time word reached Lonnie TeBeest, it was too late to say goodbye to Claire Martin.

After he retired, he and Sandra moved back to South Dakota, their heart-earth. At first, except for occasional calls from old cop buddies, he might as well have been a thousand miles and a hundred years out of the loop. At one point, the Wyoming Attorney General specifically warned that because he was no longer an agent, information about the Uden case could not be shared. The cop life had moved on without him, but he was happy to be home in South Dakota.

So it was several days before another agent called him in Spearfish with the old news that Claire had died. He missed her memorial service, too.

At first, TeBeest was a little sad, mostly because she'd died without knowing what happened to Richard and Reagan. He was very disappointed in himself that he'd retired and effectively given up on the case when he'd promised her he wouldn't—not just once, but several times.

The last time he saw Claire was when he went to her austere little apartment to tell her in person that he was retiring and a new detective—*what, the fifth or sixth?*—would soon contact her. Her face slumped. She'd heard it all before.

He didn't cry, then or now. That was Lonnie TeBeest. It was personal, not sappy or sentimental. He'd never been very emotional about witnesses and survivors. It got in the way. Death happens. It lurks in the background, biding its time, watching. He wasn't suddenly going all mushy.

Ah, but anger was different.

Most of the time, TeBeest saw himself as pretty levelheaded, but when he got angry and knew he was right, he stayed angry. He'd heard once that the measure of a good man is how long he can hold a grudge. By that standard, he'd been a very good man, even if he was mellowing.

Yes, he felt cheated out of a solution. He felt a pang that he never helped Claire feel safe and warm. He regretted that answers were always just beyond his grasp. He was sorry he let too much time pass and hated that he couldn't do anything about it now. He lamented that the mystery might have kept her alive longer, but that that might only have meant more sleepless nights. And he was relieved he hadn't seen her at the end, plugged into a wall.

But emotion? He didn't do anguish. The most he'd felt in Claire's case—besides being angry at his bosses—was when he realized Richard and Reagan were about the same age as his own two sons. He wanted to know what happened to them because if it had been his boys, he would have never given up until he keeled over dead.

In that, he felt Claire's pain, intensely and intimately. He just couldn't cry about it. It wasn't the absence of feelings. He felt something. He'd only worry when he felt nothing.

Claire's suffering was over now, anyway. It had been a long life. Some good days, more bad. She'd been a prisoner of her agony and grief, not living the free life she once dreamed. Now, she was past caring forever. She had her answers.

All part of the journey, he thought. *None of us gets out alive.*

Chapter 7

BONES AND SHADOWS

Tina Trimble was the oldest of five kids, all born to a single, under-employed, and overwhelmed mom who tended to move around a lot, just ahead of creditors. The moves were often hasty, so the whole family's worldly possessions came down to whatever could fit in the car and a few black plastic trash bags.

Tina learned early the value of organization, efficiency, and getting everybody in the car fast. Stepfathers drifted in and out, and Mom had a steady stream of boyfriends, who tended to be boozers, abusers, and jerks from all the dirtiest corners of the oil boomtown of Casper. So Tina also became a surrogate parent to her three sisters and youngest brother, whom she started babysitting when she was only six or seven. That was her life, slightly out of control, just the way it was. It'd be a long time before she understood that not everybody grew up that way.

After high school, she took a job at the local Target store. Reliable and conscientious beyond her years, Tina moved up quickly. She landed on the store's security staff, where she busted shoplifters daily, calling the occasional uniformed cop to take the hard cases away for booking. She thought cops were cool, so decisive and commanding. *Under control.*

One day, one of the cops urged her to take the test and put in an application. She studied up, took the test, and passed, even though she was only twenty years old, a year shy of the age limit. But as soon as she turned twenty-one, the Casper Police Department immediately offered her a job.

Tina spent the next five years on patrol, loving every minute. It satisfied her craving for structure and responsibility. When her chance came to join the local drug task force, headed by DCI, she volunteered.

Two years later, in 2005, an agent's job opened at DCI. They already knew her to be a trustworthy, fastidious cop, and they needed more female agents, so it was a no-brainer. She got it.

Trimble was assigned a cubicle desk on the other side of a wimpy little office wall from a crusty old investigator in the Casper field office's bull pen. Her team leader—the state's less threatening term for a sergeant—told her to learn quickly how to write reports and to read up on one of the team's particularly fascinating cold cases: the Uden mystery.

She did, and the next morning she was full of questions for her new cubicle mate, SA Lonnie TeBeest.

"When are you going to arrest them?" she asked him.

"What?" TeBeest was surprised by the question. "How do you know about that?"

Rookie SA Tina Trimble was suddenly a little intimidated. "I was told to read it."

"Yeah, well, I'd arrest them right now if I could," he said.

TeBeest never talked much about Gerald and Alice, but Trimble sat close enough to hear it unfolding. The receptionist would page TeBeest on the intercom, and Trimble would hear him on the line, sometimes very exercised, sometimes cajoling.

There were times, too, when the receptionist would page TeBeest on the intercom. She knew it was Claire. He always said the same thing: "Nothing new."

TeBeest wasn't real demonstrative, Trimble observed. He once warned her not to get too close to the task force guys who floated through the office, volunteers from other agencies who could be temporary or half-assed, both things he hated. He described them as puppies who might dash into the street at any moment and get run over. *Don't get attached,* he'd say, *and don't bother to learn their names.*

But he cared deeply about some things. He was hip-deep in the Uden case now, and just eavesdropping on his phone conversations, Trimble sensed the depth of his commitment.

She also sensed that the case was close to a break. She expected ... something. It was like an old-fashioned movie serial. She was a kid sitting in the back row of a dark theater, being held in constant suspense.

But it never broke.

A few years later, in 2009, she volunteered as a grunt on the aborted dig at the Remount mine, where she personally found a few fragments that were both meaningless (to the investigation) and tantalizing (to her).

She also saw TeBeest away from his desk, on the ground, as passionate as any cop she'd ever known. She'd been peripheral, digging in a trivial hole for a body that obviously wasn't there. He stood at the edge of a chilling precipice, believing that being there made all the difference.

He wasn't a mentor, really, because he didn't care to teach a damn thing. He wasn't a big brother, either, because he wasn't soft and cuddly that way. It made her smile to think of him as a big M&M—hard on the outside but softer deep down. OK, way deep maybe.

But not everybody with a good heart wears it on his sleeve. She knew TeBeest was at the center of a genuine storm, and he was all in. Suddenly, the Uden case wasn't just a paper chase to Trimble. She'd seen it in all its repugnant glory. It had real-life consequences for him and for people who depended on him.

She wanted to be a cop like that.

Wyoming's first Cold Case Team gathered on October 23, 2012—less than a month after Director Steve "Woody" Woodson authorized it. SA Tina Trimble was in charge.

They had plenty of work to do and no shortage of unsolved mysteries from which to choose, even in Wyoming. There were two Jane Does whose stories were entangled. There was the strange 1974 case of a confessed killer who supposedly left a dead man tied to a tree near Dubois that was never found. There was a 1989 disappearance of another

Riverton woman who was never found but whose vanishing would eventually lead cops to a serial rapist.

But the team's first case was the 2011 murder of a thirty-five-year-old Texas woman who'd recently moved to the small town of Newcastle, where she was shot one night in her home by an unknown intruder. The evidence and memories were fresher, and there were no expensive excavations. It promised a quicker score for the fledgling squad.

The Uden case was the centerpiece of the team's next meeting.

On an unseasonably tepid Monday morning in January 2013, the team gathered in the conference room of the City of Cheyenne's annex building, across the street to the north from the Hall of Justice, behind a Subway sandwich shop.

At Director Woodson's invitation, Lonnie TeBeest drove down from Spearfish, South Dakota, that morning. It was mostly a courtesy. The team already had everything it needed. TeBeest could answer any questions they might have—they didn't—but he was mostly there only to see that his case hadn't died. When they asked if he had anything to add, TeBeest underscored how Alice had always controlled her police interviews, setting the times, choosing circumstances, briefing Gerald on the questions.

For example, he told them, she defined the length of her interviews by announcing, in advance, upcoming appointments she couldn't miss. She knew if she could outmaneuver her interrogators until then, she could walk out. Rope-a-dope.

It wasn't accidental that she and Gerald were never in the box at the same time. That way, she could preview the questions and get her story straight with Gerald. So TeBeest suggested it might work best if future interrogators kept them separate between interviews.

He also delivered several contractors' rough estimates for the excavation. None amounted to the previously estimated $50,000, but they weren't free either.

TeBeest had nothing more to add. But these were smart and experienced homicide detectives, and TeBeest wasn't inclined to tell them how to do their jobs, especially on a case he couldn't close.

He had no idea if the cold-case team knew what he had tried and failed to do. Some weren't in his orbit. If they'd asked, he would have told them because he knew the story line by heart, but they didn't. Maybe they just had the same feelings about murdering children that he did.

The team knew instinctively what TeBeest had known for a long time: the Remount mine, whether it was an empty hole or a secret grave, held the next answer they needed. If it held a body (or four), the case might be cracked wide open. If nothing, the case was likely at a dead end.

The meeting adjourned after a couple hours of discussion. TeBeest's torch was passed, so he left. He drove back to Spearfish that afternoon, thinking about what he did and didn't do. Not because of that cold-case meeting, but because that's how he'd been spending his windshield time for the last several years.

While TeBeest was on the road, the team wasted no time. Tina Trimble personally proposed an idea that had been shot down a couple times in a previous DCI administration as too dangerous and too expensive: excavate the Remount mine. Find Ronnie Holtz or hit rock bottom, whichever came first. Either way, the answer they needed was in that cold hole.

Woodson wasted no time, either. This case wasn't a whodunit but a "how do we prove whodunit?" He totally agreed that the mine was the key that would unlock two intertwined decades-old cases—or slam the door shut on them forever.

He gave Trimble the green light to dig. He'd glanced at the cost estimates, but they weren't important. He wasn't going to let money obstruct justice.

He sent a clear message back to his team: *Explore all options and let me worry about the money. And make it happen . . . sooner rather than later.*

Woodson himself called TeBeest and let him know the dig was on again. After he hung up, TeBeest felt relief like a hundred-year flood. After all those years of delays and bullshit, finally somebody who knew what he was doing—and cared—was getting things done, he thought. *Maybe it won't pan out, but we have to look.*

Just like that, the wind changed direction, as it's known to do in Wyoming. Finally, instead of a hindering headwind, it blew now at the backs of the good guys.

Four months on the job, and Woodson was already making good on his vision for the Division of Criminal Investigation.

Now in their seventies, Gerald and Alice's golden years were more or less blissful. They lived on a quiet Missouri farm, doted on the occasional grandchild, sat on the porch together, generally avoided neighbors, and were pretty sure they'd literally gotten away with murder.

The cops had long ago stopped interviewing the kids and coming around. It'd been eight years since the Wyoming agents came to Missouri and revealed to Alice they knew something about Ron Holtz, but if they had anything—like, say, a body—they would have arrested Alice on the spot. They didn't.

So life moved on. Well, mostly.

Gerald and Alice owned a cat named Muffin and a faithful golden retriever, Lady, for many years. In one of their moves, they couldn't take Lady, so naturally Gerald's only option was to kill her (Muffin was spared because she was reasonably self-sufficient). But, ironically, Gerald simply couldn't pull the trigger, so he took Lady to the local veterinarian to be euthanized. He cried like a child when they bought a grave plot and properly buried her at the town's pet cemetery.

When Alice couldn't ride along on many of Gerald's cross-country hauls, he found other companionship. In a bird.

For $350, he bought a baby sun conure—a kind of parrot—that he fed with an eyedropper for several weeks. Then he strapped a cage in his passenger seat and hit the road. The bird learned a few words as it grew, and it especially liked to ride on Gerald's left shoulder, watching the passing traffic out his driver's-side window. Gerald loved his parrot, who performed little tricks and loved attention. The clever parrot's name was O. J.

Over the long winter of 2012, Gerald and Alice had the second-biggest fight of their married life (the biggest was when Gerald wanted to start drawing Social Security at age sixty-two, and Alice wanted the bigger paychecks at sixty-five). Now Gerald was almost seventy, and his roads seemed to be getting longer every day. He wanted to retire. He genuinely believed the $11,000 in his 401(k) would sustain them until they died.

But Alice protested, hard and loud. It was always about the money with Alice. Three years older, she wasn't working anymore, but she wanted more than their Social Security and Gerald's meager pension were paying. She wasn't a wasteful spender, but she apparently needed more pocket change than the average unsanctified nun who'd promised God a certain degree of poverty.

But ultimately, she agreed to allow Gerald to retire as long as their lifestyle continued without a hitch.

It didn't. Their savings dwindled, and Alice's standard of living thinned out, so she demanded Gerald go back to work. Just eleven months after he retired, Gerald unretired and hit the road again—at about the same time as DCI's Cold Case Team was considering a new strategy to literally burrow for Ron Holtz, Virginia Uden, and her missing sons.

It didn't pay to argue. When Alice was happy, life was easier. And bad things happened when Alice wasn't happy.

Almost forty years after Ronald Lee Holtz went missing . . . twenty years after Alice's tormented son Ted shared his mother's vile secret with an off-duty cop . . . four years after diggers merely scratched its repulsive surface . . . seven months after Steve Woodson gave his long-overdue blessing to a new dig, Tina Trimble and her cold-case squad prepared to dig a little deeper into the Remount mine.

From that moment, the team began laying the considerable groundwork for the complicated task of excavating a dangerous, possibly toxic hole on private property that might swallow some of them completely as they searched for a corpse that might or might not be there, using methods that were part forensics, part earth-moving project, and part hazmat emergency.

Just three days after getting the go-ahead, a DCI agent tracked down Sharon Mack in Chugiak, Alaska. Now forty-one, the wife of a commercial shrimper in a tiny village north of Anchorage, and the mother of two adult children—one of whom was severely disabled—Sharon was also the biological daughter of Ron Holtz.

She'd been six months old when her teenage mother fled the violent, drug-addled, psychotic Vietnam veteran in Colorado in 1971. So to her, Ron Holtz was a ghost in her deep past, something between a memory and a secret. Her grandfather discouraged her early on from asking too many questions about her real father. "No good could come from it," he warned.

Sharon was legally adopted by her stepfather at age five, but he died when she was twelve. That's when she moved from Colorado to Alaska with her mom, who soon had another boyfriend, who eventually left too. Then along came another stepfather when Sharon was seventeen. And there was always her grandfather, Conway Holtz, until he died in 1995. She had no shortage of father figures in her life . . . just no actual father.

Her specter-dad obsessed her, although her mother never talked about him. *Why doesn't he come looking for me?* she wondered, more than a little sad.

In 2009, Sharon's half-sister had called with an enticing, if slightly incoherent, tidbit: Some cop—*maybe FBI?*—had told her that Sharon's dad maybe had been murdered by a "black widow"—*I dunno, maybe somebody else's wife?*—somewhere—*maybe Florida?* Anyway, the cops—*I forget the name*—wanted Sharon's DNA just in case—*or maybe they found a body someplace. I just don't know.* She had no names, no numbers, no clue.

Curious, Sharon called the FBI field office in Anchorage and repeated the story, as muddled as she'd heard it. The agent sort of chuckled. He checked his computer and found only some missing persons listings from Wyoming about Ron Holtz. Otherwise, the FBI had no pressing need for her or her DNA. She just dropped it.

In 2012, the same sister told Sharon that if her mother hadn't left Ronnie forty years before, they'd all be dead. It chilled Sharon to think that the people who should have loved her father the most, particularly his own father and sister, were now his greatest detractors.

Now, a year later, a state agent from Wyoming sought a fresh DNA sample from her, the only known direct descendant of Ronnie Holtz, in case they found him dead or alive. She agreed, even though she had no realistic expectation the case was going anywhere. Her genetic fingerprint would be entered in the National Missing Persons DNA database for any future testing. A formality.

In the early afternoon on January 23, 2013, as a favor to the Wyoming DCI, an Alaska state trooper came to Sharon's house. He collected four painless swabs from her mouth, then shipped them to the University of North Texas's Center for Human Identification. She didn't know agents would soon be boring into an abandoned mine she never knew existed, much less that a lot of smart people thought they might finally find out where Ronnie Holtz ended up.

Over the next six months, while the ground thawed, the team got its ducks in a row. Some ducks lined up perfectly, others not so much.

Agents again secured the necessary permission to search the mine from the Remount's new owner, an amiable rancher named Steve Bangert, who grew up in a small Nebraska town, the son of a Korean War veteran who'd lost both legs in combat. Bangert now lived with his family at the Remount, where he tended a few hundred head of prize Texas longhorns.

A casual observer couldn't tell he was a billionaire, his day job being the CEO and founder of a big-time Denver investment bank, where he routinely wore blue jeans and shitkicker cowboy boots in the high-rise executive suite.

Dr. Rick Weathermon, the university's forensic osteologist who'd lent his considerable expertise to the fruitless pigpen and futile 2009 dig, was eager to take another shot at the Remount hole. But he knew bones, not mine safety, and DCI had learned in 2009 that they couldn't just grab a few garden shovels and start grubbing around like a khaki-clad prison chain gang.

So agents inquired whether the Wyoming National Guard might know anything about confined-space recovery operations, which often require geared-up specialists to work in narrow and constricted spaces that are dark, cold, and filled with hazardous stuff. But the Guard was deployed before their specialists could gear up.

DCI agents also interviewed Alice's oldest son, Tommy, just to see if there might be anything else they should know before they broke ground. But this son blamed his dysfunctional family's complete fragmentation on three decades of nosy investigators. He hadn't spoken to his mother in a long time, although he had heard she had some kind of cancer or heart disease. She never told him about any killing, but his sister Thea did; when he asked Alice about it later, she ended the conversation. He'd volunteered to search for the Uden boys in 1980 but got kicked off the team when cops learned he was their stepbrother. He really wasn't any help, but they had to ask.

A few new lab tests came back on several items found in the 1980 search, but none contained anything helpful.

And, of course, the agents had to juggle their usual caseloads too. Cold cases might have gained importance at DCI, but the live cases didn't suddenly become unimportant.

By midsummer, the last and biggest unknown was exactly how a motley bunch of cops were going to be able to safely gouge into a rocky slope to find—hell, just to recognize—as many as four dead humans among a hundred years of large animal remains. The prime time for digging before fall, when the first snow could fly, was slipping away.

Then somebody had a brainstorm. Wouldn't the Cheyenne Fire Department have some training and equipment for rescues in cramped spaces, like babies who fall down wells?

Why, yes, as a matter of fact they did.

The Cheyenne Fire Rescue team jumped in with both feet. After surveying the massive hole, the firefighters drew up plans for the safe insertion of trained diggers without any equipment heavier than a shovel. It was already twenty-five feet deep, and bedrock might be ninety feet down. A lot can go wrong nine stories deep in a narrow, unnatural pit of rot.

Their first priority was to keep searchers safe. They'd drape a stout canvas tarp around the walls to prevent dirt and rocks from falling onto anybody at the bottom. Air quality would be constantly monitored for unsafe levels of hydrogen sulfide, methane, and other gases. They'd be ready to pump fresh air in and bad air out, if necessary. Diggers would safely rappel into the hole and climb out on ropes anchored securely outside. And a rope-and-pulley web would be rigged directly above the opening to shuttle buckets of mud, bones, and other offal to the surface, where it could be examined closely, then filtered further as needed.

But the shaft wasn't just a hazardous hole in the ground. It was a potential crime scene that must be protected to keep pertinent evidence uncontaminated.

So Dr. Weathermon set the perimeter. He diagrammed a forensically sound, orderly work space that resembled a big target. At its center was the Hot Zone—the craggy maw, which was ten to twelve feet across—where diggers would do the real, grueling labor of shoveling.

The next circle immediately surrounding it, another twelve feet, was a no-man's-land where Weathermon, his anthropology team, and some specially trained agents would get the first close look at the bucketloads of muck, trash, and bones the hole disgorged. They'd wave a metal detector over it and rinse it; bigger items were pulled out for inspection, while the remnant muck went to the screens for further sifting. Everybody else would be asked to stay out as much as possible.

The outer ring was for the support staff who would sift the mud for smaller artifacts and bones, photograph the potential crime scene, run errands, give first aid, and generally supply the necessary grunt work.

Weathermon outfitted them with several archaeological screens that captured anything larger than a quarter-inch wide because very few human bones would be small enough to fall through. Any hidden bones that sifters found in their screens would be set aside for Weathermon to examine as he wandered among them.

This time, Deputy Director Steve Holloway, still in charge of the state crime lab, would only play a peripheral role. Weathermon and the firefighters would call the shots, and Woodson would make all the final decisions, if necessary.

In the end, the excavation team would comprise fifty professionals from Cheyenne's Fire Rescue, the Division of Criminal Investigation, the state crime lab, the University of Wyoming's anthropology department, an ambulance crew, and the Red Cross—and Director Woodson's personal guest, SA Lonnie TeBeest (retired).

Director Woodson had done something else: He thought out of the budget box. He personally appealed for help from Wyoming's Department of Homeland Security, which underwrote various major crime-fighting projects. His request was granted.

Since Wyoming's only four-year university and the Cheyenne Fire Department saw the two- or three-day excavation as both a "good cause" and an excellent training opportunity, they volunteered their work freely. The only cost to DCI would be some food and a $46 per diem to its agents.

All told, DCI would probably pay less than $2,000, far less than the estimated (and possibly imaginary) $50,000 that had constipated DCI's bean counters less than two years before.

On August 26, 2013—almost thirty-nine years since anybody saw Ronald Lee Holtz alive—Wyoming detectives embarked on their last, best chance of finding him.

In Wyoming, the end of August means it might snow at any moment, so SA Tina Trimble was eager to get started. She'd been entrusted with more than TeBeest's case. She'd inherited his fervor to close it too.

But nobody was more eager than Lonnie TeBeest to burrow into that damned hole again. He'd driven five hours from Spearfish the day before, checked into a Cheyenne motel, and rose early.

Woodson picked him up that morning in the lobby. Neither had slept well because they'd both staked a lot on this little expedition. Woodson had been pushing against an entrenched system, and TeBeest had been tugging mightily from the other side. In their own separate ways, both were expectant—and nervous about being proven wrong.

Forty-five minutes later, they stood at the edge of the Remount Ranch's McLaughlin Shaft. Even at only twenty-five feet deep, just as they'd left it four years before, it unnerved them. They circled around the hole, staying a few steps back and leaning over as far as possible to see inside, as if a giant tongue might suddenly dart out and suck them down.

The team prepared for the digging. Tarps went down all around the hole, filtering screens were erected, the overhead pulley system was suspended between the surrounding trees, and firefighters—wearing respirators to protect them from airborne dirt and stench—prepared to rope down into that cramped, vertical shaft on their bleak recovery mission. Everybody was assigned a task or two. TeBeest and Woodson were assigned to muddy grunt work on the screens.

By lunch, the first spades full of black, rancid earth were turned.

Again, that unholy sepulcher upchucked some vile slop. Various cow and horse bones, from skulls to hooves and everything between, came out in great clusters. Plumpish blobs of grave wax were everywhere. Everybody was slimed in a sticky black goo created by years of decaying meat, human refuse, pine needles, and dirty runoff water.

The stink was overpowering. Some of it was the unmistakable stench of decomposing flesh. But the pit also contained years of dead cows with bellies full of last meals. The actual stomach had long ago decayed, leaving big wads of half-digested grass and feculent gastric juices that smelled worse than black plastic bags of vomit, dog shit, and lawn clippings left sealed in the summer sun for a week.

At first, the mood wasn't as squalid as the task. Cops and firefighters exchanged plenty of playful trash talk. Moments of gallows humor punctuated the work—*What do you call a dead man in a hole? Phil.* When a salamander squittered out of the hole, Trimble captured the cute little guy with her bare hands and showed him off to everybody.

The whole system worked like an old grandfather clock, more or less smoothly except for a couple beats. They worked in shifts, so the digging never stopped. Lunch was delivered by some Cheyenne delicatessens. The buckets came up constantly. Their muck was slopped on a tarp for highly educated people to pick out the big chunks. Finally, the rest was squished, shaken, and sprayed through a metal filter to find any good stuff.

Alas, the first day ended without any good stuff. The firefighters had deepened the hole another ten feet, and nobody had gotten hurt. But among the piles of bones discarded around the perimeter, everything from cow skulls to owl femurs, there was nothing human. Nobody said it out loud, but more than a few of the searchers felt a little discouraged as the sun went down. The hole might be dry. Drinks were had.

Day two dawned more chastened than day one. The team kept its routine, moving buckets of mucky rot from the hole to the perimeter, passing through the professors' scrutiny and quarter-inch screens along the way.

Somebody reminded Weathermon of the story about the great-grandfoal of Flicka—or at least her real-life inspiration—who died and was tossed in the mine in the mid-1970s, around the same time as Ronnie

Holtz supposedly went down there. So the good doctor kept his eye peeled for the bones of a young horse. Hey, even scientists can hope.

Around midmorning, an excited digger called up from the hole. He'd found something.

A barrel.

Fifty hearts skipped a collective beat. The whole area went silent, except for the wind in the tree canopy above. Ron Holtz had supposedly been crammed in a barrel, they knew. Might this be it?

The tension built as diggers strapped the barrel securely and hoisted it slowly from more than three stories below the surface. Weathermon and the workers above got their first glimpse as it emerged from the dark hole: a rusty and crumpled metal barrel that obviously contained something.

A cowboy who stumbled on an old feed barrel would simply pry it open with a shovel or a stick, but this was a forensic operation searching for a murdered corpse. They couldn't just hack open a collapsed steel drum if it might contain crucial evidence in a homicide investigation. With some care and deliberation, trained investigators gently peeled it open to find . . . decayed antelope guts.

Everybody exhaled. Ronnie Holtz remained an elusive ghost, but the dismay was real. Nobody was more disappointed than TeBeest, who'd ridden this wretched roller coaster for twelve years: occasionally up, mostly down.

Work continued, a little more somber. Bucket after bucket came up full of wet muck, empty of smoking guns.

Just past noon, Weathermon left the cordoned work area to grab a sandwich and soda from the nearby sag wagon. He, too, felt everybody's chagrin. Nearly forty feet down in that damned pit and . . . nothing. His brain calculated a hundred fool's errands. Maybe this was the wrong hole. Maybe this was just another snipe hunt. Maybe Ronnie Holtz wasn't down there at all. Maybe he wasn't even dead.

The bone collector returned to the dig and wandered among the screeners, looking at the small bones they set aside for him. Nothing human.

Then one of his assistants from the university called him over. She'd found a bone he needed to see.

He instantly recognized it as an immature horse's humerus, a distinctive upper foreleg bone. Had it belonged to the Flicka great-grandfoal? Could Ron Holtz be near? Oh, for God's sake, was he really investing his whole scientific examination on a secondhand family yarn about a fictional horse?

Well, at the moment, yes. Weathermon had nothing else.

Before he had time to talk himself out of this foolishness, the skull of a young horse came up.

"OK, everybody," Weathermon told the team, "we need to pay attention now. The bones will be small."

But in that next golden hour, when Weathermon expected so much more ... nothing. Aside from a few more young horse bones, nothing more came up. More buckets, more glop, more sinking spirits. Everyone was briefly buoyed by the discovery of the young horse's skull, but the excitement wore off.

Around two, a digger hollered he'd found another barrel, but it was just the metal snap ring that had once held a barrel's lid in place.

TeBeest and another DCI agent who operated one of the screens knew time was running short. They kept straining dirt, filling the corner of their screen with smaller bones caught by the filtering. They worked now without much chatter as the professor wandered silently among the screens, discarding everything on the growing heap of useless bones.

As he had for two days, the bone expert stopped at TeBeest's screen and looked closely at the pile of smaller bones he'd set aside. One caught his eye. He washed it again and turned it over several times.

"Stop!"

Weathermon's shriek was loud enough to be heard back in Cheyenne. Everybody froze.

TeBeest's heart was pumping fast, but only partly because of Weathermon's dramatic screech.

"Better call the coroner," Weathermon said.

Ironically, TeBeest had found the first evidence that a human, maybe Holtz, was in that shaft. It was a human metatarsal, one of five bones in the foot, between the ankle and the toes. To the casual observer, it looked like a bone from a chicken wing; to the bone specialist Weathermon, it was as unique as a human skull.

Director Woodson, the lifelong cop, had one question for Weathermon.

"Are there any animal bones that can mimic human bones?" Woodson wasn't doubting his expertise. He was already building a case.

Weathermon snorted. "No," he replied. "This is human. No doubt about it."

The only smile bigger than Woodson's was TeBeest's. Everybody was high-fiving.

Forty feet at the bottom of the shaft suddenly became, officially, a crime scene. Woodson pulled the firefighters out of the hole and sent an experienced DCI homicide detective down there to unearth any more remains. Human bones started pouring from the hole. First, a bucket with two humeri, then more buckets with ribs, femurs, tibia, scapulae, pieces of pelvis, a pile of vertebrae.

Then a skull with a perfect little hole in the back.

That dreadful mine also belched up another little artifact of a long-ago death, a fragment of a story they once didn't know if they should believe: A dog's collar with a single name. *Jefe.*

Weathermon laid out a fresh blue tarp in the shade of the ponderosa pines, out of sunlight that might crack cold, wet bones that had spent decades below ground. Within the hour, his assistant had put them back together in what looked like an exploded view diagram of a human skeleton.

Weathermon studied the bones, which were remarkably clean and therefore not ancient. The skeleton definitely fit Ron Holtz's profile. The robust sciatic notch in the pelvis and heavy eye orbits indicated male;

the femur put his height around six feet; the pubic symphysis suggested a man twenty to thirty years old.

But something bothered the professor. Telltale features of the cranium and femur suggested this *might* be a Native American, not an ordinary white guy, but they might simply be remnants of a long-ago interracial romance, or just aberrations.

It wasn't important at the moment. They'd come here to find a dead man, shot in the back of the head and dumped unceremoniously in this deep, dark hole. They found him. This was no longer just an archaeological excavation; it was a murder investigation. The final determination of whether this was Ronnie Holtz was in the hands of DNA profilers and the medical examiner.

When the dead man's bones were packed up safely in a box for the coroner, Weathermon turned to TeBeest, who beamed under the protective shade of the pines. He shook the old cop's hand.

"You did it" was all the bone man said.

TeBeest was euphoric ... on the inside. He tried hard not to let anyone see how jubilant he was because ... well, just because. He figured Claire knew, and that was good enough.

That night, everybody celebrated.

Weathermon went home to Laramie and popped a beer. He loved his job and got a lot of satisfaction when his old bones meant something, but he hated not being able to talk about the crimes he dug up.

"Did you find what you were looking for?" his wife asked him that night. She knew he couldn't say too much.

He just nodded and smiled.

Meanwhile, the cops and firefighters met for steaks and beers in Cheyenne. They were still on a high, lots of backslapping.

Except Tina Trimble, who suddenly felt the fever and chills of the flu coming on. Her stomach ached. *Dammit.* She'd planned to attend the upcoming autopsy in Loveland, Colorado, which she expected would give her everything she needed to get an arrest warrant for Alice Uden. The flu just wasn't gonna help.

Sure enough, after a sickly night, the next day at DCI's Cheyenne headquarters was worse. She drove home to Casper, and by the time she arrived, she was doubled over with stomach pain. Then came nausea and waves of diarrhea like she'd never known. She crawled into bed and waited for things to get better.

They didn't.

Two days after Ronnie Holtz was plucked piece by hideous piece from that putrescent Remount mine, he lay on a morgue table in McKee Medical Center in Loveland, Colorado. More specifically, his bones—minus a left rib and a few small bones in his hands and feet—lay in a disarticulated pile, waiting for a morgue assistant to put them all in order, like a morbid two-hundred-piece puzzle.

His right collarbone had either degenerated or been gnawed by animals, but Ronnie Holtz was in pretty good condition for a young man, considering he'd been dead for almost forty years.

Tiny bits of his dried bone marrow and dental pulp were sent to the state crime lab to be compared to Sharon Mack's DNA profile, just to confirm this was actually Ronnie Holtz. Analysis quickly showed that this pile of bones was 1.11 million times more likely to be Sharon Mack's father than any random pile of bones. Those were good odds.

Ironically, if Ronnie Holtz's bones had been found in 1984—only ten years after he was last seen—they couldn't have been identified precisely because DNA profiling didn't yet exist in the forensic toolbox. He would have remained an unidentified adult Caucasoid male. At best, prosecutors could have made only a circumstantial case, if they went to court at all; at worst, his nameless bones would have been piled in a pine box and buried in a pauper's field under a soon-forgotten number.

That morning, forensic pathologist Dr. James Wilkerson focused on the one unmistakable peculiarity he didn't expect to see in most healthy adult Caucasoid males: a neat bullet hole in the back of his skull. He needn't have performed almost six thousand autopsies to know that was significant.

Wilkerson described the wound in the precise, court-worthy argot of forensic medicine.

> Entrance gunshot wound to the right back of the head located 3.5 inches from the top of the head and 1.5 inches to the right of the anterior midline. The hole is approximately one-third inch in dimension with inwardly beveled fractures.... Within the skull on X-ray there is a small-caliber, deformed projectile and it is recovered at autopsy.... No exit is identified.

In plain language, he might have said the poor guy was shot from behind, probably close range. The "projectile," later identified as a .22-caliber bullet, made shrapnel of his cranium, so all those tiny bits of bone did their own damage.

Bullets travel damn fast, so fast that they zip through soft brain matter faster than brain matter rips, doing extra damage by stretching and shoving biological material as they zip.

The bullet hit the inner wall of Ronnie's skull above his left eye and ricocheted around in his brainpan, immobilizing him instantaneously. His skull was fractured in several places by the force of the bullet and blast. He might have bled profusely.

But while Ron Holtz might have seemed clearly dead to his killer, he mightn't have been clinically dead for as long as thirty minutes after he was shot. If Alice had quickly loaded him into a cardboard storage barrel after she shot him, he might actually have been technically alive when she did, although he certainly wouldn't have been conscious.

The deformed bullet that killed Holtz was found stuck in some dirt, leaves, and empty insect eggs on the right inner wall of his skull, where gravity eventually caused it to rest. That meant that Ron Holtz had spent the last forty years with his head canted to the right, open in the back to any hungry bugs looking for shelter. In fact, his bones were found in a curled or folded fetal position, bunched up with his knees to his chest . . . a cramped position that might be necessary to jam a tall man's corpse in a barrel.

There wasn't much guesswork to be done. The cause of Ronnie Holtz's death was a gunshot to the back of his head. And since he probably didn't shoot himself, Wilkerson ruled it a homicide.

Ah, but as they'd say in Wyoming, the Uden investigation was snakebit.

For more than thirty years, a series of unfortunate circumstances—some avoidable, some not—had prevented devoted detectives from busting their best and only suspects, Gerald and Alice Uden. From a slow start and disgraced sheriffs to missed sightings of dead bodies and internal political obstacles, the entire case seemed to be irreparably derailed several times, but it was always brought back from the dead by dogged cops.

Now, SA Tina Trimble couldn't make the arrest because she was laid up, gravely ill. The symptoms were so bad she considered death to be her better alternative. After two painful days in bed, her husband demanded she see a doctor.

At first, the doctor suspected food poisoning. For two days at the Remount excavation, she'd eaten sandwiches catered from delis in distant Cheyenne. They might have arrived with some foodborne bacteria, or germs might have multiplied as the sandwiches sat in the summer sun, even in coolers. But forty-nine other people ate the same food and didn't get sick.

It was also possible she'd inhaled or swallowed something dangerous from the nasty, necrotic mine shaft, but again, nobody else who was there—some even closer—was sick.

"Did you handle any snakes or turtles or any reptiles?" the puzzled doc asked.

No snakes or turtles, Trimble said ... then remembered the salamander she'd caught.

A few blood tests later, mystery solved. Trimble had salmonella, and it had likely come from that cute little amphibian. At the mine, she'd washed her hands with store-bought sanitizer, but that wasn't enough to kill the powerful salmonella germs. Although some strains of salmonella are barely noticeable, others can be fatal in vulnerable people, especially when it causes dangerous dehydration.

Trimble was a long way from being cured. The doctor gave her antibiotics and twenty pills of a potent antidiarrheal medicine, then sent her home for much-needed bed rest. For a week, she was up and down so often that her husband slept in another room. She was forced to return to the doctor's office when she developed huge, painful lumps on her legs. It wasn't especially soothing to hear that they were signs of the infection leaching out of her body.

For nine days, Trimble was bedridden.

And for those same nine days, Gerald and Alice Uden lived a pleasant, unmolested life on their Missouri farm, utterly unaware that Trimble and her team had found Ronnie Holtz. Their justice had been delayed yet again.

That was about to change.

Chapter 8

WASH THIS BLOOD

Less than a month after DNA identified the Remount skeleton as Ronnie Holtz, and just days after SA Tina Trimble got back on her feet, she couldn't wait any longer. She, three of her DCI colleagues, and an FBI agent hit the long road to Missouri for what they hoped would be their last encounter with Gerald and Alice Uden on their turf and their terms.

If it wasn't, that would mean something had gone terribly wrong.

They drove two unmarked cars on the two-day journey, Trimble and DCI agents Len Propps and Loy Young in one, DCI's Andy Hanson and FBI agent Paul Swenson in the other. On the way, they plotted a careful interview strategy, knowing how the Udens had gamed their system before. They had warrants in their pockets, but they preferred that Gerald and Alice voluntarily let them search their property and come in for questioning.

On their first night in the unincorporated Ozark farming community of Chadwick, Missouri (pop. 600), the agents scouted out the isolated Uden farm, just off Missouri 125, six miles from the nearest proper town. Everything was quiet. They couldn't see Gerald's big rig, which would be there if he were home.

His absence was an accidental gift, a stroke of luck Trimble and her fellow agents hadn't expected.

The killer couple had had thirty-three years to get their stories straight, and they had always compared notes between their various interviews over the years. Trimble knew this time could be different.

Her goal remained for Gerald to divulge more than Alice was likely to admit. But suddenly, the battle plan changed. The more Trimble kept Gerald guessing about what Alice might have revealed, the more likely he'd slip up. Without Alice to provide equilibrium, Trimble hoped Gerald would spill everything he knew about Ronnie Holtz. Alice would be hopelessly tangled up in her own lies, and Gerald would have neatly tied the fatal loop around her neck.

That was the plan. But the best-laid plans sometimes go sideways.

The next afternoon, Thursday, September 26, 2013, DCI's Propps and Hanson, the FBI's Swenson, a Missouri highway patrolman, and six local sheriff's deputies knocked on the door of the Uden farmhouse.

Alice answered, fully clothed. She was now seventy-four, with thin, white, cotton-candy hair.

The agents asked if she'd allow them to search her house and property for a brown folder that supposedly contained documents—a sheaf of personal notes, letters, clippings, and photos—about the disappearance of Virginia Uden and her sons. She readily agreed but wasn't sure where it was. Maybe in the moldy shed out back. *I have nothing to hide.*

Alice also agreed to show them where Gerald kept his guns. After a quick inspection of several weapons, the cops saw nothing that could have been used in the Holtz shooting.

While the deputies and detectives searched, Alice made small talk, like a chatty grandma. *The day is warm, isn't it?* Her cockatoo, Angel, was eight years old and said "bye-bye" to everyone. Alice almost died from chemotherapy for lung cancer a couple years before. *I'm allergic to ragweed and cedar.* Her surname was pronounced "YEW-den," but she answered to "OO-den" too. *We had a big garden last summer.* Gerald was making a delivery in the Chicago area, she said, eight hours away. She wasn't sure when he'd be home, maybe tomorrow, but it all depended on whether the dispatcher had another load waiting. *Here's his cell phone number.*

"I'm getting so sick of this," she said as she sat at the kitchen table.

"Of what?" a friendly deputy asked.

"This case out in Wyoming."

"Yeah, it's been a long time," he said. "They're hopefully getting some resolution."

"I hope so because I'm tired," Alice said. "Not that I don't like talking to all of you."

While the deputies continued to search, Alice agreed to ride along with detectives to the Christian County Sheriff's Office for a chat with Special Agents Trimble and Young. *We had nice seat belts like these in a car we used to own.*

On the half-hour drive, she chattered about her beloved daddy, her five children, her late husband Prunty's many illnesses, how to move a mobile home, Social Security checks, nursing jobs she'd had, being diabetic, living as a single mother in a Cheyenne trailer park, meeting her biological family just ten years before . . . her whole biography. Minus a few meaningful details.

It was hard to think of this little old lady in her embroidered cotton T-shirt and blue jeans, telling her meaningless stories in her sweet little country voice, her cartoonish half-gallon travel mug in hand, apologizing for being a back seat driver, as what they said she was: a cold-blooded killer.

Deputies took her to a cramped interview room, hardly bigger than a half bathroom. In a few minutes, Trimble and Young squeezed in with her and politely introduced themselves. Young started by reading Alice's Miranda rights, which she'd heard more times than most never-arrested grandmothers.

Trimble didn't waste time.

"You know we've been working on this case a really long time," she told Alice. "We wanted to clear up a few things, and I think you have the answers we need."

Alice nodded helpfully. She didn't seem especially nervous—except her hands. Her fingers knitted and unknitted. At times, she unconsciously rubbed the backs of her pale, veiny hands, as if she were wiping off some invisible stain.

Trimble handed her a photograph of a bare-chested young soldier standing beside a Vietnam-era military chopper, unsmiling. He sported tattoos, dog tags, a crucifix, and a cigarette.

"You know that man?" Trimble asked.

Alice studied the photo and shook her head. "No," she replied.

"No?"

"Nope."

"Are you sure you don't recognize him?" Young asked her again.

"No, I don't. I have no idea who that is."

"You sure?"

"No, uh-uh," Alice repeated, shrugging her eyebrows in Young's direction.

Trimble pulled out another photo. Same guy, at parade rest in a buck private's uniform at boot camp.

"Here's another picture," she said. "Recognize the man?"

Alice studied it again.

"No, I don't."

In all, she denied recognizing the young man in either image at least seven times.

Trimble calmly put the photos away and swiveled toward Alice.

"Who is Ron Holtz to you?"

Now, the uneasy hands of the little old lady across from her trembled. She paused before answering.

"He was my husband for a while," Alice said.

"Where did you two meet?"

"A VA psychiatric hospital. I was working there."

"Was he a patient?"

"Uh-huh."

"Do you remember what date you got married?"

"No."

"What year?"

"1974."

"Do you recall how old you were at the time?"

"Well, I was born in 1939, and that was '74. I'm not good at math," said Alice, who would have been around thirty-five at the time.

"Do you know how old Ron was when you met him?"

"Twenty-three or twenty-four."

"So did you guys develop a relationship there at the hospital?"

Alice answered directly. "Yeah. Sort of. It wasn't much of a relationship."

She launched into a convoluted tale about how she'd already decided to quit her four-month-old nursing job at the Sheridan, Wyoming, veterans' psych ward and move back to Cheyenne when her manipulative patient Ron Holtz begged her to give him a ride to Denver. Eventually, she said, he convinced her to do more than drive. They soon slipped away from the hospital and married two weeks later in Colorado. She moved her mobile home to a Cheyenne trailer park, he got a job as a cab driver, and their married life immediately turned sour. When Ronnie Holtz became verbally and physically abusive, threatening to kill two-year-old Eliza, Alice claimed she kicked him out after less than three weeks of wedded bliss. She never saw him again.

In fact, she said, Ron Holtz was such a jerk he never called once to check on her or Eliza after he left.

Alice said she phoned the Cheyenne police once after Holtz left because she was afraid he might come back and hurt her, but they just laughed.

Alone and still struggling financially after her previous husband died and left her with $10,000 in unpaid bills—even though four of her five children lived with distant relatives—Alice moved back to her native Illinois, filed for bankruptcy, divorced Holtz, and found a new job.

Trimble listened patiently, occasionally asking follow-up questions. Alice recounted the rest of her post-Holtz life up to meeting Gerald in a Lander trailer park, a natural stopping point.

"I know a lot of stories—statements—have changed," Trimble said.

"So like I said, we just wanted to set the record straight. I'm not hiding anything here."

But she was.

Alice admitted she'd been dishonest about Holtz, but only because she was embarrassed. A nurse hooking up with a mental patient in her ward was shameful (although it had happened with Don Prunty too). She came to her senses, though, when she tossed Ron Holtz out of her trailer a month or so after running away with him.

"Well, I'm glad we cleared the air, but there's some stuff we're still kind of unclear about," Trimble said as she reached again into her manila folder and pulled out another photo. She showed it to Alice.

It was a full-color photo of an unwashed human skull.

"This is Ron Holtz," the agent said.

Alice didn't recoil or blanch. She didn't gasp. She didn't fall out of her chair again. She just examined it momentarily, as if it depicted an ordinary wildflower.

"It is?" she asked, anything but dumbfounded. "Hmmm."

Trimble leaned uncomfortably close. "We're here today to give you a chance," she said. "We know where he is because we have him now. And I know that you killed him."

"Absolutely," Alice mumbled.

Trimble persisted. "We're here to clear this up and get the truth about everything else."

"I've been telling the truth," Alice insisted, suddenly defensive. "Except . . ." She gestured limply toward the skull picture.

"The DA in Wyoming sent us all the way out here to settle it."

"You gonna take me to jail?" Alice asked.

"Yes, I am," Trimble said. "Here's what I need: if I'm to go to the prosecutor and tell him that you told the whole truth—and I know you're not telling the whole truth right now—you have to start being honest about this." She shook the skull image in front of Alice's blank face.

"I know they're looking to figure out what happened to Virginia and her boys too," Trimble continued. "I don't know if you're a religious person, but I know that at some point, you have to make your peace. You need to clear your soul. You know that."

On this point, Alice had no illusions. "That's been taken care of," she said confidently, "my soul."

She wasn't so sure about Ronnie Holtz's soul, though. Confronted with proof that he'd been found, Alice unburdened her soul and came clean:

When Ronnie came home one night after driving his cab—she didn't know the day, date, or season, really—Eliza was wailing. He hated crying babies. He always screamed about all the babies he killed in 'Nam, and now he threatened to kill hers too. Angry and freaking out, he went to Eliza's crib, and Alice grabbed her .22 rifle from its hiding place in her bedroom closet.

Just as Ronnie was lifting the bawling Eliza, Alice put the barrel of her gun against the back of his head and pulled the trigger. Ronnie slumped into the crib, dead.

"It's all so traumatic, I have a hard time remembering the details," Alice told the agents. "I'm just so upset I got Eliza into this mess. I was only trying to protect her."

Alice continued: she grabbed an empty cardboard barrel where she'd stored her Christmas ornaments, and she crammed Ronnie's limp corpse in it.

At over six feet tall and near two hundred pounds, wouldn't his dead weight have overwhelmed the rather petite Alice, who stood five-four and weighed 140, tops?

"It wasn't very easy," she said. "But I had enough adrenaline going that I made it."

Alice hurriedly swaddled Eliza in warm blankets and drove her to Commerce City, Colorado, where she dropped off the baby at her in-laws' house. She asked them to babysit overnight because she and Ron had been fighting and she was planning to "get rid of him." They understood, because they had once kicked him out too.

Then she drove back to her Cheyenne trailer park, where she backed up her Ford LTD to the trailer's back door and rolled the barrel into the trunk, which she tied down with a cord. She already had a plan: She drove west down the dark, empty highway toward Laramie, to the Remount Ranch, which she knew intimately after helping her late husband, Don Prunty, manage it. She remembered an old abandoned mine hidden up in the trees, where they'd thrown dead animals and trash. It was the perfect place to hide this trash too.

In the dark, she backed her LTD close enough that she could roll the barrel out of the trunk, down a little hill, and into the deep, dark shaft. *You know, where Flicka was thrown.*

Back at the trailer that night—or maybe early morning—there wasn't much mess to clean up, just a little spot of blood on the mattress.

"Wait," Trimble stopped her. "Did he fall on the mattress? You said he fell in the crib."

Alice's nervous fingers worried that ghostly spot again. "No ... he ... I don't know how that blood got on the mattress," she stammered. "I don't remember that part."

"Because he was standing up, right?"

"Yeah ... he kinda fell ..." She tried unsuccessfully to explain, then abruptly changed the course of her narrative: "I just grabbed Eliza and got her out of there. I felt so scared he was still alive."

Suddenly, Alice turned all pathos, although she never cried. She was the real victim. When she was a child, her mentally ill mother picked all her friends, so she'd been surrounded by crappy people all her life. Her first three husbands had been unloving louts, abusive boozers, or dope fiends who didn't care about her like they should. Ronnie Holtz's death signaled the beginning of her new, free life where she was in control, not them.

"Did you ever tell any of your kids about killing Ron?" Trimble asked.

"Yes, all of them."

"Did you ever tell Gerald?"

Alice pondered the question. "I think I mentioned it to him before we got married. I wish I hadn't."

"Was he concerned at all?"

Alice shook her head. "If he was, he didn't tell me."

Alice answered a few more of the agents' questions about Holtz.

She'd been expecting to go to jail for killing Holtz since 1974.

He was naked when she stuffed him into the barrel.

She had no idea where that Cheyenne trailer park was.

She bought her rifle after Don Prunty died and sold it to somebody in Cheyenne shortly after the shooting. She didn't know who.

(A few weeks after Ron Holtz's skeleton was found, some agents and firefighters returned to dig a little deeper for the murder weapon in case Alice had tossed it down there with her dead husband. They found nothing.)

VA records that said Ron Holtz was last alive on Christmas Eve 1974 must have been wrong, Alice said. *They often are, you know.*

She knew Kay Florita. Kay was a friend. But Kay didn't know Ron Holtz or help hide his body.

Alice never told her parents she'd married Holtz. Her insane mother, who'd once been in an asylum, would have started a physical brawl.

Yes, Alice had confessed that particular sin—shooting a man in self-defense and dumping his body in a secret hole—to her children, but only as a cautionary tale about drugs, she assured Trimble and Young. Holtz had been an unrepentant junkie since Vietnam, she said. She merely wanted to scare her kids straight by vividly illustrating how drugs can be deadly.

Like any caring mother should.

Alice's bad habits were catching up to her. She'd started smoking at ten and recently had the lower lobe of her cancerous left lung removed. She now took pills for type 2 diabetes. Her blood pressure was too high. Her legs were numbed by neuropathy. She suffered from atrial fibrillation. Her balance was bad, and she'd been falling a lot lately.

But she was tougher than her medical chart. An hour into her interrogation for one murder she admitted and three others she wouldn't, she showed no sign of emotion.

During an eleven-minute break, Alice fidgeted alone on her squeaky chair in the interview room while Trimble figured out a way to get Gerald back to town.

Pretending to be a home health aide, she called Gerald's cell phone.

She told him Alice had been arrested and was freaking out. She didn't know what to do. The cops said it was about something in Wyoming a long time ago. Gerald said he was a little freaked out too and he'd call the Christian County sheriff to find out what was happening. They hung up. The trap was set.

When the two agents returned to Alice, their questions turned to Don Prunty.

Not much to tell. Alice met him when he was hospitalized for electroshock therapy in Illinois and she was his nurse. She got pregnant, they married, and then they moved to Wyoming in 1971 to manage the Remount Ranch, where Eliza was born. Don was not just an abusive, far-gone alcoholic; his blood pressure was grotesquely high and uncontrollable at 250/190. As a nurse, Alice dispensed all of Don's drugs, and his doctor told her she'd be damn lucky if she could get his blood pressure to 180/100—still deadly. When the Ostlunds fired him from the ranch a year later, he and Alice bought a new trailer (and mortgage insurance in case "anything happened to him") and parked it at a highway rest stop, which they were paid by the state to keep clean. They made extra cash driving a rural school bus forty miles every day, picking up and dropping off ranch kids at a one-room schoolhouse. Don's condition quickly worsened. He accused Alice of cheating. He began to hallucinate about nonexistent "lumps" in the carpet and wave at people who weren't there. When his delusions grew worse, Alice took him to the Laramie hospital where she worked, but he died the next day with his phantasms, "malignant" blood pressure, and kidney failure.

Don's $5,000 life insurance policy was paid to his son from a previous marriage, but Alice claimed the new trailer, free and clear, thanks to the mortgage insurance.

"Might extra salt have made his condition worse?" Trimble asked, a veiled reference to Alice's previous admissions that she'd "put something in his drinks" to stop his drinking.

Agents TeBeest and Trimble, based on doctors' opinions of Prunty's medical records, had long believed that "something" could be salt. Excess sodium in the bloodstream makes it harder for the kidneys to filter out water. The extra water in the blood then strains the whole circulatory system, raising the pressure inside veins and arteries, especially the delicate blood vessels in the kidneys and brain. If Alice had added a little extra salt in each of her husband's drinks and meals, the effects might show themselves in a few days and would get worse fast.

Alice danced around Trimble's question. No, she didn't think the doctor restricted Don's salt intake, but he prescribed tranquilizers and pain pills so freely that it might have made things worse.

Eliza received some monthly survivor benefits from the VA because of Prunty's WWII service. Alice only got the trailer, which she moved around a little before landing in Sheridan, where she met Ron Holtz, who would eventually die in it. A few months later, she sold it in Illinois because she needed cash, since she earned only $2.25 an hour as a nurse.

During another lengthy break, Alice sat alone again in the little room, cameras still rolling. Checking age spots and rubbing her hands, she sighed deeply a couple times and muttered inaudibly to herself. About her arrest? About the pills on her nightstand? About her soon-to-be-evicted cockatoo, Angel? Nobody knows.

Trimble and Young then returned for Act Three. The climax of this four-hour tragedy would star her dear husband, Gerald, as the antihero so eager to please his shrewish wife that he'd slaughter his ex-wife and adopted sons, restoring his reign over an empire of rust and dirt. It was Shakespeare in the weeds.

Alice told them how she and Gerald had met, minus the frequent sex. While they were dating, Gerald's divorce was still pending. He talked about Virginia and tried to introduce Alice to her a couple times, but Alice refused. It wasn't right. Ex-spouses had no place in new relationships. None.

Alice's rule was so adamant that she never even knew what Virginia looked like, she said, until the local paper published a photo after the disappearance.

Alice didn't recall much about letters that supposedly were exchanged while Virginia was in New Jersey. Something about getting married again, she thought.

On the day of the disappearance, she knew something was afoot, but she reckoned it was just Virginia "playing games." Gerald had gone out to meet them, but they never showed up, she claimed.

Oh, and about that time, Alice recalled out of the blue, a calf had died on the Pavillion place and Alice needed a couple days to butcher it. Her kitchen was a bloody mess, and they were forced to remove shelves from the refrigerator to let the meat cool.

Odd, thought Trimble. Nobody asked her about her kitchen, blood, livestock, housekeeping, refrigerators, or anything remotely related.

"Do you think that Gerald is ready to tell us the whole truth about it?" Trimble asked.

"I don't know," Alice replied. "I don't have any idea."

"What has Gerald told you about it?"

"Nothing."

Agent Young was perturbed. "For thirty-seven years, every time you've talked to law enforcement, you've said you told them everything you know about Ron Holtz. Now we're asking you today to tell us what you know about Virginia and the boys, and . . ."

"I can't tell you more than I already have."

"You can!" Young said. "You can tell us. I know you don't want to, but this is the opportunity you're getting to tell us."

Again, Alice diverted the topic when it fluttered too close to the flame. "Am I going to jail in Wyoming or here?" she asked.

Young told her how it'd work—jail in Missouri until she was extradited to Wyoming to face murder charges—and Trimble drew her back.

"Do you remember how many times the boys came out visiting before they went missing?"

"Once or twice."

"Did you guys ever take them hunting, fishing, hiking, camping...?"

"I never did."

"You never went along?"

"I don't know that it even happened."

"If someone told us that you and Gerald had taken the boys out to the reservoir to go boating..."

"I think we went out there one time."

"OK, but you remember that?"

"Yeah. I was about to say that before you asked me. I remember them and Eliza in the water, playing."

"Did they both know how to swim?"

"I don't know."

"You weren't there trying to teach them to swim or anything?"

"No." Alice shook her head. "They just played outside like any kid would."

"If someone told us that when the boys were in the water, Gerald drove the boat away until one of the boys started crying, would that be true?"

"No, no, no," Alice said.

"If someone told us that when the boys came to your house, they got locked in a separate trailer or room..."

"No, absolutely not."

"What were your personal feelings about the boys? Did you know them well? Were they well-behaved?"

"They never did anything I had to get after them for."

Trimble tried a new tack: sympathy. She asked Alice if she had grand-kids. *Yes, thirteen, but I never see them.* Trimble encouraged Alice to talk about all the foibles of her dysfunctional family, the divorces, the drugs, the distance between them. Alice talked about insanity and illness in their lives but, oddly, not any good memories, if there'd been any.

"I don't know how much TV you watch, but there is so much tech-nology in the world right now, so many scientific advances," Trimble told Alice. "They've done a reexamination of all the evidence from back in 1980, and we made a lot of progress as far as being able to identify it and where it came from. I hate to see someone put in a situation that they don't have to be in. As far as the situation with Ron, I have no reason not to believe you. It's probably a big relief to get it off your chest . . ."

"Yeah, it is. I lived with that for a long time. I knew the day might come that I'd go to jail." For the only time in the entire four-hour inter-view, Alice briefly, almost imperceptibly, lost her composure for a fleeting second.

"Going to jail is going to happen," Trimble said, leaning closer. "I'm not going to lie to you or sugarcoat it. You knew this day might come, and that day is today. Just know I'm gonna be up-front and honest with you about that . . . and I hope that you'll be up-front and honest with me too."

But Alice was more concerned with the logistics of imprisonment: someone to care for the animals, how she'd get her pills, messages to her home health aide.

"When is Gerald supposed to be home?" asked Trimble.

"I don't know." Alice shrugged. "He went back to work [six months before] in February, and he was just home for the first time about four weeks ago."

"I'm concerned about what's going to happen from this point with you and Gerald," Trimble said.

"I don't want a trial," Alice said. "I admit it. I'll go to jail for the rest of my life."

"Maybe I was being too subtle earlier when I talked about this. If you have information about what happened to Virginia and the boys, about whether you participated, whether you helped afterwards to make it seem like things were OK, that's a decision you need to make about how much responsibility ..."

"I can't help you. So I'm just gonna have to go to jail."

"Gerald has some business with us as well. The score hasn't been settled yet. I think he has a lot he needs to talk about with us. We've done this work for a long, long time. Sometimes when there are two people who know about something bad that's happened, fingers start getting pointed, and sometimes they get pointed at the wrong person. Is Gerald going to tell us it was all you?"

"I don't know what Gerald is gonna tell you. He keeps things to himself."

Agent Young schooled Alice on the wealth of circumstantial evidence in the case. Things like the bogus Mailgram and letters designed by Alice to mislead Claire Martin and the cops; the boys' blood in the station wagon; Gerald's arrest outside Claire's laundry; his many odd statements about distant fires, carnivorous pigs, and more—"So much evidence that points to you and Gerald."

"Today's the day we can get all this behind us," Young said. "Part of you has made the decision that you'll just go to prison for the rest of your life. We can't make any promises, but we can tell you that we've talked to the prosecutors, and they're interested in getting to the bottom of the entire matter, not just Ron ..."

"OK."

Young leaned in closer. "If you can tell us about Virginia and the boys, it can make a difference ... to you."

Alice pushed her glasses back and spoke directly. "I can't help you. I've given you everything I know. If I could, I would, because I don't really want to go to jail, but I knew it was gonna happen sooner or later," she said calmly, then asked a peculiar question of her questioner. "Do you chew your nails?"

"Is it that obvious?" Young replied.

"Yes."

"Well, I can't hide the evidence."

Alice sighed. She resisted the urge to fill the long silences.

"I've always personally believed that some kind of redemption has to be made," Young said. "Sometimes it takes some doing to make it worthwhile. We have to pay the piper. We have to take responsibility for the things we do. Sometimes that redemption might be giving other people relief in a matter. You have the opportunity to help us do that . . ."

"Excuse me," Alice interrupted, rubbing her left eye. "I had eye surgery, cataract surgery that didn't come out too good."

Trimble found some eye drops in her purse, and Alice leaned back to administer them. But Young persisted through Alice's latest diversion.

"Do you think Virginia and the boys deserve to be laid to rest so that they can be at peace?"

"I don't think so."

The answer startled Trimble and Young, but Alice quickly caught herself.

"No, I *do* think so. Sorry, I'm upset. Obviously. I have a right to be upset."

A minute-long silence—a seeming eternity in that little box—hung like a leaden vapor. Alice sat stoic. She stared back at both of them, not defiant but cold. When Young finally spoke, it was sharp.

"There must have been a lot of animosity between you and Virginia and the boys," he said. It wasn't a question.

"No, there wasn't."

"Are you sure about that?"

"I didn't have any reason to have any animosity towards her."

"When I asked you if they should be laid to rest so they could have peace, you said you didn't feel that way."

"But I changed it."

"There's a reason that it came out that way," Young said.

"I didn't have any animosity towards her."

This time, the agents changed the subject. They wanted to know when they could expect Gerald to be home from the road, how often he got home, when Alice quit the trucking, how many trucks they'd owned, how much money they made, how many miles they could put on one truck.

"You've been married, what, thirty-seven years? Are you still pretty close?"

"It's hard to be close when you're running this way . . . but he calls me every day."

"How was Gerald as a stepdad?" Trimble asked.

"They didn't care for him."

"Was there a reason?"

"He's got some strange ideas," Alice said. "He was raised by Germans. He just had strange ideas from his upbringing."

Alice quickly recapped Gerald's life, from his Nebraska roots to his navy years.

"You know we want closure for Virginia and the boys. You know that . . ." Trimble interjected.

"I do too."

"How do we get there?"

"I don't know. I thought about that ever since this started happening. I don't know."

Trimble veered away from it. "Were you close with your folks?"

"Yes and no. My mother and I didn't get along all that well. She was kind of possessive. She was the kind of person that you had to love her and you couldn't love anybody else. There's a name for that, I can't think of what it is. She had mental problems."

"If your mother said you and Gerald were involved in the disappearance . . ."

"I wouldn't believe anything she said. She made up anything that made her more important. It was her job to be more important than anybody else."

Trimble asked Alice to think back to a time right after the disappearance, when the grand jury convened in Fremont County to consider charges. Alice had only a vague recollection, except that a lawyer had charged her $1,000 to advise her and Gerald to plead the Fifth and say nothing.

"I did what the lawyer said. Somebody asked me why I was doing that, and I said I wasn't paying a lawyer a thousand dollars to not follow his advice."

"Did you tell the lawyer that you didn't have anything to hide?"

"We told him what was going on," Alice shrugged. "He got a thousand dollars."

They rambled about Gerald's red truck and Alice's red Pinto, his mechanical abilities, finding parts in a small town, local gas stations, and whether that old Ford pickup ever broke down. The move from Wyoming to Missouri. They talked about buying and selling land. Remodeling their little shack in Pavillion by adding a double-wide trailer. Alice's two milk cows, the chickens and turkeys, their eggs.

"Back when all this started, and it was obvious that you were being looked at for being involved in the disappearance, one thing I had questions about is the lack of effort on your part," Trimble said. "If you really had nothing to hide, then why weren't you more cooperative with law enforcement and with the grand jury?"

"I was cooperative. I talked to them for a long time. I asked Gerald, and I didn't get any answers that led me to believe he did something."

"The day they went missing, you've said a couple things about what he was doing that day that are completely different from each other."

"I think he came home and went to bed, then got up in the afternoon sometime."

"Did you ever go and help look for Virginia and the kids? Were there any organized searches that you took part in?"

"Gerald did," Alice said. "He contacted the people in New Jersey to find out whether she'd been cashing her checks. I remember that much."

"Was Gerald ever violent with you?"

"No. Never. He's never even raised his voice to me more than a couple times."

"Have you ever had to get after him for anything?"

"I got after him for retiring last year. He's been fighting me since he was sixty-two to retire. He had the thought that when you're sixty-two, you're supposed to retire. I didn't have that thought . . . He went behind my back."

"So probably your views on people who take handouts and don't work for a living are negative?"

"Right," Alice grumbled, then launched on a couple chronically unemployed relatives she called "mentally ill."

She touted her own work ethic as a single mother of four kids, earning a nursing degree with the help of a government program and supporting everyone with the help of $225 a month in child support payments from her first ex-husband.

The random questions turned quickly to Gerald's work history and some problems he'd had with fellow workers at US Steel, and then to Gerald's arrest outside Claire Martin's laundry.

"He said he was watching to see if that camper showed back up, and to see if Virginia showed up after dark when she wouldn't be seen."

"Do you know why he had that weapon in his pocket?" Trimble asked.

Alice huffed. "It wasn't a weapon. It was a fishing weight. That was hilarious. People look at things and come up with their own ideas."

"Did Gerald ever tell you about going to see Claire and asking her for things while you were gone?"

"Uh-uh."

"Did he ever tell you he wanted to get custody of his boys?"

"Yeah, he did say he wanted to get custody," Alice said, but they hadn't taken it further.

"What was your feeling about that?"

"I thought if he wanted them, that was fine. I really didn't want more children because I was on my fifth one, but for his sake I would have taken them. It's like taking somebody else's dog. They've been raised a certain way, and they have bad parts that you don't want. I know we're talking about children, but children pick up things too."

"Do you watch any of those crime shows on TV?"

"Sometimes."

"DNA is like the big thing," Trimble went on. "It's getting easier and easier to find it, and you can get it from stuff that was touched now. A lot of that stuff was collected in 1980, but it didn't mean as much then as it does now. We've been in here talking about this for a long time, Alice, and we really just need to get the whole thing put to rest. We know that you have information to help us, and today is the day we need to talk about that. Get it all out. It's not gonna get any easier. The ball's in your court."

"Right. I told you everything I know."

"Gerald needs to answer for the things he's done."

"Did they find him?"

"It wasn't hard. They'll give him an opportunity to come clean. It's not a question in anyone's mind who's responsible. The question is whether it was a cold-blooded, calculated thing that happened, or was it something else? That's why we're talking to Gerald, and that's why we're talking to you. We're going to take Gerald to jail."

Alice never blinked. "There goes that paycheck."

Trimble was leaning so close that Alice pulled back.

"Are there things that you think happened?"

"I try not to think about it," Alice said, squirming. "I want it to go away."

Trimble touched Alice's knee. "I know you don't want to think about it. That's what I'm telling you."

Alice recoiled. "Your hands are cold," she said.

"If you can feel it through your jeans, that means it's really cold," Trimble said.

"I'm getting warm."

"I want to be able to do the right thing. You have kids, you're a grandmother . . ."

"They don't have much to do with me."

"But it doesn't mean that you don't care about them. No matter what kind of heartache Gerald had with Virginia, because I'm here to tell you, looking at some of the things that she said and did . . ."

"She wasn't a real nice person," Alice said.

"She wasn't, and I can't say that she was," Trimble said, seizing the moment to sound as if she empathized.

"I never met her."

"I can understand an adult-to-adult conflict, but what a jury will try to understand is who could hate those little boys so much? Was it a mistake, or was it malicious?"

Alice had nothing to say.

"Gerald's going to have to answer for what he's done. I just don't want to see him drag you down with him."

"I just can't tell you any more. I told you everything I know."

Trimble stared at Alice for a long time, maybe a minute. Nothing. "When Gerald came down from the mountain, did Gerald talk to you?"

"Uh-uh."

"Witnesses saw him on the mountain," Trimble said.

"Really? Hmm. He didn't say anything about it. Gerald's a pretty private person."

"There's privacy, and then there's stuff you can't really keep private." Alice shrugged. "Well, I didn't hear about that."

"Remember when I asked you about Virginia and the boys getting peace?"

"Yes, I do. I think they deserve to be at rest."

"I think you can help us make sure they get peace."

"I don't think I can. You've pretty well picked my brain—what's left of it."

"You seem pretty lucid," Trimble said.

"Well, I remember certain things. Certain other things . . . you don't pay attention because you don't know somebody's gonna pick your brain about it."

"But there are so many things about that incident that you kept records about," Trimble said. "There's nothing you can recall that might help us out on this?"

"I've racked my brain over all these years. I don't know of anything I haven't already told you."

"You've told us different stuff over the years. Not all of it's the same."

"My memory's not the same either."

"One thing you're sure of is that you've told us the truth about what you know and what you were involved in?"

Alice nodded, coughed, and took a big swig from her oversized mug but said nothing.

"I can't arrange for you to actually talk to Gerald, but I know it's comforting for one person to be able to communicate and say, 'It's time,' or 'Let's get this over with.' If you were to write a note to Gerald and said, 'I told them the whole truth'—because you're telling me you told the whole truth—do you think he'd be comforted by that note and know that he didn't have to hide anything about Ron Holtz?"

"I don't know what he would do," Alice replied. "I've never been able to figure out what he's gonna do."

"But I know he's naturally going to try to protect you."

"I'm not even sure about that. We were out in California on a great big street we had to cross. Gerald ran across and left me stumbling behind. I asked, 'Why didn't you wait for me?' He said, 'I didn't want to get ran over!'" She giggled about it.

"But would you be willing to write the note to him so he doesn't get put in that spot where he's hiding information that he doesn't need to hide?" SA Young piped in.

"I think he needs to do what he needs to do. If it sends me to jail, that's fine. I've been waiting for it since 1974."

"Yeah, well, we're past that part, Alice," Trimble said.

"I just can't. It's hard to say how he'd take that. Yeah, I don't know. I don't know."

"How else could he take that?"

"I don't know. Gerald thinks differently than everybody else does. He might not even know what that's all about. He's got a terrible memory. I don't want to put him in that position."

"To tell the truth?"

"To worry about me or anything else."

"He's going to worry about you. He's also going to be curious about what you say. Because . . ."

"He knows from the last time where I stand. He should be fine with it."

"But the truth sets you free. You've heard that."

"Yeah, but I don't trust him. I don't trust him with my money. Some of the decisions he's made, I don't trust. He wasn't considering me. He thinks about himself . . . I'm kinda selfish. I want to keep money for myself that I can go spend for myself and I don't have to say why. It works for us."

After a water break, the agents brought some pepperoni pizza for dinner.

"We just got a brief rundown from our agents out in Chicago with Gerald," Trimble said. "The bottom line is they say things haven't been that great between you and Gerald."

"Just the last few years."

"That's what he said also. They said he was holding back a little bit, but from the information they have now, it's plain that we have more to talk about."

"You and me?"

"Yes," Trimble said. "You're putting a lot of faith in believing Gerald's not gonna tell everything he knows about you. You need to look out for Alice, because Gerald's looking out for Gerald."

"I figured he would."

"He is. Just like that street in California. You've got to speak up for your side. If your story is never heard, it's only going to be Gerald's story."

"I don't have anything else to say."

"But you really do," Young said.

Alice only wanted to talk about other things. Again, her memory was vivid on many inconsequential details but vague on things most people would remember to their dying days.

"So if Gerald tells us a different story than you told us about the disappearance and murder of those three people, who's lying?"

"I think he would be."

"You think we should believe your story and not his?"

"Yes."

Except Alice had told no story. Over more than four hours, she confessed to killing one husband, teased about another, catalogued her various maladies and their corresponding pills, calculated the cost per acre of land she hadn't owned in decades, disparaged her husband's financial smarts like an angry accountant, recalled the nuances of color between long-sold vehicles, said "I don't know" a hundred different ways (none convincingly), diagnosed half of her relatives as mental defectives, rubbed the back of her hand raw—and, ironically, explained how chemotherapy ravaged her memory.

But chemo had not just cured her cancer. Maybe it taught her a lesson about mortality too. Or maybe just escape.

"I would think about how it'd be if I just didn't wake up," she told the agents. "Everybody's afraid about dying, that it might hurt. That would have been an easy way out. I wouldn't have known it was coming, and it wouldn't hurt."

A little past six the next morning, Alaska time, somebody knocked on Sharon Mack's front door.

She recognized him. It was Christopher Long, the investigator from the Alaska State Troopers who'd swabbed her for DNA the previous January.

She asked him in, and they sat in the living room.

"Sharon, I've got some news for you," he said somberly. "Down in Wyoming, they found some bones in a mine shaft. With the DNA I collected a few months ago from you, investigators positively identified the bones as your father, Ron Holtz. They've made an arrest in the case, too."

Sharon was shocked . . . and at the same time, lost, relieved, sad, and blessed.

"Are you OK?" Long asked.

"Yes," she said. "I guess you are prepared but really never fully prepared."

"Can I do anything for you?"

Nothing, she said, except to thank all the cops who'd done so much for her. She walked him out to his blue, unmarked car and waved as he left. She went to her husband's shop out back and told him they'd found the father she couldn't remember. He hugged her and said he was sorry for her.

She was sad but not sorry. She felt blessed to be the best part of Ron Holtz's befouled life.

Mostly, though, it gladdened Sharon to know her father hadn't abandoned her after all. He hadn't chosen his absence.

By the time guards locked Alice in her cell for her first night in jail, Gerald was hunkered down in an Illinois truck stop, addled about his next move in this cockeyed chess game.

The day before, he'd picked up a load of paper at a mill in Ashdown, Arkansas, and headed for Chicago. Chadwick wasn't far off his route, so he parked his eighteen-wheeler at a truck stop in Strafford, Missouri, just two hours away from their farm. Alice picked him up and drove him home to Chadwick for a home-cooked meal and a good night's rest in his own bed.

The next morning, they rose at dawn and drove back to the truck stop so Gerald could be back on the road by eight.

Gassed up and ready to roll, Gerald and Alice told each other to be safe on their separate roads, then kissed goodbye. He spent a few minutes inspecting his rig, catching up his electronic log, and checking his overnight messages from the dispatcher. Then he hit the road.

He was accustomed to long days. He stopped for lunch and fuel in Effingham, Illinois, then headed north on I-57 toward the heart of Chicago.

His cell phone rang just outside of Champaign, eight hours into his day. Alice's number flashed on the display. She never called while he was driving because it was against company rules, so maybe there was an emergency. He answered.

It wasn't Alice. The woman on the line said she was a physical therapist who visited the house to help Alice with her exercises. She was frantic. The sheriff had arrested Alice. Something about a case a long time ago in Wyoming. She was freaking out and didn't know what she should do. Was there a relative who could come right away?

Gerald gave her the names and numbers of family in the area, then hung up. He was a little freaked out too.

A half hour later, the phone rang again. This time, it was an FBI agent. He wanted to know exactly where Gerald was. The agent then demanded that Gerald return to Missouri right away to discuss "Alice's legal troubles." Gerald explained he was under a load and couldn't possibly return until he had delivered it. The agent objected, but he couldn't exactly turn the truck around himself.

"When can you get back here?" he asked.

"Tomorrow afternoon."

Gerald shut down his rig in Monee, Illinois, an hour south of Chicago. Sleeping on the streets of Chicago was a little too dangerous, even for a triple killer. He'd drop his load in the morning, before rush hour, then hightail it for Missouri.

That night, at the Monee truck stop, his mind raced about Alice's arrest, his crimes, his own story . . . He'd always known he might be arrested too, even if the chances had grown slimmer with every passing year—until now. *What did they know?* For more than thirty years, he'd lied to everybody but Alice about Virginia's disappearance. It was time to make things right with his family and save Alice, if he could . . . but how?

He started to shake.

When he'd calmed down enough, in the wee hours of Friday morning, he composed a "family letter." For thirty years, Gerald, his sister Linda, some cousins, and an aunt kept a quaint tradition of writing a single letter that was mailed to one of them, who then scribbled something extra and forwarded it to the next one on the list. No Uden had ever spent a night in jail, and now he might spend the rest of his pathetic life in prison. As heavy as his heart was, he wanted them to hear it from him.

Sept 27 2013

Dear Ones if you are reading this it means this will be the last family letter I will write. It will also serve as goodby [*sic*] and fare-well. Alice and I have been arrested and charged with the murder of Virginia and the boys. Alice is innocent of any wrongdoing. However sadly I am not. I'm sorry for the lies and will pay the price probably with my life.

I never had any idea growing up things would turn out this way. I don't think anyone does. I can make all kinds of excuses for this but in the end knew it was wrong. I'm hopeing [*sic*] after my death I'll be creamated [*sic*] and my ashes scattered to the wind and no marker to show I was ever here. I do not want anyone to grieve or feel sorry for me and if anyone asks about me say He died in Prison, always said he would come to a bad end.

I don't have Linda's adress [*sic*] or phone nbr. Last I knew she was back in Billings Mt. Tried to call her oldest daughter Annie but no luck there either. So suggest if family letter is to keep going don't send to Linda unless sure of her adress. Alice and I have many fond memories of you all and wish you all the best.

Love Gerald & Alice

He delivered his paper freight the next morning and hightailed it south toward Missouri. The dispatcher wanted him to pick up another shipment and head to Texas, but he refused. He needed to get home, no detours.

A few hours later, his phone rang. It was Eliza, and she demanded to meet him at a Flying J outside of St. Louis. There, she parked her car in front of his truck, left her twenty-year-old son inside, and crawled up into Gerald's cab. She wasn't happy.

"What did you do?"

He started to tell her the whole sordid story, but she shut him down. "I don't want to know!"

But she really did.

He tried to explain how Virginia and Alice battled, how he had to solve the problem or lose Alice, how he shot them all and dumped their bodies where nobody would find them . . . and how he, not Alice, should pay the price. He'd do anything to protect Alice. He'd even tell them she never knew anything. It was all him.

He'd rather spend the rest of his life in jail than disappoint Alice.

And he already knew what he'd do next.

A little after five p.m., Gerald pulled into the farm. Eliza got there just ahead of him. He started cleaning out his semi, giving most of the stuff to his grandson. Before the cops got there, he'd bequeathed his trucker boots, two guitars, fishing gear, and a few guns. Another tender family moment, if one overlooked the looming prospect of murder charges and prison.

He placed his family letter in the mailbox out by the road, to be mailed by the first relative who received it to the next, who'd mail it to the next, and so on.

Around six, an unmarked car came up the road. Gerald watched four men get out. A state trooper and deputy waited at the car while the other two walked up to the porch. He met them at the door, and they identified themselves as FBI Agent Paul Swenson and DCI SA Andy Hanson from Wyoming.

"C'mon in," he said. "I've been waiting for you."

Inside, they made small talk and settled in at the kitchen table.

"Gerald, we're out here doing an investigation," Swenson said. "And you know a little bit about that investigation from what . . ."

"What I heard from my daughter Eliza today is that my wife has confessed to a whole lotta stuff," Gerald said brusquely. "That true or not?"

"Ordinarily, we're not gonna talk a whole lot about what other people did or didn't do," Swenson said, "but in this particular case, I think your daughter's pretty accurate in her assessment, OK?"

Swenson started to explain why the FBI was involved, that he knew Gerald had already talked to cops several times over the years, that he really appreciated Gerald coming in from the road to talk.

Gerald interrupted. "I have made arrangements for my company to pick up my truck tomorrow at five o'clock," he said. His voice was weary but resolute. "I have cleaned out the truck because I have anticipated that you guys didn't come here on a social visit. Now let's not fool each other, all right? I don't know what you've got or what's changed, but I'd really like to know that, if there's any way . . ."

Swenson tried to lower the temperature a bit. *Take it slower.*

"For right now, we're here just to talk to you. We don't have an arrest warrant for you at this point . . ."

"That surprises me."

"Does it? How come?"

"Well, because . . ." Gerald sighed deeply. "I don't know how Alice could know anything about it. She had nothing to do with it."

"We got a lot to talk about, and we've got as much time as you're willing to give."

Yeah, he knew what they wanted to talk about. They knew about Virginia and the boys, and they were just circling like hungry wolves around a wounded animal.

"I've thought about this," Gerald said. "My youngest daughter confronted me about this today. She came right out and said, 'Dad, did you kill all those people?' I looked at her, and I said, 'Yes, dear, I did.' But I said, 'Your mother had nothing to do with it,' and I'm gonna tell you that right now."

Swenson and Hanson were dumbfounded, but they couldn't show it. *This guy is confessing to a crime we haven't asked about! Say . . . something!*

"OK," said one. "Yes, sir," said the other.

"Alice had nothing to do with it," Gerald continued. "I don't know why they even arrested her. I don't really understand that at all. I thought maybe it was because they wanted me to come in, which, all they had to do was ask."

"We appreciate that," Swenson said, eager to keep Gerald talking. "You're great. You drove all the way from Chicago today. You let us in your house. You're talking to us voluntarily. We appreciate all of that."

"Now that you guys are here, I've got to assume that you either found some bodies or something else," Gerald continued to spill. "I gotta tell you, if you found bodies, it's a miracle, because I'm here to tell you right now, the place where I put those people would be just about as impossible for anybody to find as any place could possibly be. I'll say that up front, right now."

"OK."

"As a matter of fact, if you took me out in that area, I could only point in the general direction and say, 'They're out there,' because they're not buried on land."

"Yes, sir."

"I was in the navy, and I had a boat. On the fifth of November that year, those people and I took a long ride. We went out to the West Coast, we launched the boat, and went off the bar of the Columbia River, where the depth drops off. They sleep with the fishes. Now who you got now? I don't know."

Yeah, that part about Oregon was a lie, he knew, *but I'm not ready to tell that particular truth.*

"Is that Washington?"

"Yeah, that area," Gerald mumbled.

Gerald's confession came gift wrapped in a conspiracy theory.

"I told my daughter today I don't want and won't accept a lawyer. I'm gonna plead guilty, and I'm gonna tell the judge that for a long, long time, I have felt this was more about money than anything else. The court system and the lawyers have decided that Mr. Uden here has got too much assets, and we want some of it. Sorry, boys, you ain't gonna get none. I am gonna plead guilty, and I want life in prison or a death sentence. You must understand, I may be stupid, but I'm not crazy. Everybody wants to live, but nobody—including you boys—is gonna live forever. I have made my peace with my god, and if I'm sentenced to death, then I am not afraid. People are gonna say, 'You're crazy.' I'm seventy-one years old. I've lived ten years longer than my father. I got no complaints. That's just the way it's gonna be."

"Yes, sir. And that's fine. What we could do—if it's all right with you, sir, I would like to back up to that day. Could you just kinda tell us what happened, how it happened, why it happened?"

"Yeah, I can and I will."

"Thank you," Swenson said. He didn't know what else to say. This had turned surreal.

"Virginia Uden. They gave her a name. They call her a predator. By that, I mean she went around to men and got them to do things."

He told how she'd hoodwinked him with an old gun that she knew he'd love. It was all just a subterfuge, he said, to trick him into supporting her and her kids.

"One thing led to another. I'm in bed with this gal, and not too long after that, I'm getting married."

She duped him into adopting her boys, he told the agents, then six weeks later filed for divorce. Suddenly separated, Gerald hooked up with Alice, who'd been married and divorced a few times and was a veteran of custody wars. She became his adviser on how to deal with Virginia, whose erratic behavior threatened to chase off Alice, his true love.

And Virginia was skilled at getting under Alice's skin by insisting she be allowed to visit the Udens' home with her boys. The notion sent Alice into rages.

"I'm trying to juggle two women, and it ain't flying," Gerald said. "So finally it just went off. I said, 'I'm gonna solve this problem,' and I did. I'm a fan of Mafia books, and one of the things is that you never let the victim know you're coming."

He told them how his murder plot burst into full bloom that day at the hospital with Richard when Virginia told him she needed a trailer. He invented a generous neighbor who'd lend her a trailer and made arrangements to meet the next day for a little target practice with the boys. She could see it then. *Bring your mom's gun*, he told her.

So they met the next day, just like he'd told all the investigators before, and they drove to the secluded bend in the road, near the drainage canal.

"Virginia was there, the gun was there, I was there . . ." he recounted. "I shot her right square in the back of the head, and she went down."

Then Richard, who never saw it coming. Then Reagan, who saw it coming and fled in terror before he died. *Ten seconds*, he said, *and they were gone*.

He loaded their bloody corpses in his truck, drove to the middle of nowhere, and dumped them in the Lewiston gold mine. Six weeks later, he got nervous because he was attracting too much suspicion. He retrieved their decomposing remains from the mine—alone—on his fifth wedding anniversary, put them in barrels, and drove them to the Washington coast to toss them from his pleasure boat into the deep, dark sea near Astoria, Oregon, seventeen hours away in twelve thousand feet of water.

"If you got 'em, you got somebody I don't know about," he said.

But Gerald's wild story wasn't done.

He considered putting the corpses in US Steel's blast furnace, he said, but he feared his coworkers might smell burning flesh. He dismissed other ideas before settling on the old mine. Disposing of the car, on the other hand, was a good idea gone bad.

"They found the car up on the switchbacks, because I had taken it up there. I tried to roll it over the damn cliff, but do you think it'd go over?"

"Not so much," Swenson answered.

"Not so much!" Gerald replied as if he were telling a sea story. "If that damn car had gone over the cliff, we might not be having this conversation. Well, the sheriff out there fancied himself a little bit of a psychological guy, I guess, and they tried to trip me up about the car, but the problem was, the first job I had after the navy was working for the Forest Service, and I knew those switchbacks."

He also knew the spots where he killed Virginia and the boys, and where he dumped the car, were Indian land, which made it all a federal crime scene.

"I understand why you're here," he said to the FBI agent. "And that's the whole story."

At that point, SA Andy Hanson slipped out of the house and called Trimble's cell phone. She'd been waiting anxiously for any word about their chat with Gerald. She hoped he'd tell everything he knew about the murder of Ron Holtz, bolstering her case against Alice. But the cell service out here was crappy, and she wasn't sure she'd hear from them at all.

Until her phone rang. It was Hanson on the other end.

"Oh my God, Tina, he's confessing to everything."

"Are you shitting me?" She wanted to know more, but Hanson had delivered his headline.

"I gotta get back to this," he said as he hung up. "I'll fill you in later."

Back inside at the kitchen table, Swenson was drilling deeper into Gerald's story.

"How did the station wagon get up there?" he asked.

"I took it up there."

"How did you get back?"

"I walked. I was, at one time, a pretty active guy. Twenty-some miles. Five miles an hour, four hours."

"When did you take it up?"

"In the dark."

"That same night?"

"Yeah."

"What about the gun? Where did that end up?"

"In the slag heap. I took it apart and took it to work and set it to the torch. There is no gun anymore. A funny thing: nobody ever asked me about that gun, and I was sure they would."

Swenson asked about Gerald helping Claire search for Virginia that night, even though he knew her body already lay in a remote, abandoned mine with her two dead little boys.

"It's a hell of a thing to admit," Gerald said, "but I probably would have killed Claire too. But it just so happened she had a friend named Marie, and Marie had a baby, and they were all there at the Laundromat. I just lost my stomach. I'd done enough killing for one gol-damned week . . . Claire lucked out."

"Claire ended up with a cut telephone line . . ."

"That was me," Gerald quickly confessed. "I had ideas of taking her out. At that point, I think I was a little crazy."

Out loud, he contemplated his particular insanity. The killings weren't business or sport. He derived no special pleasure from them, "but it stopped the child support, and that was gonna come to about $16,000, so you could say that was a motive."

"What about when you were there at the laundry a week or so later? What was your intent?"

"Well, I'm not sure," he said, laughing a little. "Somebody walking by saw me and called the Riverton police."

Gerald's description of the "weapon" he carried launched him on a long, confusing description of the mining processes at US Steel and the life of a maintenance mechanic. Swenson and Hanson let him ramble a while, then dragged him back to the subject at hand.

"There were a couple of Mailgrams that were sent to Claire as if they were from Virginia," one of them brought up. "Alice had those sent. It looks an awful lot like Alice running interference on a police investigation. You tell me, is that what was going on?"

"Well, I'd have to say probably, yeah. I don't know why we decided to do that. But, yeah, it was some interference."

"Was that Alice's doing or your suggestion?"

"Probably Alice's. I never would have thought of it."

"Did she do it more than once?"

"She might have. That's something I don't know. I don't understand her sometimes. With me, she has always been as loving and kind as any human can be with another. Yet there are times . . . she can be vindictive, if you push her hard enough."

"You kinda had each other's back. Did she know what had happened to Virginia and the boys?"

"I think she did."

"Can you tell me any other parts of this case where she was actively involved?"

Gerald eluded the question. "You're gonna do whatever you're gonna do, but I'd just like to see her come home."

"Alice told us to tell you that she told the truth. She said to tell Gerald, 'I told the truth, and I feel better.' That includes the thing with Mr. Holtz."

It was a lie, of course, but it didn't matter. Gerald had already spilled more beans than anybody ever expected. Certainly more than Alice expected.

"Thank you for sitting down with us and sharing this whole story," Swenson said, still outwardly courteous. "I have to be honest with you:

other than a few of the specific details, I really don't know that you told us anything that we didn't already have some basic knowledge. It speaks volumes about what kind of person you've become."

But Gerald wasn't done.

"One of the things I was most proud of: I started trucking in 1984," he said, followed by another convoluted story about his life on the road and the high value of even his cheapest loads. "In all of those years, I've never taken so much as one dime of somebody else's stuff. . . . I could have stayed in Canada. I didn't."

How cute. The killer who'd lied about everything for more than thirty years was proud of his honesty.

"At what point did Alice find out about all the goings-on?" Swenson pressed into tricky territory.

"I don't really know," Gerald fumbled around. "That memory's a little fuzzy."

In the interview, Gerald recalled precisely the number of grains in his favorite bullets, his favorite comedians and the names of their best comedy routines, the tidal habits at the mouth of the Columbia River, his 102-year-old aunt's address, the exact models of his guns, the year they were made and their book value, the industrial chemistry at US Steel, and a variety of insignificant dates and times.

But he couldn't remember when his wife—who also had a prodigious memory for the right things—learned about his three murders.

"You know the name Ron Holtz?"

"No," Gerald said, but he could only name two of Alice's three prior husbands. The agents told him number three was Ron Holtz.

Gerald seemed to be digging around clumsily in his foggy, cluttered memory. "The only thing I know about him—she was very upset—she told me about shooting this guy. Maybe after we were married. He was beating her and beating Eliza. That name's not familiar. She said she had put him in a gold mine out there on that ranch."

"What ranch is that?"

"Um . . . Remount."

"Alice told you she'd shot him?"

"She started crying and said, 'I suppose you're not gonna love me anymore,' but I said, 'That's not the way it's gonna be. I don't care.' I tried to comfort her. I told her I done worse. Anyway, we have been together for thirty-seven years, and in all that time, I have never, ever feared for my safety. Never. I don't care what she did. I will always love her."

"That's the definition of love," Swenson said.

"We're not here to question that, that's for sure," Hanson said.

"Maybe I should have went to the authorities and said, 'Hey, I got a killer for a wife.' But as far as I'm concerned, that was self-defense."

Most days, Gerald said, he was glad he killed Virginia, Richard, and Reagan because it was "the only way" to make peace with Alice. Some days, not so much. But despite his ambivalence about the actual killing, he told the agents he often congratulated himself for evading arrest for so long. Alice knew, Eliza knew, and now two agents from Wyoming knew what he'd done—nobody else. He wouldn't even trust a priest with that particular confession.

Gerald had long ago decided that, no matter how provoked, he'd never do anything like it again. He'd outgrown his killing.

He offered to write a letter to any living relatives of his victims, not knowing there were none. But he didn't want to do it right away.

The rambling, ninety-minute interview dwindled down to a few follow-up questions, some logistics, some sidelong cracks among guys. In an hour and a half, Gerald had mellowed from a surly long-haul trucker to an affable uncle whose jokes weren't as funny as he thought they were.

"Is there anything we didn't talk about? Any questions you have for us?" Swenson asked.

"Am I staying here tonight," Gerald wondered, "or am I going with you?"

"Well, things have changed in this conversation"—*no kidding*—"so we have to call the sheriff."

"One thing, and I don't want anybody to take this wrong, but I'm on one side of the law, and you guys are on the other. That makes you not my friend. It doesn't make you my enemy, but you're not my friends."

"Fair enough," Swenson said. "It doesn't mean we can't be respectful to one another."

"Just so you know that I understand you guys are just doing a job . . ." Gerald launched into another long-winded story about how he always wanted to be a Navy SEAL but couldn't swim. The moral of his digression? If he could swim, he might have been killed while fighting "gooks" in Vietnam, or he might have made a career in the navy . . . but he wouldn't be under arrest today for three murders.

He'd clearly spent too much time pondering life's unintended consequences, and maybe not enough on free will. Stupidity *and* insanity played roles too.

In reality, he wouldn't be under arrest today if he hadn't presumed—incorrectly—that Alice was jailed for her role in Virginia and the boys' disappearance. The cops hadn't tricked him; he tricked himself. If he'd told the same tired bullshit story he'd told a dozen cops over the past thirty years, he'd be sleeping in his own bed tonight.

For that matter, he wouldn't be under arrest if he hadn't killed three people in the first place.

But what's done was done. His confession was an unexpected gift.

A Christian County deputy slapped handcuffs and leg-irons on Gerald Uden, loaded him into a patrol car, and took him to jail. Like Alice, he was under arrest for first-degree murder. After booking and a strip search, he was stuffed in a holding cell with several other prisoners, none alleged killers like him. Through a small ballistic-glass window, he could see the booking area.

He spotted Alice out there, passing through. She didn't see him, and he couldn't get her attention. Then, as quickly as she appeared, she was gone.

He didn't know how this had all happened so fast after so long. He didn't yet know Alice had her own crimes to answer for.

But he knew their perversely charmed life together was over.

He knew that goodbye peck in a truck stop the day before was probably their last kiss.

And he knew he'd likely never see her again, except like this, a ghost beyond his reach.

A day after Gerald's arrest, Alice had second thoughts about her story.

In a second interview with agents Tina Trimble and Loy Young, she waived her Miranda rights and clarified her accounts of both her and Gerald's crimes.

For one, she confessed, Ron Holtz hadn't been threatening baby Eliza when Alice shot him. In truth, she'd waited until he fell asleep, then put the barrel of her .22 rifle against the back of his head and fired once. He died facedown in bed, leaking blood all over the mattress.

She killed him, she said, because she was terrified of him. She didn't say, however, why she was changing her story now.

Was it possible that Gerald had driven a thousand miles to Astoria, Oregon, to dump Virginia and the boys in the Pacific Ocean, Trimble asked? Alice admitted they'd visited Gerald's mother in nearby Longview, Washington, on the Columbia River, but they didn't bring their boat. And she couldn't recall when.

More important, she admitted to seeing Virginia's car at her house on the day of the disappearance, but she was too busy butchering her dead calf in her blood-splattered kitchen to care.

Yes, she knew at that moment that Virginia and her boys were dead.

Yes, she later contrived the bogus Mailgram and letters to cover Gerald's tracks.

Yes, she had kept that secret until now.

No, most incredibly, she still didn't know why Gerald did it.

Lonnie TeBeest knew the cold-case team was in Chadwick. Before they left, they'd given him a heads-up that they might call if they needed information. They never did.

Instead, one of the agents—an old friend—called to tell him Alice had confessed. A few hours later, Trimble called with the official news: Alice Uden had admitted she killed Ron Holtz, and she'd been arrested on suspicion of first-degree murder. Trimble shared the high points of Alice's story, which was a lot about Holtz and nothing significant about Virginia and the boys.

TeBeest wished out loud he'd been there to watch. He'd had his shot with Gerald and Alice once and failed. He still thought about what he might have done differently. It was always an internal argument: Truth was, he didn't think he'd have changed a thing, knowing what little they knew at the time, but Wachsmuth never agreed with the rough way he handled Alice. He might have been right.

His cop's mind still churned. He advised Trimble to put a hold on Alice's calls from the jail so she couldn't communicate with Gerald or Eliza. *Keep him in the dark*, he told her.

On Friday, he and Sandy drove to Colorado. At the end of the day, they checked into a Holiday Inn and went to bed. TeBeest turned off his phone, a luxury after years of being on call and tethered 24-7 to the station, and fell asleep.

The next morning, he had two texts.

The first was from Director Woodson and said only, "Call me ASAP."

The second, also from Woody, said, "He confessed!"

He read them several times. He wasn't sure they really meant what they said. Gerald once told TeBeest he'd never give up a secret. *Never.* Nobody expected Gerald to admit anything. At best, they hoped Gerald would fill in a few details on the Holtz murder.

TeBeest congratulated Woodson for keeping the case alive and told him to tell Trimble she was a hero. He had invested a lot of blood, sweat, and tears in the case, but it wasn't his. It was theirs.

After they hung up, TeBeest was both delighted and dejected. Happy—tickled shitless, really—that this wretched case would finally be closed, sad that Claire wasn't here to see it. She'd never found out what happened to the boys, but a part of him thought maybe it was better that she died with a tiny flicker of hope for them.

Lonnie TeBeest kept those two texts in his phone for a long time.

They always made him smile.

Chapter 9

THE HANGMAN'S HANDS

Eager to confess to his killings, Gerald Uden quickly waived extradition back to Wyoming.

His mission was to reassure anybody who'd listen that Alice had nothing to do with the slaying of Virginia and the boys. He alone—or so he said—had planned and executed three merciless murders and then secretly disposed of the corpses *twice* without his wife's knowledge, inspiration, or help. He wanted to control the dubious narrative that Alice was utterly innocent. In his mind, the faster he could blurt it all out and get to prison, the less likely cops would delve deeper.

Less than two weeks after his arrest, Gerald was in the Fremont County Jail in Lander, playing spades and dice games with his fellow inmates, watching television, and generally impatient to get his day in court.

Back in 1980, Gerald's original plan was to tell only one lie so as to avoid getting tangled up in a web of his own deceptions. But growing, thirty-year-old deceptions required regular feeding, so his lies multiplied geometrically. What was one more?

When a local defense lawyer named Sky Phifer—retained by Eliza with Gerald's pension money—came to see him in jail, Gerald retold the same story he'd told the agents, including the warped saga about how he'd deep-sixed their bodies in the bottomless Pacific Ocean off the Oregon coast. When he finished, Phifer said he planned to discuss a deal with prosecutors: in exchange for the whole truth and nothing but the truth, would they take the death penalty off the table?

Gerald hadn't expected a plea bargain, but why not? At seventy-one, any lesser penalty he might get for one count of first-degree murder—

never mind three—was a life sentence, so it didn't matter much to him. He just wanted to tell his Alice-less story as soon as possible.

Phifer worked fast. A day later, he returned to the jail with good news. Gerald wouldn't be executed, but he must tell a judge exactly what he did. If he lied about anything, the death penalty would be back in play.

Oh, shit. One lie too many.

He had planned to die without ever telling the truth about where he really dumped Virginia and the boys. Or that he'd killed them at all. But he'd spilled those beans. A man's word was his bond, and Gerald felt a queer compulsion to come clean. After all, he was about to shake on it. For the man who'd lied about everything for so long, honesty was now all-important.

Instead of the Oregon coast, he told his lawyer he'd heaved them into the glacial abyss of Fremont Lake.

Phifer was livid with Gerald, but the deal stood. Gerald, Phifer, and county prosecutor Michael Bennett signed the plea bargain on October 24, 2013, just twenty-seven days after his arrest in Missouri. At the earliest moment, he'd tell a judge what he'd done and take what was coming to him before going straight to prison.

But before he went to court, Gerald's sister Linda visited him in jail. She, too, was livid. He tried to calm her by explaining why he'd killed three people and never told her or anyone else. He begged her not to worry about him and made light of his extraordinarily evil situation.

"One nursing home is as good as another," he told her.

A week later, Linda died of a stroke in her sleep. The sheriff asked Gerald if he wanted to attend her funeral, but the embarrassing prospect of appearing in shackles and an orange jumpsuit eclipsed his grief.

On November 1, 2013—thirty-three years and six weeks after he'd massacred three people who'd once loved him—Gerald Uden walked into District Judge Norman Young's courtroom to tell his story again and accept his punishment. The gallery overflowed with fifty or more spectators, including some friends of Claire.

First, the judge asked Gerald if he was guilty or innocent.

"Guilty, Your Honor."

The judge then invited Gerald to explain his crimes. Point by horrid point, Gerald recited, in a chillingly confident voice, what he'd done, from the ruse that brought Virginia and the boys to "the corner" on September 12, 1980, to sinking their decaying corpses in Wyoming's Fremont Lake—not the Pacific Ocean—seven weeks later.

"When you met Virginia and the boys at 'the corner,'" Judge Young asked Gerald directly, "was it your intention to take them out and murder them?"

"Yes."

"And it was basically over the child support and visitation?"

On that, Gerald wanted to split hairs.

"It wasn't about the money, per se, because I had the money to do that," he said. "It was the fact she was trying to break Alice and I up. It wasn't that Alice said, 'Look, you got to choose' . . . but her actions were giving me a lot of grief at home. I had to get rid of the grief.

"I finally wound up having to make a choice because Alice was giving me a hard time about it and Virginia was giving me a hard time about it, so I made a choice. I decided I would love Alice, and Virginia was intolerable."

"And your solution to that problem was to get rid of Virginia?"

"Yes."

"The two boys as well?"

"Yes."

A chill fell across the silent court. The prosecution had nothing to add that could have possibly made Gerald look more wicked than he made himself look, and the defense couldn't make him look any better. So Gerald himself burnished his own wickedness.

"I don't know whether the court wants to know," Gerald interjected, "but Virginia is buried in Fremont Lake, at the bottom. And I could not go to the lake to point and say where, because it was dark. But that's where they are."

After a few minutes of legal throat-clearing, the judge asked Gerald if he had anything to say before his formal sentencing that would most assuredly imprison him for the rest of his life, however much time he had left.

"Once upon a time, I was in the navy," Gerald calmly told the judge. "When asked a question, there were only three proper responses: Yes, sir; no, sir; or no excuse, sir. I will accept the third response. There is no excuse."

"I agree," the judge said tersely.

Judge Young explained that court rules required him to consider probation, "but it is as obvious as it ever will be that it is not appropriate in this case."

With the death penalty off the table, the judge affirmed the plea agreement, accepting Gerald Uden's guilty pleas to three counts of first-degree murder and sentencing him under 1980 laws to three concurrent life terms, $150 to the state's victim compensation fund, and twenty bucks in court costs. No fine or restitution was assessed.

In Wyoming, then and now, life was life. Under Wyoming law, lifers are never eligible for parole unless the governor commutes their sentences, and it was unlikely Gerald would live long enough to see that kind of mercy.

Was there more?

Fremont County Undersheriff Ryan Lee, a young Riverton native who could trace his law enforcement pedigree back to his coroner grandfather, feared local law enforcement might never know some of the details of Gerald Uden's killings if he disappeared into the prison system before somebody asked. So he got permission to spend a few days driving around with Gerald, revisiting the key sites and hearing some of the lesser-known details, just a couple guys on a road trip. Maybe, he thought, it would shake loose some overlooked memories that might lead to the still-missing bodies of Virginia and her boys . . . if Gerald would do it.

So Lee met with Gerald in the jail and proposed his expedition. It'd take a few days, he said. Gerald would be shackled, but he could wear civilian clothes and pick any lunch place he wanted (as long as it had a drive-up window). Lee would pick up the tab.

Lee was playing an old cop's game. He wanted Gerald to see him as a new friend helping him through a tough time in his life.

Gerald happily agreed. "Show and tell," he called it. He didn't need civvies, and he understood the shackles. He didn't care. It'd likely be his last breath of free air, and he knew it.

"You can't offend me," the confessed triple killer told his new buddy. "Ask anything you want."

A day later, Lee showed up at the jail in his three-quarter-ton, unmarked pickup. A deputy helped him load Gerald into the passenger seat, and they headed out to Pavillion for their first stop: Gerald and Alice's place, which was never much to look at but now was as forlorn as a scab.

On the way to Williams Road, they chatted like a couple of drinking buddies. Gerald was a bottomless spring of information. He knew every neighbor, every fence line, every dry creek, every crossroad . . . everything. Lee made a mental note about how vivid Gerald's recall seemed to be.

Gerald pointed out where the houses and sheds once sat. A dirt two-track still meandered onto the parcel but just stopped out in the scrub. As old men do, he told a few stories that had nothing to do with anything except whatever strange movie looped in his brain.

Then they drove out to the murder site, the wide spot where a lonely dirt road crossed an irrigation canal. Gerald got out of the truck and walked to the spot where Virginia and the boys came to their end. He made a gun with his fingers and coolly acted it all out. *Pow, one shot in the back of Virginia's head . . . pow, one shot behind Richard's ear . . . and pow, one shot in Reagan's screaming little brain.*

Lee asked a few questions, but mostly Gerald told his story as calmly as if he were remembering a pleasant outing with his family, not a methodical slaughter.

"Ten seconds," Gerald crowed. "They didn't suffer. But I had no idea the human body contained that much blood."

They backtracked toward town and Gerald pointed out the dusty creek bed where he buried the fancy stock of the murder gun. Still shackled securely, he kicked the dirt where he said it was, and Lee rooted around but found nothing. It might be nearby, Lee thought, or Gerald might be lying, but they didn't have time to waste digging holes.

Back in town, Lee kept his promise to buy lunch anywhere Gerald chose. He picked Wendy's, his favorite burger place.

That was it for day one. It had exhausted Lee to pretend to be unfazed while listening to Gerald maunder about his life and demonstrate his bloody crimes so casually. He never interrogated Gerald, just let him tell his stories. Some of his tales were exaggerated, and some were exceptionally self-centered at times, but on the whole, Gerald was mostly credible, Lee thought.

On day two, they drove to the Hidden Hand mine, an hour into the middle of nowhere, "the perfect hiding spot" where Gerald said he first stowed the bodies.

Again, Lee was struck by Gerald's nearly photographic memory. He knew every bend in the highway, the mile markers, the unmarked boundaries between federal and state land, which shacks were new, which gates were bastards to open. At one point, he immediately recognized that the road had been moved slightly by the Highway Department. A couple times, the old trucker even told Lee how to drive. He might be lying about everything else, Lee thought, but when he was talking about details, he wasn't BSing.

His memories about the bodies were slightly more frayed. Gerald was fairly sure, but not absolutely certain, it was the Hidden Hand mine where he'd stuffed them. He couldn't recall which boy had worn green tortoiseshell glasses (or what he'd done with them). He wasn't terribly clear about how he'd gotten into the mine or out of it.

But some details came into sickening focus. Gerald remembered that when he returned to retrieve the decaying bodies, they were sunken, gnawed, and rotted. At the time, Gerald had never learned to back up a trailer, so he had a hitch on the front of his truck, which he used to hoist the bagged remains out of the hole. The desiccated bodies were much lighter in death than in life and easier to compact into his barrels. And they wouldn't float because the decomposition gases had long ago dissipated.

Lee was sickened by it, but he showed no reaction. His only goal was to find the victims, and he didn't want Gerald to stop talking. The actions Gerald described would be difficult, but not impossible. The behavior was hard to believe, but the known parts of his story were hard to believe too.

When they were done, Lee drove Gerald back to town, where they could grab a McDonald's meal at the drive-through before returning to jail. They talked all the way about paltry things. Out there on the road, Gerald teared up a couple times for a strange reason: It was Ryan Lee himself, his new friend. It saddened Gerald that they'd never see each other again.

Lee outwardly palavered and prattled with Gerald, but was inwardly troubled . . . maybe even pissed that he was no closer to finding Virginia and the boys.

The third and last day of Gerald's tour would be Fremont Lake. First, he was transferred to the Sublette County jail in Pinedale, much closer to Fremont Lake. The next day, Lee and a fellow deputy drove Gerald out to the lake, where they met Special Agent Tina Trimble and several members of a local search and recovery team. They asked Gerald to lead them to the approximate spot where he'd tossed the bodies over the gunwale into the water.

First, Gerald directed them to the landing where he vaguely thought he'd shoved off. *Past the marina. No, too far. Back down. Near that bay . . .*

At the ramp, they shackled Gerald, then bundled him in an exposure suit and enough life preservers to save four drowning people. They didn't want him to fall or jump overboard and cheat the warden.

It was mostly fruitless from the moment they pushed off.

It had been pitch-black that night. Gerald had no reference points, no reliable lights in the distance. He'd merely motored out far enough in the darkness to a spot where his sounding line stopped dragging on the bottom, then stopped the boat, dropped the rope into the water, and pushed the barrels overboard—just like he told them. Gerald had no idea where he was at the time.

"Are you BSing me?" a frustrated Lee asked.

"No bullshit," Gerald responded. "I want to be right with God, so I have to tell the real truth. This is where the bodies are. No bullshit here."

So they puttered around out there, dropping some search equipment in the cold water to no avail. The local searchers marked a few interesting blips on their sonar, but after a few hours in the sharp wind and cold, they gave up, promising to come back for a more intensive search next summer after the lake thawed.

After loading up for the short trip back to the Pinedale jail, Lee and Gerald stopped for prepackaged sandwiches at the marina and ate their lunch at a roadside picnic table. They talked about his memory, his life, and all the people they knew in common. For Lee, it was all part of the game—acting like a casual friend, hoping the faked closeness would induce Gerald to drop his guard.

"I think that at the time, I was insane," Gerald admitted. "I don't know about now, but at that time, I was insane to think I could get away with all this."

At the end, they had no better idea about Virginia and her boys than when they started. If Gerald was guarding a secret, it stayed guarded.

Back at the jail, Lee handed Gerald his card and wished him well as he went back inside forever.

"Take care," he said.

Gerald's reply chilled him.

"Watch your back," he told Lee. "Be careful out there. One of these days, you're gonna meet somebody just like me, only not as nice as I am. I don't want to read about you in the paper."

Ryan Lee began to wonder who'd been playing whom.

Don Prunty had been a ghost for more than forty years, but he'd only been haunting Tina Trimble lately.

How many times is the average American personally brushed by a single murder in a lifetime? she wondered. *Once? Maybe?*

Yet she knew without a doubt that Alice Uden was connected intimately to *four*. She had murdered one husband and was indirectly involved in three other homicides, including her husband's ex-wife. The marital theme leapt out. Suddenly, the premature death of another husband warranted a second look.

SA Lonnie TeBeest first suspected it, and a doctor who examined Prunty's medical records had raised the specter of foul play. But finding Ron Holtz was a surer bet at the time.

Now Trimble had Ron Holtz, and she had Alice's confession. She also had accounts from two of Alice's children that Alice had put "something" in her alcoholic husband's beverages to end his drinking. If Alice's confessions to her children led to Ron Holtz's bones, it wasn't far-fetched to think they might reveal another killing.

Shortly after returning from Missouri, Trimble's team collected Prunty's medical records and death certificate for Dr. James Wilkerson, the Colorado medical examiner who'd autopsied Ron Holtz. They also compiled a summary of Alice's various admissions to her children about the mysterious "something" with which she dosed him. And they asked if an exhumation was likely to prove anything after four decades.

Two weeks later, Dr. Wilkerson responded:

The medical record demonstrates malignant hypertension, kidney failure, and encephalopathy. While these symptoms are attributed to hypertension, they could also be seen in poisoning, specifically, with ethylene glycol. After the blood pressure was controlled he continued to have kidney failure with a blood urea nitrogen of 68 mg% and creatinine of 6.6 mg% [both elevated]. He continued to remain confused and lethargic and had severe electrolyte abnormalities with a sodium of 121, chloride of 69, and a potassium of 2.4% [all grossly unbalanced]. He remained encephalopathic and by the morning of 7/23/1973 he was much less responsive than when he was admitted on 7/21 and subsequently expired.

These findings are similar to those that would be observed in ethylene glycol poisoning. Ethylene glycol is the principal ingredient of most automobile anti-freeze solutions, particularly in 1973. Its metabolites are toxic. Upon ingestion, individuals can develop neurological, cardiorespiratory, and renal symptoms. Neurologic symptoms develop within 12 hours after ingestion. Cardiorespiratory manifestations occur 12–24 hours after ingestion.

Mr. Prunty has been reportedly buried in a steel casket. If the remains are dry, it is possible that ethylene glycol could be detected in the tissues. Certainly if kidney tissue remains, oxalate crystals can be seen in renal tubules and sometimes in the brain. I would be happy to assist with the autopsy should an exhumation occur.

Ethylene glycol is the primary compound in ordinary automobile coolants and antifreezes. In the past century, it has also been a favorite poison—especially for husband-killing wives, according to forensic data—because it's in every garage, it's colorless and odorless, it tastes very sweet, and its toxic effects can be misdiagnosed as something else.

Like its distant cousin ethanol, the stuff in booze, ethylene glycol is a moderate neurotoxin that causes slurring and stumbling. But its real damage is done by the human body's chemistry, which breaks it down into oxalic acid in the bloodstream. That acid combines with calcium to form sharp-edged calcium oxalate crystals that slice and dice cells in the kidneys and other organs.

Its fast-acting effects include seizures, slurring, and headaches. Over time, the neurological effects can include symptoms of dementia, delusion, and significantly disrupted movement and speech.

Ethylene glycol poisoning fit Don Prunty's case history better than a salt overdose, Wilkerson believed.

That was enough for Trimble, who immediately contacted the funeral home that prepared the forty-six-year-old Prunty's corpse for burial. The mortician confirmed he'd been buried in a sealed steel casket and probably embalmed with formaldehyde, the only chemical used in Wyoming in 1973. The manager of Laramie's Greenhill Cemetery told her there were no water table issues. Don Prunty's body should be reasonably preserved. If so, and if he had been poisoned, modern science would likely see it.

The likelihood of definite answers was all Trimble needed to get a search warrant to exhume Donald Prunty.

On the frigid Monday morning of January 13, 2014, gravediggers opened the grave. Trimble and a handful of DCI agents, the county coroner, and the funeral director all watched as the vault was removed and the casket lifted into the open air and sunlight for the first time in forty years.

And that's when things started to go wrong.

The badly rusted casket was partly collapsed. Water had penetrated the seals and generally corroded everything except the stainless steel handles.

Back at the county coroner's office, the corrosion was so bad that the mortuary's universal casket key—or "end crank"—wouldn't work, so they used a reciprocating saw to rip the coffin open.

Inside, it was a god-awful mess. The casket and its seals had failed miserably. A lot of water and mud had seeped in through gaps and busted gaskets, and a thick layer of dirt had settled in the bottom. They found wriggling earthworms in the muck and live spiders in the remnants of a dirty, decaying liner.

What they didn't find was anything recognizable as Don Prunty.

The skeleton was mostly mired in mud. No soft tissues remained, although a small patch of skin clung to the skull, with its hair still neatly combed and parted. His once-white shirt and green suit were mostly decayed.

Dr. Wilkerson carefully collected the remains and took them back to Loveland, Colorado, for a closer examination. The rusted, useless casket was left behind to be junked.

The body was so degraded that some investigators surmised that he hadn't been embalmed at all, a sneaky mortician's way of saving money; the funeral director argued that once water gets inside a casket, even the best preservative can't forestall the rot. Both theories were plausible.

Alas, the bright lamps of Dr. Wilkerson's morgue shed no new light on Don Prunty's ending. Except for that patch of hair on his skull, he was skeletonized. Even with his moldering clothing and a crust of mucky bug husks, he weighed only twenty-three pounds. The autopsist collected fingernails, hair, and debris for toxicology; although none of them would show ethylene glycol, they might contain other strange substances. (Ultimately, they did not.)

When Wilkerson opened the skull, there was plenty of mud and water inside, but no brain.

The ME also found Prunty's gold wedding band, still encircling the bones of his sludgy left ring finger. It was offered to his son Joe and daughter Rachel, but they didn't want it.

In fact, when the autopsy was done, Prunty's son and daughter from his previous marriage wanted to cremate his remains and rebury them in Illinois, as he'd wished, but they weren't his next of kin. Alice was. Although she was awaiting a murder trial in the Cheyenne jail, she and Eliza demanded that her late husband be reburied in Laramie. The state of Wyoming, which had torn apart his first casket, picked up the cost of a new one, and Don Prunty—minus his wedding band—went back into the same wet hole he'd occupied since Nixon was president. (The ring was found years later in a coroner's file cabinet, overlooked somehow in the reburial.)

In the end, the exhumation signified nothing. Don Prunty wouldn't be any help in solving the riddle of his own premature death. And his exhumation certainly didn't provide enough information for criminal charges.

"Based upon the history and autopsy findings," Wilkerson wrote in his final report to DCI, "it appears that Donald Prunty most likely died of his heart disease. However, poisoning cannot be entirely excluded. The remains are too degenerated for definitive testing. The manner of death is undetermined."

With Don Prunty—or what little was left of him—back in his grave and Gerald claiming the full blame for Virginia and her boys' slayings, Alice now had only to answer for one untimely death: Ron Holtz.

Alice Uden's trial for the first-degree murder of Ronald Lee Holtz began on Thursday, May 1, 2014, in Cheyenne, nearly forty years since anyone had seen the deeply troubled kid alive. Her fate was in the hands of five men and seven women.

A criminal trial is a construct that only approximates reality. Citizens assume that juries hear *all* of the evidence against accused criminals, but that isn't generally true, and it certainly wasn't true in Alice Uden's case. They hear only what the judge thinks is *enough* evidence.

In pretrial hearings, Alice's court-appointed defense lawyer, Don Miller, argued vehemently that Gerald's crimes—even though they'd been publicly confessed—could only pollute the case against Alice. The jury, Miller asserted, might be so disgusted by Gerald's murders that they transferred their anger to the question of Ron Holtz's killing. In short, they might base their decision on the "wrong" case.

The judge agreed. There'd be no mention of Gerald's crimes, even if Alice played a role.

The prosecution had bigger worries.

In court, the state must prove who, what, when, where, and how . . . not why. Motive usually isn't necessary, so prosecutors needn't prove the defendant's purpose. Nevertheless, ordinary people—juries, for instance—want to know *why*. In Alice's case, the prosecutors' challenge, then, was to at least offer a plausible explanation for killing Ronnie Holtz, even if it wasn't required by the law, or they risked making the jury feel unconvinced or betrayed.

And the *why* of Ron Holtz's slaying was still murky. Maybe Alice was erasing a bad life choice, or exerting her ultimate control, or planning a convoluted career move, or covering up a busted scheme to steal some veterans benefits. Or something else. There was no clear motive.

The strategy that most worried prosecutors was that the defense might sway jurors with a strong argument that Alice was simply defending her baby from a crazed, drug-fueled Vietnam-killer wacko.

And much had changed since 1974. Mostly Alice.

Jurors didn't see the dark-haired, big-bosomed, curvaceous seductress. What they saw now was a bespectacled seventy-five-year-old grandma in a wheelchair, her wispy white hair combed straight back, her face withered. She wore a wireless listening device and matronly clothes off the rack, which made her seem all the more feeble.

Assistant District Attorney Leigh Anne Manlove, who'd be Alice's chief nemesis, had started as a part-time prosecutor of domestic abuse crimes. The daughter of a judge, she was passionate about protecting victims of family violence, mostly women and children. But if Alice succeeded in using the law to justify the cold-blooded shooting of Ron Holtz, it would damage the legal prospects for real battered women and kids.

This was an execution, not self-defense. Alice was a predatory, manipulative, greedy, and ruthless survivor who did whatever was necessary. It wasn't by accident that she had gotten away with murder for forty years.

Manlove knew about the Prunty suspicions and presumed Alice played a starring role in Gerald's dramatic murders as well, even if they couldn't be used in court. But, she wondered, had there been other "instant partners" just like Ron Holtz whom she dispatched and left where they'd never be found?

But this case could be about one victim, and only one victim: Ron Holtz. Manlove painted the broad outlines of the prosecution's case in her opening statement.

The evidence would prove, Manlove promised, that Alice shot Holtz in his sleep around Christmas Eve 1974, crammed his dead body in a storage barrel that had held holiday decorations, rolled it into an abandoned mine, and did her best to disappear without a trace. Jurors would hear it all—and hold Holtz's skull.

"And you will have the opportunity to see the bullet hole at the base of it," she said.

"If there is one word that describes everything you will hear and see in this case," Manlove told the jurors, "it is 'cold.' Cold because this was a cold case, a largely unknown homicide unsolved for almost forty years. Cold because the evidence will prove the manner in which Ron Holtz was killed was calculated and malicious. And cold because after Alice Uden murdered her husband and covered up her crime, she just moved on, no remorse."

Naturally, the defense had a much different thesis, and it began with time travel back to 1974.

"Nixon just resigned," Don Miller said in his opening. "Gas was fifty-five cents a gallon. Vietnam just ended. In Cheyenne, we dialed just five numbers. There was no mall. There also was no abuse shelter.

"If you called police to tell them, 'This man is beating me,' they would tell you, 'Let us know when he's actually doing it because it's just your word against his.' People would tell their daughters, 'Go home and make your husband happy—that's your duty.' There was no 9-1-1. There was no stalking law. There was no place to hide."

Miller portrayed Alice as a desperate single mother in 1974, already once divorced and once widowed. She had a trailer, five kids, and insurmountable debts. The VA psych ward in Sheridan hired her to talk to patients because she wasn't trained to do much else.

"She met a young man named Ron Holtz, and she did her job: she talked to him and tried to help him through whatever he was going through," Miller said.

He led jurors through Alice's version of the tawdry romance that followed: falling in love with a handsome, well-built, likable—and much younger—guy ... her protective feelings for Holtz, as if he were a stray puppy ... the hasty-hot wedding ... the demons that soon showed themselves.

He didn't just abuse Alice physically and mentally, Miller argued. When Ron raged, he destroyed anything he touched. Bit by bit, he wrecked Alice's mobile home—"the one piece of security she had."

And Holtz was irrationally disturbed by crying babies, Miller said. When little Eliza wailed, he freaked. "Shut the kid up!" he'd scream. "I'll kill her!" He reportedly told Alice about a crying five-year-old Vietnamese girl he'd killed. "I can kill this one too," she remembered him saying. "It doesn't make a difference to me."

One morning, while Ronnie Holtz slept off whatever high from the night before, Eliza began to cry. Alice was in the kitchen when she heard Ron get up. She sensed trouble, but when she rushed to calm Ron, he punched her in the back and stormed toward Eliza's room. Alice grabbed her .22 rifle from the closet and followed him.

As Ron reached for Eliza, Alice raised her gun. She pointed it at the back of the crazed man's head and pulled the trigger. He slumped, dead.

"She didn't have a choice," Miller said as his dramatic story ended. "She didn't have time to think. Ron never got his hands on Eliza, but he wasn't there to burp her. He wasn't there to read her a bedtime story. He was there to do harm. And Alice stopped him."

The stage was set for an emotional, gut-level struggle: Did Ron Holtz die in an act of self-defense or self-indulgence? Was his murder a trailer park siren's calculated depravity or a mother's instinctive protectiveness?

The prosecution's first witness was DCI Special Agent Lonnie TeBeest (retired).

TeBeest led jurors through the entire history of the stop-and-go-and-stop-again case. How Alice's son Ted had first revealed his mother's private confession about killing Holtz. How Alice twice had a chance to justify her killing but completely omitted Holtz from her list of husbands and the psych ward from her long list of jobs. How DCI had dug at the Remount mine, finally finding Holtz's bones forty feet down that awful hole in 2013.

"Nobody ever reported Ron Holtz missing, right?" Don Miller asked TeBeest on cross-examination.

"Yes."

With that, Miller entered Ron Holtz's thick pile of medical records, including his violence, insanity, and drug abuse.

The next prosecution witness was Thea Thomas, Alice's daughter and second-oldest child. She was no longer a child but now fifty-five years old and haunted. She hadn't spoken to her mother in years.

Thea described a rootless childhood that bounced between her father's Illinois home and whichever crappy trailer Alice happened to be hauling from town to town. She had good memories about moving from Illinois to the Remount Ranch, even hauling a small horse in their U-Haul trailer . . . and checking every few hundred miles or so to see if it had suffocated back there.

A significant break between mother and daughter happened in Thea's sophomore year of high school, she said, when Alice left Thea to babysit Eliza while she rode with her then-boyfriend, a trucker. When Alice returned to find Thea sick and the house a mess, Alice flew into a rage. She tried to paddle her teenage daughter with a metal spatula. Thea left.

A couple years later, Alice came to Illinois to help Thea sew a prom dress. The two of them—mom and high school daughter—were drinking at the kitchen table. Thea asked about Alice's latest husband Ron, whom she'd never met.

Oh, Alice casually told Thea, she'd shot him while he slept. She packed him in a cardboard barrel like Thea's grandparents used to store canning supplies in the basement, then dumped him on the Remount Ranch.

Their matter-of-fact conversation wasn't a big deal for either of them, Thea said.

"I don't remember any drama. It just was," she told the jury. "Considering my whole life and things that happened with my mom, it was just one of those things. . . . I just wanted out of there. It was like, *Really? Could that have happened?*"

Whether it was momentous or forgettable, Thea only talked about it with her brother Ted a few times and never told another soul until a Wyoming detective, Dave King, asked her about it in the 1990s.

The defense had few questions for Thea.

The next witness was Ted Scott, Alice's middle son. He barely recognized his own mother sitting at the defense table, but it had been more than thirty years since he last saw her. His testimony had been delayed because he'd shown up drunk the day before.

Like Thea, Ted also loved his Remount years. "I could think of no better place to live," he told Manlove. "I had a two-thousand-acre playground."

But he, too, recounted the countless moves and a childhood constantly on the brink of calamity, never settling long under anybody's roof.

Life was just weird for the kid. For example, when he was sick, Alice—a trained nurse—would ask the local veterinarian for penicillin, ostensibly for her animals, then inject it in Ted's butt.

He testified that he never met Ron Holtz, who was "just another guy in my mom's past."

Then, in seventh grade, he moved with his mom to Laramie. She was supporting herself and kids as a barmaid in tiny Buford, twenty-five miles east. Although he was only twelve or thirteen at the time, it was his job to accompany her for the night shift, then drive her home every night while they shared a filched six-pack of beer.

One night while they were driving back to Laramie, both a little buzzed, Alice just blurted it out.

"She just—out of the blue—just kinda flat-out told me how she had got up one night and got a .22 and shot Ron in the head," Ted told the silent courtroom.

She told him the same story about the barrel and the Remount mine, adding only one detail: she had sought the help of a friend.

"Apparently, he was a bigger guy, and she couldn't get him loaded up by herself," he told Manlove. "That's when she got help. It was the owner of the Buford store at the time, Kay Florita. Then they drove to the gold mine and dumped the body in there . . . it was the ranch burial ground."

"Why did she tell you this story?" Manlove asked Ted.

Ted shrugged.

"I've asked myself that question for years and years," he said. "I have no answer. I don't know why a mother would tell her children that she killed somebody. I don't know. It's haunted me for years."

Privately, Ted had told Manlove that on that dark, drunken drive, he had confronted his mother—he only called her Alice, not Mom—about her poor parenting skills. She responded with her story about killing Ron Holtz. He took it as a threat to him, not a tender moment of motherly vulnerability. She didn't know why he couldn't bring himself to tell that same story to the jury now.

"Did you ever tell anybody?" she asked.

"I've told everybody I ever came in contact with over the years," he said, starting to lose whatever fragile glue held him together. "I've told sheriffs, bosses, spouses. I've told everybody, trying to rip this demon out of me."

He explained how he'd first told the late Riverton cop Jack Coppock about Alice's confession nearly twenty years before, then showed Agent Tom Wachsmuth the location.

"Nothing got done. Nothing got done," he repeated. "Nothing got done."

The hushed courtroom wasn't ready for what happened next.

Subtly, Alice silently mouthed to Ted, "I love you."

Ted erupted.

"I hate you!" a seething, red-faced son yelled at his mother, who sat stoically beside her lawyer. A long second passed; then Ted shouted again across the courtroom: "I hate you!"

The angry judge recessed for both sides to collect their wits. Manlove calmed Ted down and told him to face the jury, not Alice, for any remaining questions.

When court resumed, Miller cross-examined Ted, who admitted that Ron Holtz might have been abusive; that he didn't like Lonnie TeBeest; and that over the years, parts of his story became Thea's, and vice versa. He was shocked when he first discovered Alice had told Thea because he half hoped, half feared he bore that burden alone.

Ted's questioning was done. The judge excused him, and he left the witness stand.

"I hope it was all worth it," Ted muttered to Alice as he passed her on his way out of the courtroom. She just stared forward through her wire-rimmed glasses.

Next up was DCI Special Agent Tina Trimble. District Attorney Scott Homar, who had no intention of letting Alice off the hook without a fight, led Trimble through the crucial last few years of the investigation. She focused on the three abortive excavations in or near the mine and finally the successful dig in 2013. She showed the jury the circular metal ring of the barrel lid, and she described the discovery of the young horse's bones, Jefe's collar, and Ron Holtz's bones.

There was no cross-examination.

The next few witnesses, all largely unchallenged by the defense, included the Cheyenne Fire Rescue chief, DCI's crime scene unit boss, and Dr. Rick Weathermon, who all described the messy process of finding Ron Holtz forty feet below the surface of the prairie.

ADA Manlove intended to put Ron Holtz's daughter, Sharon Mack, on the stand by telephone from Chugiak, Alaska, but Miller angrily objected.

"She didn't want to talk to me [before the trial], so I'm not exactly sure what she's going to say," Miller told the judge. "She's never met Mr. Holtz. She has some pictures. I don't see any way this could be relevant. I'm concerned it would be more prejudicial. Things like 'Gee, I miss my daddy' or 'I never got to see him.'"

Mack's testimony was ultimately allowed, but it added very little. She explained her lineage and confirmed she'd given DNA, not much else.

One of Ron Holtz's younger sisters, Karen Lash, then took the stand. She told the jurors about family life with her brother, who was constantly seeking his father's approval. She described a boy who could be affectionate to his sister but cruel in every other way. She had met "big and mean" Alice when Ronnie brought her home to meet the parents.

When Alice and Ronnie took off to Illinois to meet her family, they left little Eliza with her parents for six weeks. The babysitting chores fell to Karen, only thirteen, who took Eliza to church on Sundays and slept in a bunk bed with her.

When they came home and fetched Eliza, that was the last Karen ever saw her brother.

A DNA expert confirmed that Mack and Lash were directly related to the bones found in the Remount mine. The chances that those bones weren't Ronnie Holtz were a million to one.

Next, Dr. James Wilkerson, the veteran Colorado medical examiner, described his autopsy. Ronnie Holtz died of a classic bullet wound in the back of his head. Back to front, slightly right to left. He probably lost consciousness immediately, was immobilized, and bled profusely, but he was not necessarily technically dead.

The defense was more interested in whether the bullet hole could possibly indicate whether Holtz was standing or lying down, awake or asleep, when he was shot. Dr. Wilkerson admitted it couldn't.

DA Homar began his redirect questioning by handing Dr. Wilkerson a box.

It contained Ronnie Holtz's actual skull.

Dr. Wilkerson illustrated the bullet's trajectory by poking a rod through the hole to the spot where it ricocheted off the inner wall of Holtz's forehead over the left eye. Holtz was shot while his head canted slightly down or because the shooter fired from a lower angle, but there was no way to know for certain.

The prosecution closed its witness list by bringing SA Trimble back to the stand. She recounted Ronnie Holtz's mental health history in excruciating detail: suicidal thoughts at sixteen; debilitating father issues; paranoia that nobody cared for him; thirteen hospitalizations since his premature discharge from the army; diagnoses of character disorder, high blood pressure, drug dependency, depression, lack of impulse control, aggressive tendencies; fears of being locked in anywhere; admission to the VA psychiatric ward in Sheridan; and falling for his nurse Alice.

In less than two months, he and Alice both fled the psych ward, marrying only eleven days later in Colorado.

During her first interview in Missouri, Alice first told Trimble that she shot Holtz at Eliza's crib, but she couldn't explain bloodstains on their mattress. When she was questioned two days later, though, she admitted she'd shot him while he slept.

With that, the prosecution rested.

The defense wasted no time.

Don Miller's first witness was Alice Uden herself. The bailiff wheeled her to a spot near the witness stand, very near the jury box.

In a sweet, soft voice, Alice catalogued her mean history: an unwanted baby, moving around constantly with her military father, pregnant and married at sixteen, four kids, divorced, married again with a fifth child, widowed, adrift, doing any work she could find.

That's when she met Ron Holtz.

She told the court she had reservations about him, but she married him anyway because he seemed like marriage material. Even at thirty-four, Alice claimed to be naïve and easily manipulated. Although she met him in a psychiatric ward, she claimed she didn't know he had mental problems. She felt sorry for him. They were intimate fairly quickly.

Yes, she dumped Eliza with Ron's parents while the two of them went east to find work. They lived with her parents until they moved back to a trailer park in Cheyenne, still out of work. Ron got a job as a cabbie, but his abuse and rampages escalated.

She told the jurors—who'd already heard several versions—that she shot Ron at midmorning over Eliza's crib, not while he slept in his bed.

"I tried to stop him," she said. "He knocked me down and ran into her bedroom. I was by the mop closet, and I had a gun in there. I followed right behind him. He had already entered her room. I came around the corner and saw him reaching for her."

"What happened next?" Miller asked.

"I shot him," Alice said. She had no emotion in her voice.

"Can you explain what you felt?"

"Fear," she said. "I was scared. Scared he wasn't dead and he would turn on me—beat me up or kill Eliza."

"So you were committed the moment you touched the gun?"

"Yes."

After calming the two-year-old and taking her to the Colorado in-laws, Alice came home to Cheyenne three hours later to clean up her "mess." She retrieved a cardboard barrel from her closet and slowly shoved Holtz's naked, dead body into it. When his trunk was mostly inside, she stood the barrel on end to fold his limbs in. She latched the metal lid on it, then rolled it to her back door, where she had backed her Ford LTD up to the porch. She wrestled the barrel into the trunk. She tied down the unclosed lid and drove to the Remount in midafternoon.

Getting the heavy barrel out of the car required a lot of grunting, but when she finally did, she rolled it under a protective barbed-wire fence around the old mine and into the hole. Alone.

The next day, she snatched up Eliza from her in-laws. She put her mobile home up for sale, sold the murder weapon, paid her bills, and fled to Illinois in a U-Haul containing her worldly goods and the bloody mattress—*crib* mattress, she corrected herself—for her mother to take to a county dump, three states away.

Before she killed Holtz, Alice said she called the cops to report Ron's abuse, but they couldn't help. After he was dead, she didn't call the cops because she had the important job of raising a child and couldn't afford to go to prison.

DA Homar seemed slightly incredulous as he cross-examined Alice.

On the day of the killing, when she heard the baby cry and a commotion in the back room, why did she reach for a gun instead of rushing to the baby first?

By "mess," didn't she mean "the dead body on the floor"?

If the safety and rearing of baby Eliza were paramount in Alice's motherly mind, why did she allow her twelve-year-old son to drink and drive? Why did she tell her children she was a murderer at all?

She testified that she confessed to her kids because she felt guilty, but she had told Agent Trimble that she wanted to scare them off drugs. Which was it?

She feared being homeless if Ron destroyed her trailer—yet after she killed him, she sold it and moved in with her parents?

If Ron Holtz fell dead in the crib with a bullet in the back of his head, how did blood leak on it?

"And about the bloody crib mattress, aren't most crib mattresses waterproof?" the prosecutor asked.

"I don't know," Alice replied, her voice slightly more forceful now.

"It's funny, but you said in your divorce papers that you couldn't find Ron Holtz," Homar said. "I'm sure you couldn't. That wasn't a lie to the court?"

"In my mind, it's not."

"You say you sold the trailer and it paid all your bills," Homar pressed. "So why file for bankruptcy?"

"I had more bills than money."

On redirect, she admitted telling three of her children that she shot Ron Holtz while he slept, but it was just a fake story.

"Why did you say you shot him in bed?" Miller asked.

"Because I thought they already had me," Alice replied. "I wanted it over with. Just tell them what they want to hear and get out of here."

The defense had only one more witness, a professor who was both a former cop and a domestic abuse expert. He explained how in 1974, law enforcement wasn't dealing well with spousal battery. The first shelter for beaten women in Wyoming, he said, opened in Cheyenne in 1979, five years after Alice killed Ronnie Holtz. But Manlove pointed out that Wyoming wasn't a misogynistic Wild West: it had already ratified the Equal Rights Amendment in 1974 and was one of the few states that had codified battered woman syndrome.

Both sides rested.

"It really is a simple case," Homar said in his closing remarks to the jury. "On that day, did Alice Uden get out of bed and shoot Ron Holtz in the back of the head while he lay sleeping? So started almost forty years of lies, deceit, and, as you saw, family anguish."

Nobody denied Holtz's unpredictable explosions or his horrid behavior, but if Alice felt threatened—a big "if"—killing him wasn't her only option. It's more likely that she simply wanted something else and needed to wipe her slate clean.

"Ron Holtz was mean. She didn't want him around anymore, so she took care of it. She didn't tell anyone until she told her kids. She covered it up, and she held it tight for forty years. There's no self-defense, nor is there defense of others.

"He was asleep," Homar ended his passionate speech. "*He was asleep.*"

Miller came out equally passionate. He explained Alice's many discrepancies and inconsistencies as the fog of memory over four decades. "Forty years is a long time to remember things, especially when you're trying to forget them," he said.

He warned jurors they must travel back in time to 1974 and consider the killing of Ron Holtz in the context of its moment. Alice had nowhere to turn. Wyoming was a hard place that required hard people to solve their own problems. Sometimes those solutions were harsh and looked unfairly harsher under brighter lights two generations later.

"Alice made mistakes," he admitted. "There is no doubt about it— she made a lot of mistakes. She told you after her husband died, she was lonely. At that point, here comes this handsome, attractive man. She made a mistake from the get-go: he was extremely violent, unpredictable, and impulsive.

"But if you look at the situation she was in, I think you'll see it was reasonable for her to be terrified of him."

DA Homar stepped up to the jury box one last time on rebuttal.

"You saw her reaction on that screen [during her videotaped interrogation in Missouri]," he said. "She didn't make a lot of mistakes. She wants you to think she's weak-minded. They want you to think she can be talked into things, manipulated easily . . . That's not Alice. She does what she wants to do. Weak-minded? No."

Homar dismissed the wheelchair-bound granny in front of them.

"That is not the woman who shot Mr. Holtz," he said.

He held up a picture of young Alice instead.

"*This* is the woman who shot Mr. Holtz. And less than a year and a half later, she was happily married again, moving on with her life."

Homar made one last emotional plea.

"Alice lived her life," he told jurors. "Ron Holtz didn't get a chance. He didn't have a chance to get better. He didn't have a chance for anything. He spent the last thirty-nine years in that hole. She shot him when he was asleep. Thank you."

For the jury, the case wasn't as simple as Homar would have it.

A quick poll at the start of deliberations showed seven jurors ready to convict Alice of premeditated first-degree murder and five who saw Ron Holtz's killing as merely manslaughter. First-degree murder carried a mandatory life sentence. They all agreed she had committed a crime, but the defense's battered-wife theory was powerful for both male and female jurors. They also had to work hard to imagine frail grandma Alice as buxom, young, street-savvy, and ambitious.

As discussions unfolded, jurors slowly migrated to the first-degree side, until only one insisted Alice was guilty of nothing more than manslaughter. Deadlocked after thirteen hours—and coming perilously close to a mistrial—the lone holdout agreed to a compromise: she would accept second-degree murder as a compromise. They agreed.

The jury declared Alice Uden guilty of second-degree murder, which might still land her in prison for the rest of her life.

At her sentencing, an angry letter from Ron Holtz's only child, Sharon Mack, was read into the record.

"I believe you are a very disturbed individual yourself," Mack wrote directly to Alice. "You do not deserve to be alive in my eyes. . . . Justice has been and will be done. Know you are not forgiven for your sins."

DA Homar requested that Alice serve a minimum of twenty years in prison, effectively a death sentence for the infirm septuagenarian.

"We don't want to send a message to society that if you cover up a crime long enough, you'll get away with it with very little punishment," he said.

Defender Donald Miller asked the judge for mercy. He suggested Alice be given probation because her daughter Eliza, now in her forties, reportedly had breast cancer and was expected to live only six more months.

District Judge Steven Sharpe said he weighed all the possible mitigating factors, including Alice's lack of a criminal record. Suspicions about Donald Prunty's death weren't discussed; her participation in Gerald's triple murder and cover-up never came up. But this one brutish act couldn't be explained away easily.

"This was very much a cold, calculated murder," Sharpe said. "The jury heard all of the evidence that was before the court, and the jury rejected the defense that it was self-defense."

Alice, who lied to the end, deserved life in prison, the judge decided.

As with Gerald, there would be no parole unless the governor intervened.

But parole was likelier than an honest explanation of why four separate murders—six years apart—were so eerily similar. What were the chances that two supposedly unconnected killers would both shoot their victims in the back of the head with .22-caliber rifles; dump their bodies in lonesome, abandoned mine shafts; and transport them in barrels?

The question was its own answer, but since neither Gerald nor Alice would ever breathe free air again, it was irrelevant.

ADA Leigh Anne Manlove counted it as a win, but it was sometimes hard for her to feel like she'd won. Claire was gone. Virginia and the boys were still missing. There was no chance that Ron Holtz's family would ever be whole again. But Manlove and Homar won. It was better than losing, even if the difference were sometimes indistinct. She took comfort where she found it.

Gerald and Alice would both die in prison. That would have to be enough.

Chapter 10

BLACK AND DEEP

Fremont Lake is no ordinary lake.

On the western flank of the Wind River Range, ancient glaciers clawed elongated, gnarly finger-shaped trenches and pushed gargantuan piles of boulders—called moraines—ahead of them. With moraines acting as natural dams, the glacial trenches soon filled with runoff from the rocky spine of North America, thousands of years before humans named it the Continental Divide.

Fremont Lake is one of those glacial lakes. It sits at roughly 7,400 feet. It is eleven miles long but only about a half mile wide. The bottom is flat, but its boulder-strewn sides plummet at forty-five-degree angles.

Locals call it "The Deep" because it is not just Wyoming's deepest body of water—it's the seventh-deepest lake in the continental United States.

At its deepest, Fremont Lake is just over six hundred feet. Two Statues of Liberty, one atop the other, would stand completely hidden beneath Fremont Lake's serene surface. Wyoming's tallest building—the two-hundred-foot White Hall dormitory at the University of Wyoming in Laramie—could comfortably fit three high into Fremont Lake.

In the summer, a thin layer of water on the surface can warm to the upper sixties, but the deepest 550 feet is rarely warmer than thirty-nine degrees Fahrenheit at any time of year. The lake freezes in mid-January, and the ice breaks up in mid-May.

So there's good news and bad news for the people who have searched Fremont Lake extensively for Virginia and her boys.

With no measurable coliform bacteria and minimal oxygen, chemical and biochemical processes are markedly suppressed. There are no fish nor other obvious life—or light—below 250 feet.

In plain language, nothing on the bottom decays very quickly. If Gerald's barrels settled on the cold, anaerobic floor of Fremont Lake, decomposition would be imperceptibly slow. It is likely that even forty years later, the remains inside would be essentially unchanged from the moment they went down.

At the moment of death, a human body becomes food. Bacteria, insects, and animals begin to recycle dead muscle, fat, fluids, and other tissues into their own life-sustaining nourishment. They don't allow a proper interval for grief, meditation, or cooling. The bacteria are already inside, mostly in the intestines, and they don't die when their host dies. Outside, insects and wild animals might take a little longer to find a dead body left in the open, but usually not more than a few minutes.

In this case, Virginia and her boys' already-decomposed soft tissue would soak off in the water, and some maggots might survive for a time, but not long.

The decay is stalled by frigid temperatures, immersion, and oxygen. Bacteria grow best at about one hundred degrees, poorly at fifty degrees ... and barely at all at forty degrees. In deep, cold water, decomposition can be halted almost completely, like keeping a raw roast in a sealed, water-filled bag in a refrigerator.

That's the good news. The bad news is more troublesome.

Depth is one problem for searchers. Altitude is another. Even at sea level, a human diver can only go down about 130 feet; at Fremont Lake, even a skilled, well-outfitted diver would hit the danger zone less than 60 feet down—540 feet too shallow to search for Virginia and her boys.

The pressure is a killer. A diver would be crushed before ever getting close to the bottom of Fremont Lake. And out in the arid West where scuba diving isn't a big pastime, if a diver got into trouble with decompression sickness—"the bends"—there aren't a lot of emergency responders with the right knowledge to help. The nearest hyperbaric chamber is a two-hour plane flight away.

So the search must be conducted with very expensive, very technical equipment like side-scan sonar and Remote Operated Vehicles (ROV), keen-eyed tethered underwater robots. The equipment is scarce, and skilled operators are scarcer. Lines get tangled; gadgets break. And getting those sophisticated machines in place—and back to the surface—can consume valuable time.

Luckily, Fremont Lake is reasonably clear, with little silt. Glaciers deposited countless boulders on the bottom a hundred thousand years ago, but the silt layer on them is only a half inch thick. So any barrels dropped in 1980 would likely lie openly on the moonscape floor, easily identified, with little more than a dusting of sediment. But anything that settled in the rocky sides—even a hundred barrels—might be so well camouflaged as to be virtually invisible to even robotic eyes.

Rust never sleeps, even in dark, deep, fresh water. Even at anaerobic depths, metal dissolves or corrodes. The galvanized barrel would resist corrosion better, but depending on its coating, it still might have deteriorated completely—or not at all. Nobody really knows.

And finally, at that altitude in the Rockies, squalls can strike faster than a rattler on meth. Air temperatures are moderate in summer, beastly in winter. Hypothermia can happen in water as cold as seventy degrees—which is warmer than Fremont Lake ever gets. Water access and emergency care are limited. So search time is limited, and searching itself can be dangerous.

No matter how heart-wrenching the story is, no matter how badly the searchers want to find these innocent victims, it's not worth another death.

But here's the real kicker: It might be the wildest of wild-goose chases. Almost from the start, cops didn't believe Gerald's story about Fremont Lake.

He lied before, and there was no obvious reason to believe him now. In fact, there were logical reasons *not* to believe him.

If the Udens were committed to a water burial, they lived one mile—two minutes—from the larger (though far shallower) Ocean Lake and less than an hour from the huge Boysen Reservoir. Since these were much closer than Fremont Lake, three hours away, dumping the bodies in either would have exposed the Udens to much less risk of discovery in transit. Both lakes had also already played ominous roles in this bleak story: Boysen was where Gerald and Alice took the boys for a "swimming lesson"—maybe a miscarried murder attempt designed to look accidental—and Eliza remembered Gerald motoring off alone in his boat at Ocean Lake the day after the disappearance.

Maybe the lake was just another lie.

Maybe Gerald and Alice did something so literally unspeakable to the bodies that they didn't dare reveal it. Burned them piece by piece in a trash barrel? Chopped them up and fed them to their pigs?

Alice had unexpectedly divulged that she'd been butchering a sick calf in her bloody kitchen on the day of the disappearance. Might she have been chopping up humans instead?

And in a perverse conversation with his stepdaughter, Gerald suggested the best way to hide a body was to feed it to pigs—which he owned when he killed Virginia and his boys. Then he lied about dumping them in the Pacific Ocean and changed his story to Fremont Lake for sketchy reasons.

No, there were good reasons to think Gerald was lying about Fremont Lake too.

But the art and science of crime solving is mostly the elimination of possibilities. Most alleys are blind, but they must be explored. Investigators had to look in Fremont Lake, if only to rule it out.

After the ice thawed in the summer of 2014, the Sublette County sheriff's Tip Top Search and Rescue team made its first foray into "The Deep" for Virginia and the boys.

These weren't a couple guys with a boat and a fish finder. Employing side-scan sonar equipment that most auxiliaries could only dream of owning, the team identified several curious anomalies on the lake bottom and marked them for a closer look. But that would require bigger and badder equipment, maybe just this side of the military.

So Director Steve Woodson of Wyoming's Division of Criminal Investigation then hired Cross Marine Projects, a Utah-based company specializing in unusual underwater challenges around the world, to continue the search at the bottom of Fremont Lake.

Jim Cross had founded Cross Marine Projects in 1975. In the 1940s, his father was an early explorer of the Colorado River, collecting specimens for museums and helping map the river for the US government. As a teenager, Jim worked for his dad as a guide, taking tourists deep into the Grand Canyon and hiking parts of it that are now under Lake Powell. He soon became a paramedic and a diver for his hometown fire department before launching Cross Marine.

Cross Marine opened as a commercial diving and marine construction outfit that helped government and private companies with large-scale underwater work, from inspections, engineering, and surveying to salvage, dredging, pipelines, and dam repairs. At first, the notion of a diving company in the arid interior of the American West caused some consternation, but it quickly faded when news of the company's extraordinary successes started to circulate.

Cross had partnered with treasure hunter Mel Fisher in the mid-1980s to recover two famous Spanish galleons—the ill-fated *Atocha* and *Santa Margarita*—both of which sank off the Florida Keys in a 1622 hurricane. He was also hired to search for Korean Airlines Flight 007, shot down by Soviet fighters near Sakhalin Island in 1983. For almost forty years, Jim Cross's company had worked behind the scenes of many world headlines, from tragic US Air Force crashes in the ocean to the 1985 earthquake in Mexico that killed up to forty-five thousand people.

By 2014, Cross Marine had been hired by the Japanese government to help stanch the flow of about seventy-two thousand gallons of radioactive water from the tsunami-damaged Fukushima nuclear power plant into the Pacific Ocean every day. And it had just finished a research project for the US Navy with Johns Hopkins University.

But Cross Marine took on some of the world's biggest underwater jobs so it could afford to do more of the kind of humanitarian work that touched Jim Cross's heart: rescue and recovery of people few had ever heard about, from sunken fishing boats to missing swimmers. Once, Cross even dispatched one of his divers to find a distraught new bride's missing ring in a Utah lake—and the diver did, within minutes.

Cross did all those jobs for little or no money because he felt a debt to the universe, or something. He was single-minded like that. He had a right to be: he had never failed to find what he was looking for.

Now he would launch his flagship, an insanely customized pontoon he had christened the *Charity Eden*, onto the treacherous Fremont Lake to hunt for three more people the world never heard of: Virginia, Richard, and Reagan Uden.

Cross and his seasoned crew, with all their sophisticated electronics and support equipment, planned to spend up to a week searching, for little more than their expenses. In truth, though, Cross didn't think it would take that long, and this particular story moved him.

He was a father too.

On September 3, 2014, Jim Cross started his search with a briefing by the local search team. They had briefly interviewed Gerald Uden and had already done a cursory sonar survey of the lake surrounding the spot where Gerald guessed he rolled the barrels overboard in 1980. Many "blips" cropped up.

Cross was confident that the barrels containing Virginia and her boys were within his primary search zone, shore to shore inside a mile-long box centered on Gerald's presumptive dump site.

With "targets of interest" identified by the local searchers, the *Charity Eden* set out.

Fremont Lake's bottom is littered with the rubble of eons, both natural and unnatural: columnlike boulders rolled smooth by advancing glaciers, the intact carcasses of unlucky bull elk and deer that fell through the ice, 1950s beer cans (the kind that required a church key to puncture the top)—somebody even told a story about how the Pinedale city hall might have dumped its old rotary phones there. The lake's flat floor is a strange kind of history museum where humanity's paltry contributions to the primeval landscape are preserved.

It worked like this: While the *Charity Eden* motored slowly in a methodical pattern, its sonar—high-powered sound pulses—scanned the terrain below, picking up contours and shapes in surprising detail. When Cross's team saw anything of interest, the boat's underwater robot could be deployed by the magic of GPS to inspect any peculiar artifacts up close, sending high-resolution video back to the surface.

On sonar, everything stands out. Any cylindrical or circular shapes, such as those ancient stone pillars or five-gallon bait buckets, got special attention, but nothing was overlooked.

Much of what tickled the sonar was plain old rocks. Occasionally, can-shaped rocks that sometimes featured highly reflective quartzlike bands quickened the hearts of sonar searchers—but they were still just rocks.

As the ROV crept just off the bottom, it spied round underwater springs and vents that spewed subterranean water and gas into the lake. During one pass, the ROV actually captured a faultlike fissure unzipping across the lake bottom. Unbeknownst to the team at the moment, a moderate earthquake had just shaken western Wyoming.

The bottom was mostly firm and unsilty. Somebody described it as looking like a driveway. But sometimes the searchers deliberately tested the surface to find scattered, soft pockets that were three or four feet deep. They were widely dispersed, but theoretically, they might hide a drum that landed just right.

Just south of the spot where Gerald Uden estimated he'd dropped his sounding rope and jettisoned his grim barrels, *Charity Eden* found a rope or cable tangled on the bottom. It didn't appear to have any kind of weight on it, and it probably wasn't as long as he described, but there was no way to know if it might be Gerald's depth-finding line or simply a lost water ski or towrope.

Beverage cans of all kinds were numerous, a testament to high-country litterbugs. Here were a couple fishing poles and bait boxes, there a beer bottle. Here, a dead trophy trout, there some enormous elk antlers still attached to the skull. On one pass, the ROV even spotted a cell phone that somebody dropped (or maybe threw, since cell service at Fremont Lake is spotty at best).

They also found remnants of a seaplane that crashed in 1994 in a reasonably shallow margin of the lake—a mere 120 feet deep, just fifty yards from shore. A young pilot and his instructor were killed, but their bodies were recovered shortly after the crash, along with most of the wrecked fuselage and wings. Some debris, enough to send Cross Marine's sonar wild, was left behind, never to be recovered.

But no barrels and no bodies.

By Jim Cross's calculations, the chances were slim that they were merely overlooked. If those barrels went overboard where Gerald said, they would stand out.

For the first time in his career, Jim Cross hadn't found what he came for, and it bothered him. He left the *Charity Eden* tied up at Fremont Lake for several weeks after he left, just in case. He even started to think, privately, about another expedition, just him and his team without a paying client.

It's still a possibility.

In his final report to DCI, Jim Cross summarized his unsuccessful hunt. He offered only three explanations:

As unlikely as it seemed, the barrels could still be someplace else in the lake, beyond his big search area.

Against the odds, they might have settled into the lake's few "soft spots" and sunk out of view.

Or Gerald's story is wrong, maybe even a lie.

The next summer, local searchers led another sweeping exploration at Fremont Lake, using two sonar rigs and ROVs. Again, they found discarded cans, lost boating items, big rocks, and . . . nothing else. The team leaders concluded that the likelihood of there being two metal barrels containing Virginia, Richard, and Reagan Uden on the barren bottom anywhere near Gerald's estimated drop zone was small, and only slightly more possible in the rocky sides.

At any rate, the personal risks and the cost of looking further outweighed the chances of finding them. Without any new information, the local searchers were done.

Life—and death—are filled with unanswered questions. Sometimes the answers are there, but nobody sees them. But sometimes answers simply aren't there.

Epilogue
TIME AND THE HOUR

Remembering and forgetting can be equally painful.

Or equally comforting.

Choosing between them would be as impossible as favoring the heartbeat or the instant between. If the things we carry and the things we let go are both meaningful, which is more necessary right now?

Time will tell.

Today, Gerald and Alice Uden occupy the same prison, but they're not together.

After pleading guilty in 2013, Gerald was incarcerated at the Wyoming Medium Correctional Institution in Torrington, a farming town in the eastern grasslands. After Alice's second-degree murder conviction six months later, she was sent to the Wyoming Women's Center in Lusk, another farm town an hour north of Torrington.

But Alice's age and colorful array of medical maladies likely would have landed her in a nursing home on the outside. So they simply landed her in a nursing home on the inside. She was transferred to the Wyoming Department of Corrections geriatric ward, which happens to be in the same medium-security prison where Gerald is now an inmate.

Like the mythical Babylonian lovers Pyramus and Thisbe, separated by a wall, Gerald and Alice fall asleep every night within yards of each other, separated by the prison's concrete walls. They haven't touched each other since that little kiss in a Missouri truck stop in 2013, and they likely never will again, according to prison rules. They may write letters, but they aren't even allowed to talk on the phone.

And it is somehow prophetic that the myth ends with Pyramus falling on his own sword when he presumes (mistakenly) that Thisbe is gone, just as Gerald fell on his sword when he presumed (mistakenly) that Alice had been arrested for her part in his crimes.

Gerald's old navy crewmates might have said he broke deep, sprung an invisible leak below the waterline. Until he met and married Alice, he was a clod, not a murderer. Was he simply a three-time loser obsessed with not failing a fourth time? Was he bewitched by a psychopath who was willing to manipulate his compulsion? Was he simply madly, passionately in love with the wrong woman . . . or was she his idea of the perfect woman? It's difficult to know.

Alice refuses all interviews. Gerald occasionally transfers money from his inmate account to hers, still functioning as her "paycheck." Early on, she handcrafted rosary beads as gifts to other inmates until prison rules shut her down. She no longer wears her Carmelite scapular, and her condition in the prison's convalescent block is listed unofficially as "cranky."

I corresponded with Gerald for more than eighteen months preparing for this book. He wrote me dozens of prison letters, all addressing some element of his crimes. From his boyhood to his vivid recollections about the murders to his interior reflections about their causes and effects—no topic was off-limits. We also met face-to-face in a prison visiting room for two days of interviews. He seldom missed a chance to lament his separation from Alice.

A deal was proposed: if he would reveal what really became of Virginia and her boys—and remains were recovered—authorities might allow him a brief visit with his beloved Alice.

Gerald shrugged. "I got nothing to deal. I told the truth. They're in that lake."

But when the famed forensic psychiatrist Richard Walter—who doesn't believe the three victims' bodies were dumped in Fremont Lake—heard that Gerald declined the possible deal, he wasn't surprised.

"For some reason, Alice doesn't want the story told," Walter said.

"And Gerald fears disappointing Alice more than he fears never seeing her again."

Other than his longing for Alice, Gerald exhibits little remorse and much hubris.

"It might sound cold, but I've read a lot about people having nightmares and people they killed coming back to haunt them," Gerald said in our prison interview. "But, honestly, I never lost a night's sleep over it.

"In fact, we wouldn't even be talking today if my idiot stepson [Ted] hadn't opened his mouth."

Maybe so. But in the end, we're only as sick as our secrets.

For the rest of Sharon Mack's life, she will care for her developmentally disabled daughter and worry about a son who resembles his dead grandfather Ron Holtz in too many ways.

Her heart once wondered why her father never looked for her and maybe fantasized him as something more princely. Then the reality of his tawdry life in the outer rings of hell was unceremoniously heaped in her lap, along with full-color photos of his punctured skull.

Now she squirms about what she should remember and what she should forget.

"I'm sorry he was a creep, jerk, asshole, or whatever," she says. "If I met him now, I'd probably tell him to fuck off. I wouldn't like him. I'd give him a chance, but he'd better have the right answer."

Still, she also imagines Ron Holtz on the "other side" helping other lost spirits find their place. He knew what it was like to be lost. She reckons she'll meet him someday, and there'll be plenty of answers, but until then, it makes her smile to think of him as a butterfly.

For now, Sharon stashes his ashes in a box on a shelf in her shed out back. She shrouds them in a blanket, just for warmth, even if he's past caring.

Someday, she wants to scatter Ronnie Holtz's ashes in the Colorado mountains, maybe near the lake where he once fished with his father. Someday. Not *in* the lake, though, because he would sink, and he's spent too long below.

Claire Martin died just seven months before Gerald Uden confessed that he killed her only daughter and two grandsons, although we cannot know whether knowing part of the story would have calmed her troubled heart or caused more turbulence. Not all answers are a comfort.

Who did it? She was ready to believe Virginia's conflicts with Gerald and Alice caused her death, but she probably wouldn't have accepted— most don't—Gerald's story that he acted alone.

What happened that day? Later in life, Claire assumed Virginia had been murdered, but the boys? She couldn't imagine the depravity required to kill two innocent children. When she started to talk about them in the past tense, maybe she had surrendered her illusions, but she still might not have been ready to hear they were shot in their heads too.

Where are they? She certainly wouldn't have known what became of her dear ones because only two people in this world know. In the end, that was all that mattered.

If Virginia, Richard, and Reagan are ever found, an empty grave still awaits them in a tiny cemetery in Glendo, Wyoming. Some of Claire's ashes will be buried with them because it was not just her wish but her fervent hope to be with them again.

How was it done . . . and did they suffer? Gerald's gruesome account is bad enough for a mother to hear, but every day they can't be found in Fremont Lake, more people believe he's covering up a literally unspeakable crime. He sticks to the lake story, they say, because the truth is more horrific than he can admit.

Claire's old Country Squire station wagon, which she believed might contain a clue that future science might find, has never been junked. Today, it sits in a storage yard owned by her friend Marie Roskowske's family in Riverton, Wyoming. Waiting.

Why?

Because the universe loves a stubborn heart.

ACKNOWLEDGMENTS

For more than two years, I immersed myself in a landscape and mindscape that were both familiar and foreign to me. I grew up in Wyoming, and it remains my heart-earth. Now I see those times and those people through the gauze of memory, and they haunt me.

The pages you've just read contain the names of dozens of people who helped me tell this bizarre story of Shakespearean proportions. I cannot repeat all of them here, but the reader must understand that each of them contributed crucial perspectives and unearthed memories that they'd just as soon have kept buried. When you read their names in this book, know that they were asked—and usually answered—some very unsettling questions. I am grateful to them all.

I logged thousands of miles, dialed hundreds of phone calls, interviewed more than a hundred people, sent countless emails, and walked every key site in this true story. Along the way, I had many true guides, including Glen Berghaus, Dr. David Burleigh, Amber Cabading, the late Rusty Collins, Bruce Corbett, Dr. Vincent Di Maio, Dr. Diane France, Diane and Marc Florita, Melvin Gustin, Dan Hausel, Susan Layman of the South Pass City (WY) State Historic Site, John Linn, Todd Matthews of NamUs, Vickie Vance Meredith, Damen Morrison, Marcia Murdock, Brian Oram, Mary Ostlund, Joe and Diane Prunty, Andres Rodela, Don Sammons, Tom Schingle, Joseph Smith, Bill Sniffin, Roger West, and Rusty Whiting.

The dialogue in this book is not a figment of my fevered imagination. It is reproduced faithfully from thousands of pages of court and police transcripts, audio and video recordings of interrogations, personal interviews by me, Gerald Uden's handwritten 250-page "autobiography," and other official records where one or more of the key participants detailed the conversations for investigative and research purposes. Among the many who gave me transcripts or recordings, or enabled interviews, are the Wyoming Division of Criminal Investigation, Laramie County (WY) Clerk of District Court Diane Sanchez, Fremont County (WY) Sheriff Skip Hornecker, Dee Herdt and Mark Horan of the Wyoming Department of Corrections, and US Attorney Christopher "Kip" Crofts.

You wouldn't be holding this book if not for my literary agent, Linda Konner, and editors Steven L. Mitchell and Jacqueline May Parkison at Prometheus Books. Early on, they saw this story's potential and stuck with me through some difficult moments.

Then there's the support team, who were always there with expert advice, a meal, a beer, a bed—or a willing ear. Sometimes all of the above. I owe more than thanks to Dr. Stacia Daniel, Bruce Moats, Dan Perala, Sandy TeBeest, and Bill Vandeventer.

And to my family, who understands the obstacles surmounted to assemble these words in just the right order. To my wife, Mary; daughter, Ashley; and son, Matt . . . my heart always belongs to you, even when it appears the occasional story might steal it away.

NOTES

CHAPTER 1. A CRUEL SEASON

1. The names of Alice's five children have all been changed to protect their identities.

CHAPTER 3. TOMORROW . . .

1. Blood typing was the only tool available to forensic scientists in 1980. DNA profiling was first used by forensic scientists in 1986. When the 1980 blood samples were finally analyzed in 2006 by DNA scientists, they found that the samples also contained blood from Richard or Reagan, or possibly both. The chance it belonged to anyone else was an improbable one in forty-three million.

2. Grand juries are usually secret proceedings, but as the investigation of Virginia, Richard, and Reagan Uden's disappearance dragged past twenty years, SA Lonnie TeBeest asked that it be opened. A district judge declared this grand jury proceeding had public interest and investigative value. In 2001, the judge signed an order opening the grand jury's transcript, videotapes, and evidence files.

CHAPTER 4. . . . AND TOMORROW . . .

1. The so-called Battered Woman Defense arose in the 1970s. The famous "burning bed" case, in which an abused Michigan housewife torched her tormenting husband's bed while he slept, then was acquitted by a jury, highlighted battered-wife syndrome in the United States, but at the time of Ronnie Holtz's alleged murder, it was still three years in the future.

2. Mary O'Hara, *My Friend Flicka* (Philadelphia: J. B. Lippincott, 1941), p. 102.

3. This entire 1996 interview lasted two hours. It appears here in a highly condensed form that's faithful to the original interview.

CHAPTER 5. . . . AND TOMORROW

1. Ed Pilkington, "Vidocq Society—The Murder Club," *Guardian*, March 3, 2011, https://www.theguardian.com/world/2011/mar/03/vidocq-society-cold-case-murders.

2. Michael Capuzzo, *The Murder Room: The Heirs of Sherlock Holmes Gather to Solve the World's Most Perplexing Cold Cases* (New York: Gotham, 2010), p. 10.

3. "Rick Weathermon," Department of Anthropology, University of Wyoming, http://www.uwyo.edu/anthropology/directory/r-weathermon.html (accessed January 3, 2019).